Praise for *Fundamentals for Becoming a Successful Entrepreneur*

"Most books on new venture creation are relentlessly performative, giving guidance on how to complete a business plan. Brännback and Carsrud take a different approach. Adopting the voice of an experienced and wise mentor, they guide the would-be entrepreneur/new venture creator through the start-up process, emphasizing what they need to know and why they need to know it. Engaging and scholarly without being dry and demystifying the start-up process, this is a must-read for the manager/employee interested in entrepreneurship as a career option."

—**Professor Richard Harrison**, Chair in Entrepreneurship and Innovation, University of Edinburgh Business School, Edinburgh, UK

"Brännback and Carsrud present an engaging and wide-ranging approach to starting and growing businesses that covers context, mindset, and the type of behaviors necessary for being entrepreneurial. The authors also draw from a global selection of examples to show the universality of many entrepreneurial practices along with a set a recommended exercises to help the reader on their way."

—**Professor Patricia Greene**, Paul T. Babson Chair in Entrepreneurial Studies, Babson College, Wellesley, MA

"Finally a book on entrepreneurship for the rest of us. A book not bound by the myths of the Silicon Valley, but rather a book that speaks to the entrepreneurial spirit in all of us. Brännback and Carsrud have put together a very practical book that is perfect for students, aspiring entrepreneurs or 'any person with a desire to pursue an opportunity and to achieve a goal.' This is a book for real people looking to create real businesses and real careers that meet their goals, not create mythical 'ventures.' This book is going on the syllabus."

—**David L. Deeds, Ph.D.**, Sandra Schulze Professor of Entrepreneurship, Opus College of Business, The University of St. Thomas, Minneapolis, MN

"Reading this book was a valuable refresher to my MBA coursework—and a reminder of some of my many mistakes. If you are considering starting your own business, save yourself time and money by reading this first!"

—**Chris Jarvis**, author of *Wealth Secrets of the Affluent* and founder of Jade Risk

FUNDAMENTALS FOR BECOMING A SUCCESSFUL ENTREPRENEUR

From Business Idea to Launch and Management

Malin Brännback
Alan Carsrud

Publisher: Paul Boger
Editor-in-Chief: Amy Neidlinger
Acquisitions Editor: Charlotte Maiorana
Editorial Assistant: Olivia Basegio
Cover Designer: Chuti Prasertsith
Managing Editor: Kristy Hart
Project Editor: Elaine Wiley
Copy Editor: Cenveo® Publisher Services
Proofreader: Cenveo Publisher Services
Indexer: Cenveo Publisher Services
Manufacturing Buyer: Dan Uhrig

© 2016 by Malin Brännback and Alan Carsrud
Published by Pearson Education, Inc.
Old Tappan, New Jersey 07675

For information about buying this title in bulk quantities, or for special sales opportunities (which may include electronic versions; custom cover designs; and content particular to your business, training goals, marketing focus, or branding interests), please contact our corporate sales department at corpsales@pearsoned.com or (800) 382-3419.

For government sales inquiries, please contact governmentsales@pearsoned.com.

For questions about sales outside the U.S., please contact international@pearsoned.com.

Company and product names mentioned herein are the trademarks or registered trademarks of their respective owners.

Printed in the United States of America

First Printing November 2015

ISBN-10: 0-13-396681-X
ISBN-13: 978-0-13-396681-7

Pearson Education Ltd.
Pearson Education Australia PTY, Ltd.
Pearson Education Singapore, Pte. Ltd.
Pearson Education Asia, Ltd.
Pearson Education Canada, Ltd.
Pearson Educación de Mexico, S.A. de C.V.
Pearson Education—Japan
Pearson Education Malaysia, Pte. Ltd.

Library of Congress Control Number: 2015950136

Contents

Introduction

Why This Book, What It Is All About, and Who We Are

The Why

It is always good to begin at the beginning. First of all we have long loved the field of entrepreneurship. Since 2013 we had wanted to write a new book aimed primarily at would-be entrepreneurs. Then in 2014 we were approached by Charlotte Maiorana, a long-time friend and editor in the publishing world. She asked us if we would consider writing a book for Pearson. She was scouting for a book on entrepreneurship aimed at the would-be entrepreneur, the MBA student, or an executive looking for a career change. She was familiar with many of our more research-oriented books done for other publishers. She also knew of an earlier professional book we had done aimed at the individuals considering starting a new venture. Hers was a challenge that we willingly accepted as we felt most of what was available to the reader was either way too academic, or aimed at undergraduate students as a textbook, or too highly focused on technology entrepreneurship to the detriment of other areas in which entrepreneurship occurs. We also felt that much of what was available in book form did not reflect the current contexts in which most would-be entrepreneurs exist nor did they reflect the latest trends in marketing and finance. We thus accepted her challenge and this book is the result.

Unlike many individuals, especially academics, who have written books on entrepreneurship, we have actually started ventures so we have a perspective different from many of our colleagues and other individuals writing on the topic. Through all this endeavor to write this book, we have been joined together by our mutual love for entrepreneurship and our profound respect for the many entrepreneurs we have met around the world. The area of entrepreneurship has been our personal passion as teachers, researchers, consultants, and entrepreneurs. We hope in this book that we can bring to the reader a sense of the excitement of creating a new venture, the joy of making your first sale, the challenge of hiring staff, the pains of growing, the fear of failure, the agony of planning, and the ultimate satisfaction when you look at what you have created as an entrepreneur. This is a journey, like none other. We hope, in the following pages, you will like the adventure we are suggesting you take to become a successful entrepreneur. Remember one of the joys of becoming an entrepreneur is that sometimes you cannot only challenge the rules, but sometimes also get a chance to break them. As Anglican Bishop Alan Wilson has noted:

> If nobody ever experimented with going ahead of the rules, the rules would never change and that's the evolutionary process. . . .

One of the important reasons we are able to do this book is all of the entrepreneurs and business owning families with whom we have worked over the years. They have shown us how much entrepreneurship has evolved over the last three decades. We want to thank them for the reality and practicality they have provided to our thinking. Likewise, we also owe a great deal to our many students around the world who have gone on to create a wide variety of firms and/or to teach entrepreneurship. Much of the research work that underpins this book is not just our own, but also the work of hundreds of our colleagues who have built the academic foundation of this field since we first entered it over 30 years ago. Without their research and insights, this book would be just a collection of old wives tales.

To keep this book from being a boring academic tome, we have chosen not to cite every piece of research work that is meaningful (and useful) in the field. We owe a lot to the research studies that can be found in the primary journals in the field: *Journal of Small Business Management, Entrepreneurship: Theory and Practice, Journal of Business Venturing, Entrepreneurship and Regional Development, Journal of Small Business Economics, Family Business Review*, and *Journal of Enterprising Culture*. We realize how much this field has grown since we first entered it. Today there are over 100 academic journals in the field and thousands of universities around the world with programs and courses in entrepreneurship.

No institution has influenced the field more than a 35-year-old research conference focused on the field. Thus we want to acknowledge the Babson College Entrepreneurship Research Conference (BCERC), which has long been the place where the best research and new theories have been presented. In fact, this book is being wrapped up while at the 2015 BCERC meeting in Boston. We are also indebted to the International Council on Small Business, the oldest professional organization for those interested in entrepreneurship, which founded the oldest journal in the field over 50 years ago and remains a significant source of information on entrepreneurship of a small business management. These groups are among the academic foundation stones for this book.

Next, we feel we must acknowledge the financial support of the following organizations. First we want to thank the Kauffman Foundation of Kansas City, Missouri, then The Åbo Akademi Foundation, and finally TEKES (The Finnish National Technology Agency) for their support to some of our work over the years. Finally, we want to thank our families (and pets) for their support to our efforts and the reality check they constantly provide us when it comes to what is important in life. This reminds us to say every successful entrepreneur will have to constantly deal with balancing work-life issues.

The What

We will begin this book by covering in Chapter 1 on what entrepreneurship is and its various roles in world's economy. We look as well at its historical and philosophical underpinnings. We then discuss some of the characteristics of an entrepreneur and the various contexts in which entrepreneurial behavior occurs. This includes some discussion on various theories about entrepreneurs and entrepreneurial behavior. We do this because we believe challenging your preconceived assumptions with research-based theory will be useful. Using both mini-cases and short vignettes, we provide examples of some of those characteristics and the importance of acting upon the intention to become an entrepreneur. Finally, we provide you with some exercises to do.

In Chapter 2 on fundamentals we have a lengthy discussion on what is success and what it means to become a successful entrepreneur. This includes looking simply beyond making money to helping you, the reader, to develop your own personal definition of success for the venture. Using a mini-case and several short vignettes, we explore the various meanings of both success and failure in a new venture. We also give you some exercises in the chapters, which we hope will encourage you to action. Sometimes taking action will bring success, and at other times they will bring failure. We try to make it plain that failure does not mean the end of becoming an entrepreneur, but that is only a part of the learning process of creating a new venture. To us, motivation is a key to being a successful entrepreneur and knowing yourself. In this a key task is goal setting, both short and long term.

In Chapter 3 we get to the "core" of the new venture creation process. We discuss how you find a good idea and how to exploit an opportunity to create a new venture. We think this is often the most underappreciated aspect of the process. While a poor idea with a great team pushing it can sometimes be a viable business, the better option is a good-to-great idea being led by a great entrepreneurial team. To achieve this business concept requires knowing not only what is happening in the external environment but also in terms of what you bring to the venture as the would-be entrepreneur. We discuss a variety of topics including creativity and innovation, and provide you with some examples via mini-cases and examples.

Moving on Chapter 4, we discuss everything we think you ought to know about marketing initially. You will need marketing to develop your products and services in terms of characteristics that customers want. We will direct you to understand your market in terms of their needs, wants, and fears. Using a variety of examples, including cases, we talk about how an entrepreneur needs to do market research and effective and inexpensive methods to do this work. We also discuss the feared topic of "how to sell," something most books on entrepreneurship ignore but which we feel is exceptionally important. If you are afraid to ask for the cash, or the contract, you are going to need to get over that fear.

Next we turn to a more detailed discussion in Chapter 5 on your core business concept in terms of what is your product or service and how to develop them. We discuss the importance of using marketing data in the development of your product/service regardless if you are doing a piece of technology or creating a new dish for your eating establishment. Developing a prototype is now so much easier with 3D printers and menu testing. We think this area, well known in technology entrepreneurship in engineering schools, is a core skill every entrepreneur needs to know and practice in an ongoing basis. Once again we provide you with some mini-case examples.

Then we turn to a discussion in Chapter 6 on fundamentals of building an entrepreneurial organization. We include the seemingly boring, but highly critical, topics of hiring, firing, and retaining your entrepreneurial team and employees. We discuss how organizational structure is built in a new firm, including the pros and cons of outsourcing. We then turn our attention to why every entrepreneur needs to have legal and accounting advice in the process of the formation of the new venture to ensure appropriate tax treatment. We also discuss the role of governance of the firm and the need for buy-sell agreements and intellectual property protection as well.

In Chapter 7 we turn to entrepreneurial finance and the search for capital. While everyone thinks this is the most critical part of creating any new venture, we argue that it is only after you understand what you are doing other things first. Do you really understand your business concept? What are your markets? How to reach these markets? Then and only then can you discuss how much money you need and where to get it. We put emphasis on the use of bootstrap financing and achieving profitability as frankly this is what 98 percent of all entrepreneurs will ultimately use to start their venture. We then discuss the importance of cash-flow management as the very essence of entrepreneurial finance. We acknowledge and discuss angel, venture capital, and hedge fund financing but note the true rareness of these as tools. We acknowledge that most entrepreneurs will have little or no access to significant outside resources in starting their ventures.

Next we turn to the fundamental area of growing your new venture and managing that growth in Chapter 8. We spend some time discussing the myth of high growth firms and why profitability is the primary financial goal for any new venture if success is a goal. We also discuss further issues of having family members in the business. We examine the issues of growing beyond one location and moving into international markets. Once again we provide examples and mini-cases to show the issues that are encountered in growing a business and managing it. We believe you have to learn to manage growth or it will kill your venture.

Finally, we turn to the fundamentals of planning in Chapter 9. We explore the planning process for the venture and the execution of your intentions regarding the business. We discuss when you need to have an actually written plan. We discuss when you do planning in the process of creating a new venture and what should be included in those plans or parts of plans. We comment on who will most likely want to see your business plan and why they want to see it. We then discuss why concept pitches to investors are a form of plan and why impression management in plans is important. In this final chapter we go through the planning process in some detail along with examples and how to see plans as a roadmap through the uncertainty of starting a new venture. We also address some of the ongoing issues you will have in running an entrepreneurial venture, be it for-profit or not-for-profit.

The Who

Before moving on the topic of entrepreneurship, we feel it may help you understand our position on topics by knowing more about the two of us. Collectively we have been involved in entrepreneurial activities for nearly 60 years and family businesses for over a half century. We have worked together as colleagues over 15 years, despite being separated by thousands of miles, living on two different continents, and having two different native tongues. Malin's first language is Swedish, her second is Finnish, and she is highly fluent in English. On the other hand, Alan's only language is a strange form of English, known to some as *Texan*. Despite the translational issues (wink), we have managed to overcome the barrier of being divided by the common language of English (a challenge Winston Churchill often mentioned). Both of us are only children and are very familiar with each of us having our own way. This has meant that if we were to be successful as research and writing colleagues, we had learned to cooperate, a skill we find every entrepreneur needs to learn if it is not already a part of their personality.

So that you have some further idea of who we are, you will find in the following text some information about our individual professional credentials and careers. Hopefully this information will let you understand how we blend in this book our experiences with entrepreneurial ventures with a rigorous understanding of the research that underpins this book. As we have said earlier, we want to thank our families for being supportive of our collaboration over the years. We have seen kids and pets grow up in our families and we sometimes think of each other as siblings as much as research colleagues. Yes that sometimes means we sometimes fight and frequently disagree, but from those interactions come clarity of thinking we have found useful.

Malin Brännback, D.Sc., is Chaired Professor of International Business and Dean at Åbo Akademi University from where she also received her doctoral degree in management science in 1996. She also holds a B.Sc. in pharmacy granted in 1986, also from Åbo Akademi University. After she completed her doctoral degree, she was appointed Associate Professor in Information systems at University of Turku. In 2000 she was recruited to Turku School of Economics and Business Administration as Professor in Marketing and became the founding head of the Innomarket research group. Innomarket's focus was to support start-up biotechnology companies in their commercialization processes. In 2003 she was appointed Chaired Professor in International Business at Åbo Akademi University. She has served as Vice-Rector of the university as well. Currently she is Docent at the Turku School of Economics where she taught prior to returning to Åbo and she is Docent at the Swedish School of Economics and Business Administration in Helsinki (Hanken). She has been Visiting Professor in Entrepreneurship at Stockholm Business School (Stockholm University) since 2012. She has been on the boards of several biotechnology and IT start-up firms. She has held a variety of teaching and research positions in such fields as information systems, international marketing, strategic management, and pharmacy.

She has 200 publications in areas such as entrepreneurship, biotechnology, marketing, and knowledge management. She has co-authored seven books with Alan Carsrud, some of which are *Entrepreneurship* (2007) Greenwood Publishing; *Understanding the Entrepreneurial Mind: Opening the Black Box* (2009) Springer Verlag; *Understanding Family Businesses: Undiscovered Approaches, Unique perspectives, and Neglected Topics* (2012) Springer Verlag; and *Handbook of Research Methods and Applications in Entrepreneurship and Small Businesses* (2014) Edward Elgar. In addition, she has published three case books with Alan Carsrud on family business with Springer Verlag. She, Alan, and Niklas Kiviluoto recently published *Understanding the Myth of High Growth Firms: The Theory of the Greater Fool* (2014) with Springer Verlag. She is on the review board of *Journal of Small Business Management*. Her current research interests are in entrepreneurial intentionality, entrepreneurial cognition, and entrepreneurial growth and performance in technology entrepreneurship, as well as use of social media and the role of culture and language in business.

Malin resides just outside Åbo (Turku), Finland, in the south-west Finnish archipelago with her husband (Patrik), their three children (Anton, Anna, and Axel), and their two dogs. She is an avid and accomplished chef along with her husband. She enjoys any food with lemons and wine (especially Italian). She loves to knit, can throw a mean clay pot on a wheel, and enjoys working in her garden when it is not freezing (yes there are hot summers in Finland). She adores sitting in the sun on Santorini in the summer as well as enjoying a long weekend in Rome with her husband.

Alan L. Carsrud, Ph.D., Ec.D., was reared in his family's Texas and Ohio ranching and farm business. His father was a clinical psychologist and Alan followed initially in his footsteps. He holds a Ph.D. and M.A. in Social Psychology from the University of New Hampshire, a B.A. in Psychology and Sociology from Texas Christian University. He did postdoctoral work in Applied Industrial Psychology at The University of Texas at Austin. He holds an honorary doctorate in micro-economics from Åbo Akademi University in Finland. Today he is Managing Director of Carsrud & Associates, a consulting firm for entrepreneurs and family-owned and managed firms. His consulting clients have included government agencies like NASA and the Republic of Palau, the Los Angeles Unified School District, large firms like IBM and Ernst and Young, as well as numerous family and entrepreneurial firms in the United States, Finland, Australia, Turkey, India, Mexico, Japan, and Chile. He has been involved in over 200 start-ups in industries such varied as retail, wineries, accounting, food, airlines, biotechnology, the Internet, computer technologies, and even university-based entrepreneurship programs.

His current academic position is Visiting Research Professor and Docent at Åbo Akademi University in Turku (Åbo), Finland. His prior academic positions include holding the inaugural Loretta Rogers Chair in Entrepreneurship at the Ted Rogers School of Management at Ryerson University in Toronto, Canada; Clinical Professor of Entrepreneurship, Professor of Industrial and Systems Engineering, Professor of Hospitality

Management, and Founding Executive Director of the Eugenio Pino and Family Global Entrepreneurship Center at Florida International University. He has been Senior Lecturer and Academic Coordinator of the Price Center at the Anderson School at UCLA and Senior Lecturer in Electrical Engineering at the Samueli School at UCLA. He has also been on the graduate faculties of the Australian Graduate School of Management, Bond University (Australia), Durham University (UK), Anahuac University (Mexico), Nanyang Technological University (Singapore), University of Southern California, Pepperdine University, The University of Texas at Austin, Texas A&M University, and the State University of New York at Brockport.

He is a Fellow of the Family Firm Institute (FFI) and has served on the board of directors of FFI and the United States Association for Small Business and Entrepreneurship. He is Associate Editor of the *Journal of Small Business Management*, and co-founded *Entrepreneurship and Regional Development*. He also is on the Review Boards of the *Family Business Review* and the *International Journal of Entrepreneurship and Innovation*. He founded the UCLA Venture Development and Global Access Programs, which help create new, technology-based ventures in Australia, Chile, Finland, France, Italy, Mexico, and the United States. In addition, he created the Family and Closely Held Business Program at UCLA. He has published over 230 articles and chapters on entrepreneurship, family business, social psychology, mental retardation, and clinical psychology. He has co-authored with Dr. Brännback seven books on entrepreneurship and family business, and they have three additional books under contract.

Alan resides outside Austin, Texas, in the Texas Hill Country with his husband of 14 years, Danny, and their three cats (no he is not *a cat lady* yet as that takes four cats) and a half dozen hummingbirds. He and Danny are an avid collectors of Australian aboriginal art, Cuban surrealist paintings, Mexican cubist works, Chinese and Japanese antiques, various antiquities, as well as African sculptures and masks. When not working with Malin on various books and research articles, he is usually found on the patio tending his rose bushes with a glass of wine, or a Chilean pisco sour, in hand.

What Is This Thing Called *Entrepreneurship?*

1.0 Introduction

Pick up any newspaper or business publication anywhere in the world today, such as the *Financial Times*, *New York Times*, Singapore's *Straits Times*, the *Sydney Morning Herald*, or the *Economist*, and you are likely to find an article in which a politician or an economist is stating how important entrepreneurship is to the nation and that we need more entrepreneurs to ensure economic growth and prosperity. In these same publications you will also find other stories about entrepreneurs themselves. Most of us will ignore the economist's or politician's pontifications and focus our attention on those compelling stories about the valiant entrepreneurs and their uphill battles to create successful ventures. We also sometimes enjoy the stories of the great failures as well. These are also the stories that frequently are seen as documentaries on TV and even award-winning movies (e.g., *The Social Network* in 2010 about Facebook or *Jobs* in 2013 about the founder of Apple). As the Kauffman Foundation of Kansas City, Missouri recently has stated:

> We have a myth in our heads of what the prototypical startup founder is, and that myth is an early- to mid-20s white male who studied computer science at an elite school and dropped out.

1.1 The Entrepreneur

These myths and stories usually come in two forms. One story type is a tale of somebody who had an idea that very few understood or believed in, but who with determination and perhaps sheer luck was in the right spot at the right time and *voilà!* What a wonderful success story, with some drama thrown in for good measure! Quite often, it is a story on a successful entrepreneur who has traveled from rags to riches through hard work and an ability to make the right decisions at the right time. But the college dropout has not always been the entrepreneurial myth. We will explore some other models of the would-be entrepreneur. For example, Hollywood has found great movie scripts in the entrepreneurial tales of the lives of Henry Ford and Thomas Alva Edison. Yet Hollywood has yet to tell the stories of some famous female entrepreneurs like Madam C. J. Walker who turned her homemade recipes for hair and scalp care products into a business empire that made her the United States' first self-made black female millionaire in the early 1900s.

The alternative story type is the story of a local or national entrepreneur celebrating an anniversary for being in business half a century and now handing over the firm to the next generation. You most likely will read these two types of stories because they are spectacular and entertaining. We may also be personally familiar with their products or services. You may even know these entrepreneurs personally. These stories are intriguing because they often capture some of "how dreams come true." Have any of these entrepreneurs served as personal role models? Ask yourself whether reading any of these stories or seeing these movies made you dream that you could be an entrepreneur? You do not have to be a dropout of a top college to have these dreams. Nor do you have to be under 60, or be independently wealthy to be an entrepreneur as we demonstrate in this book.

1.2 Entrepreneurial Dreams and Their Outcomes

Even Sigmund Freud would admit that both dreams and words can have various meanings. As with all words and dreams, they come with both good and bad connotations. The word "dream" is most likely related to the Germanic *draugmus*, (meaning deception, illusion, or phantom) or the Norse *draugr* (ghost, apparition), or even the Sanskrit *druh* (seek to harm or injure). Have you ever wondered whether your entrepreneurial dream could become one of these stories? Elias Howe (1819–1867) was reported to have said that the inspiration for his invention of the sewing machine came from a dream about being attacked by cannibals bearing spears that looked like the needle he then designed for his machine. Similarly Nikola Tesla is said to have been able to imagine a device in his mind's eye and then build it without ever having to write anything down, certainly an interesting form of "day dreaming."

Biographies of entrepreneurs who became self-made billionaires are frequently best sellers much for the same reason. They tell stories of dreams coming true. One only needs to think of the recent biography on Steve Jobs and the dramatic events at Apple or the movie about Mark Zuckerberg and the drama behind the founding of Facebook. We also see many of these stories focused on men, but one cannot ignore the stories of famous women entrepreneurs like Coco Chanel (fashion), or Madame C. J. Walker, Elizabeth Arden, Dame Anita Roddick, and Estée Lauder (cosmetics), or Olive Ann Beech (aircraft), Oprah Winfrey and Martha Stewart (media), or Ruth Handler (who gave us "Barbie" and co-founded *Mattel Toys*).

How many of you are familiar with famous entrepreneurs from around the world who you most likely *don't know that you know?* Consider Sweden's Ingvar Kamprad (retail), or the Netherlands' Gerard Adriaan Heineken (brewing), or Chile's Don Melchor de Santiago Concha y Toro and his wife Emiliana Subercaseaux (wineries), or Japan's Takeshi Mitarai (electronics). In all these men and women one sees a picture of the entrepreneur as a person who is visionary, hardworking, risk taking, ambitious, having exceptional leadership skill, one who never gives up, and a great source of inspiration. We like to describe them as having *an entrepreneurial mindset* (Brännback and Carsrud 2009). What all these men and women have done is to show that these qualities, in combination with a brilliant idea and the ability to market, results in a great company that ultimately made the entrepreneur very wealthy. However, is wealth the only definition of success? For many of these people, success was changing an industry or creating something that was sustainable and enduring as a business over generations.

To most of us, many of the companies cited are examples of successful entrepreneurs and entrepreneurship. They are enduring *brands* created centuries ago that we still use. Successful entrepreneurship is not only about what is created here and now. It is not only about computers and Internet business (Apple, Dell, Amazon, or eBay). It is also about sustainability over time. For a thorough discussion on lasting brands and their entrepreneurs, one needs to read Koehn (2001).

1.3 There Is No One Narrative

The great engineer and scientist Nikola Tesla, who gave away many of his patents and was often a "loner," is also a great example of someone using his own unique definition of success. While making money is one way you know that selling that idea is creating value for customers, it is not the only definition of success. There are many ways to spell SUCCESS. This is what we consider successful entrepreneurship and how we often describe a successful entrepreneur. Success is very much in the eye of the beholder and depends on the goals the entrepreneur has set for themselves. We have more to say about both the entrepreneurial mindset and success later in this book.

If you were to name a few successful entrepreneurs today, you are likely to mention Steve Jobs, Michael Dell, Martha Stewart, Mark Zuckerberg, Oprah Winfrey, and perhaps Henry Ford because you know or even own and use their products. Not all of you will know who Peter Thorwöste, Josiah Wedgwood, Erling Persson, Billy Durant, or Anita Roddick are. However, many of you know or own products from companies for whom these were the founders: FISKARS scissors, Wedgwood china, H&M clothing, General Motors, or the Body Shop cosmetics.

Consider Peter Thorwöste, who founded Fiskars Ironworks in 1649, which today is known as *FISKARS*, the global company manufacturing not just of the scissors with the orange handles (see Figure 1.1) but also garden tools, ceramics, and boats. Fiskars is today a leading global supplier of branded consumer products for the home, garden, and outdoors. Brands like Fiskars, Iittala, Royal Copenhagen, Rörstrand, Arabia, Buster, and Gerber all belong to the Fiskars brand palette.

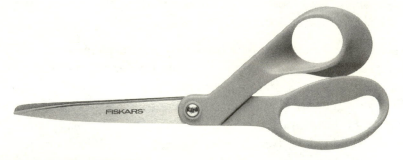

Figure 1.1 Fiskars scissors.

Figure 1.2 Wedgwood pottery.

Then there is Josiah Wedgwood, an English potter who founded the Wedgwood pottery firm in 1759. This firm's products are still selling, and the brand Wedgwood china (along with its Waterford Crystal line) is known worldwide for its quality (see Figure 1.2). While writing this book, we learned that Fiskars on May 11, 2015 agreed to acquire the WWRD group. In addition to Wedgwood, other luxury brands in WWRD include Waterford, Royal Doulton, Royal Albert, and Rogaška. These brands are now part of this very same Finnish family firm. This is a great reminder of how successful entrepreneurs can create ventures and products that continue to impact business and the lives of consumers several hundred years later.

So is Heinz, today most well-known for its ketchup. Few of us may know that their breakthrough product was pickled horseradish. Their well-known logo '57 Varieties' created in 1896, and was the first electric sign on Manhattan lit in 1900. Recently H. J. Heinz has been purchased from the founding family by Warren Buffett's Berkshire Hathaway and 3G Capital. Then there is the Henry Ford and the Ford Motor Company that changed not only manufacturing processes but also the automotive industry. The firm still remains largely in family control through a complex ownership structure.

1.4 Collective Dreams

We all dream and some of us even hallucinate. Dreams are a part of many inventions. If we think of technology, then Thomas A. Edison often comes to mind. He was an "inventor" and entrepreneur who brought electric lights into homes and founded electric generation companies that still bear his name, even General Electric (GE) was founded by Edison. However, the story of electricity would not be complete without acknowledging Nikola Tesla who many say was the first to develop alternating current (among many other numerous breakthrough inventions) while Edison's team focused on direct current.

As with all breakthrough inventions, many people are involved. For example, there were 22 others ahead of Edison in inventing the light bulb, but it was Edison who knew the power of marketing and branding. That is, pioneers in an industry like Tesla are often not the ones who win the prize or the wealth and acclaim, but those who came after them and understood how to develop a business model to exploit that invention. Success is not always about being first, or as some say, one gets "shot by other pioneers coming up behind you." Part of the task of any entrepreneur is to get those on their teams to have similar dreams, if not buy into the one of the founder(s).

1.5 Why Entrepreneurship Became Important

Here we are going to get a bit academic, so forgive us. You should realize that the terms *entrepreneurship* and entrepreneur have been around for centuries. Some consider Cantillion in 1755 as having been the first to mention the phenomena in a published work. Still others claim Say (1803) was first. Regardless, Hoselitz (1951) finds early traces in historical dictionaries to the Middle Ages in the normal course of development of the French language. The most general and probably the earliest meaning is "celui qui entreprend quelque chose," which literarily means "he who gets things done," in other words an active person. The preceding discussion shows that the term has stirred up considerable academic debate for quite some time even though Schumpeter (1934) is often considered to be the intellectual father of the modern field of entrepreneurship.

It is our considered opinion that entrepreneurship became important in contemporary life in 1987 to be precise. In that year entrepreneurship came to be regarded as a significant factor in *national* wealth creation, not just personal wealth creation. It thus entered the awareness of the wider, modern, audience. In 1987 David Birch published his book *Job Creation in America*. This book was the result of a longitudinal study carried out at MIT (Massachusetts Institute of Technology) between 1969 and 1986. The study traced 12 million individual business establishments during this period of time. The raw data was from Dun and Bradstreet (D&B), single unit stand-alone companies; a store, a small plant or a law firm. In 1986 the establishments employed 95% of all non-governmental workers in the United States. The complete files of D&B were tapped regularly during this time period. The files had information on employment rolls, age, and location of each establishment.

Birch's study showed that small start-up firms were responsible for more than 80% of all new jobs created in the United States and that large corporations in fact decreased employment. Small firms are more likely to expand than large organizations. If large firms were to create new jobs that would take place through *a new business unit*, not a new firm. To be blunt: large firms create new jobs through the formation of new business units. Mom and Pop Delis open up a second store managed by the owner's daughter. Statistics from the U.S. Small Business Administration has over the years remained fairly stable and the same holds for most Western countries; 99.5% of all firms in a country are classified as small firms. This holds for the United States, Australia, Chile, India, or Finland. In 2015 there is evidence from the United States that 310 new entrepreneurs per every 100,000 adults were added each month. This is up from a monthly average of 280 in 2014. This indicates entrepreneurial levels have returned to a more normal pattern since the great recession of 2008. Of equal interest is that in 2013, 23 million people were self-employed, according to the U.S. Census Bureau. For whatever reason, more and more individuals are choosing different paths to being an entrepreneur.

1.6 Challenging Assumptions—Entrepreneurship Is for All

That is, the results from the study by Birch challenged the long-held assumption that large organizations were the engines and drivers of a national economy in terms of job creation, innovation, and growth. A follow-up study to Birch's was presented by Bruce Kirchhoff and Bruce

Philips in the same year, but with different data. That study confirmed the findings by Birch. Both studies included recessions. Kirchhoff and Philips discovered that during recessions the job creation effect was extremely high, in fact 100% during 1980–1982. While we know that it is during recessions that large organizations lay off people, this evidence seems to have come as news to the general public and to politicians in particular.

These results caught the attention of politicians and legislators and as pointed out by Brännback et al. (2014) that each president since Ronald Reagan has endorsed growth and entrepreneurship in major addresses. The European Union (EU) signed the Lisbon treaty in 2001, which specifically states that the EU will provide substantial support to entrepreneurship as a way to create economic growth within EU. The word *entrepreneur* has been so widely used in recent years in the United States and in Europe that you often wonder who is *not* included. We discuss who is an entrepreneur later in this chapter.

One of the myths that we want to challenge at the very front of this book is that entrepreneurship is only for a few, or that it is a male career, or that most entrepreneurs are wealthy to before they start a firm. Another myth is that successful entrepreneurship only happens among those with a technology background. While there is some evidence to support that men outnumber women as entrepreneurs, that statistic is rapidly changing in the United States and worldwide.

Likewise, the number of entrepreneurs among the poor and disabled has been increasing in recent years. One reason is reflected in the work of Noble Peace Prize winner Dr. Muhammad Yunus, a Bangladeshi economist from Chittagong University. Professor Yunus created the Nobel Peace Prize winning Grameen Bank (www.GrameenFoundation.org) with the focus on women. He recognized that women were the ones usually in charge of the family's money and were far more likely to repay loans than were men who typically would waste money on drink and other women. What Yunus was building on was the fact that women are less likely to waste money on highly risky ventures and as evidenced by Grameen's success. However, they were more likely to create sustainable businesses and support their families. Another group that has exploited the same concept is Women's World Banking (www.womensworldbanking.org). Interesting immigrants in the

United States have a higher incidence of new venture creation than nonimmigrants.

Technology entrepreneurship has been all the rage for decades and increasingly more and more women are becoming involved in starting technology firms. There are programs to foster technology firms and these exist worldwide. These programs have fostered firms like Google that came from work done at Stanford and fostered by the Stanford Technology Ventures Program (www.stvp.stanford.edu). In the United States there are programs for returning military veterans at Syracuse University and UCLA, for social and "green" entrepreneurs at Colorado State University, and for the disabled at the University of Illinois at Chicago, to name just a few. The point we want to make here is that entrepreneurship is for everyone regardless of gender, race, sexual orientation, location, personal wealth, or physical health. In this chapter we hope we will challenge you to think of people from all walks of life who have chosen an entrepreneurial path for their lives and have made a difference. Perhaps what these programs show is that there are a variety of environments in which entrepreneurship can exist and in which entrepreneurs can thrive.

1.7 Entrepreneurial Environments

Birch's study also showed that new firms, which take the place of older ones, tend to relocate and use a different workforce, and other resources such as needs of capital, transportation, governmental services, education, recreation, and energy. In fact, Birch's study offered a preview of where next "business hot beds" were likely to emerge. One such was Austin, Texas, which discuss later in this chapter regarding an interesting mix of technology and artistic entrepreneurship. Birch showed that small firms and entrepreneurs were important for economic development of regions and subsequent studies confirmed this finding as well. Some of the best known examples are Silicon Valley and Route 128 that became models for similar examples worldwide. We are seeing entrepreneurial revival in rust belt cities like Detroit who have had to reinvent themselves.

For a thorough discussion encounter of the importance of regional developments in these areas, please read Saxenian's (1994) book *Regional Advantage: Culture and Competition in Silicon Valley and Route 128.*

Regional agglomerations of business activities and communities exist everywhere and tend to be specialized to certain industries or eco-systems. For example, today these even have their own annual trade shows like SXSW (South by Southwest) attracting all major actors in the industries of internet, interactive digital technology, music, and films. Another is the Consumer Electronics Show held annually in Las Vegas where cutting-edge technology usually launches. One need only think of how the Detroit Auto Show still dominates the automobile industry or how the Paris Air Show does in aircraft.

1.8 National Innovation Systems for Entrepreneurs

The development of national innovation systems was also a result of Birch's findings. These are governmental initiatives on a macro level aimed at institutions. It has always been claimed that national innovation systems are for the benefit of individual entrepreneurs, but research results are not conclusive here. In many cases national innovation systems remained abstract and distant to the everyday entrepreneurs. It is important that we as individuals realize and recognize that entrepreneurship significantly impacts our lives, not just about job creation but also as a source for developing effective and innovative solutions for environmental and social problems. In many countries cultural institutions such as libraries and concert halls, universities, and foundations carry the names of successful entrepreneurs who have been significant donors to these organizations.

It is also important to understand that entrepreneurship is not only about small firms. In fact, large organizations can be extremely entrepreneurial. This is often called *corporate entrepreneurship*. The entrepreneur may be missing, but usually the champion is then called an *innovator*. In that context entrepreneurship and innovation—or entrepreneur and innovator—have come to mean the same. Yet, following Kirzner (1973) and different from Schumpeter's (1934) ideas, entrepreneurship does not always require what most people would think of as innovation.

Since the publication of the study by Birch, entrepreneurship and firm growth have been firmly on the agenda, be it government policy, academic research, or public press. There are those who firmly believe that entrepreneurship and growth are synonyms. They are not, as we show in our book (Brännback et al. 2014), and which we discuss later in this book. They are not synonyms and neither entrepreneurship nor growth is always good or successful.

What we have shown in this discussion is that entrepreneurship is a critical element for the economic improvement of an individual, a family, a firm, a region, and a nation. To us this means that entrepreneurship can exist in small firms as much as in large organization. It exists in for-profit firms and in nonprofit social ventures. Growth and innovation are often associated with entrepreneurship and entrepreneurial firms, but not always. As we show in the following text, personal wealth creation is not always what drives an entrepreneur. It can be a desire to work independently, but also more altruistic ambitions like solving social problems.

1.8.1 Incubators and Accelerators

At this point we want to make some comments on the role of new venture incubators and accelerators. Both of us have been involved with these programs and have worked with firms in these programs in a number of countries. We have seen incubators aimed at wireless technology, cell phone apps, biotechnology, agriculture, and even new food products. Hundreds, if not thousands, of these organizations exist all over the planet. Every major research university either has one on campus or there is one located nearby. Just look at Silicon Valley or Route 128 outside Boston to see evidence of such activities. Cities with a desire to attract or retain technology talent have fostered these activities which may be either for-profit or not-for-profit in form. One only need to look at the American television shows like *Shark Tank* and its spin-offs in Canada and elsewhere to see the desire to have both financial and professional support that these institutions can provide.

However, the evidence to day is at best inconclusive if incubators really help new ventures become successful. The same outcome may well be true of accelerators. Certainly, many of these groups can claim successful firms among their graduates, but many successful firms are generated without any such supporting organization. It really is a matter of hard work on the part of the entrepreneur. We are trying to say that it takes more than just being in a program like a new venture incubator. Being accepted is not a guarantee of success. Be aware there are scams even in this industry.

1.9 Entrepreneurs: Made or Born

As human beings we like to nurture these stories because they tell us that it is possible to become a financially successful entrepreneur and because most of these are well-known. What we tend to forget, or even realize, is that all of these companies started small and the path to that success was anything but assured. With these stories, we try to discern the fundamentals of who an entrepreneur is or in some cases collective entrepreneurs or entrepreneurial teams. We assume if we can define who an entrepreneur is, we will then be able to identify these people and encourage them. We fail to realize those same skills are used to be successful in any profession.

We also must remember that success for many is not defined by money, but often filling another goal like Jonas Salk and his desire to eradicate polio. His focus was developing a safe and effective vaccine as rapidly as possible. He had no desire in personal profit. When asked who owned the patent to his vaccine, Salk said, "There is no patent. Could you patent the Sun?" His goals were not monetary but included founding the Salk Institute in La Jolla, California, which carries on his vaccine work even today. Some consider Salk an early social entrepreneur long before the term appeared in the media.

1.10 Who Is an Entrepreneur?

This leads us to start a discussion on who is an entrepreneur. According to the *Global Entrepreneurship Monitor* (GEM), there are those who become entrepreneurs by *necessity* (no income, starving, etc.) and those who are *opportunistic* (exploit a need, market, invention, etc.). Most of the following discussion focuses on the latter group, the *opportunistic entrepreneur*. It should be noted early on that the distinction is not a pure one and includes a great deal of overlap. That said, there is increasing evidence that at least in the United States there is a significant increase in the number of new entrepreneurs who are starting their own businesses because they see an opportunity, not because they are out of work and unable to get a job (*necessity entrepreneurs*). This may explain why immigrants in the United States have higher new venture creation rates than nonimmigrants, but most of these new firms are actually more opportunistic. These *opportunistic entrepreneurs* now represent nearly 80 percent of total new entrepreneurs an increase from the numbers found in the years following the Great Recession. Now let us turn to the defining who is an entrepreneur in more detail.

In the late 1980s academics tried to define who an entrepreneur is and what is entrepreneurial. William Gartner's article "Who is an entrepreneur? Is the wrong question" was published in 1988. Our friend Bill questioned the idea of "an entrepreneur." He argued that the *why* question tends to be answered with a description of *who*. Later other researchers tried to reframe the research agenda and define *what* an entrepreneur does, *why* they do, *how* they do, and then *who* this doer is. It has been argued that if we could find the answers to these questions, we should be able to design targeted educational programs to create more entrepreneurs. Completing an exam in entrepreneurship, or majoring in entrepreneurship at a university, would then be a rational solution to creating entrepreneurs. But, most of us know that this is not exactly the way it works. Certainly entrepreneurs have existed for millennia and certainly long before anyone developed a course on how to be one at universities such as Texas, Harvard, Stanford, New South Wales, Helsinki, or Oxford.

If one cannot make people into a functional entrepreneur, we rationalize that entrepreneurs are really born, that entrepreneurial behaviors are genetic—often using family firms as examples. But, anyone in a family business will attest that succession in family firms is among the most difficult tasks to carry out. Not all children are interested, willing or even able to take over the firm. Sometimes none of them are. And the ones who may be interested are not the ones the present owner wants as successor. Some children have no desire to live the life of a "constantly-on-the-job" parent who is an entrepreneur. While the parent's hardworking may reflect the cost of being successful, not all children see that as desirable for themselves or as a factor in being a successful parent.

1.11 The Entrepreneurial Personality

Then there are those who will argue that becoming an entrepreneur and a successful entrepreneur is all about personality. We do believe having a personality compatible with entrepreneurial life is critical. But that compatibility often is contextually bound, depending on the idea, the market, and the culture in which one finds oneself operating. Frequently, it is argued that entrepreneurs are risk takers and innovators, but in many cases that is not the case. We acknowledge that there are certain personality types and motivational styles often associated with entrepreneurship in Europe, the United States, and some of the former British Empire. We also know that Persian Jews turned to entrepreneurial activity as that was the only one available to them in a conservative Muslim environment.

These personality factors, however, may not be consistent in their impact in other cultures such as Asia, Latin America, or Africa. There is some indication that there are even gender differences across cultures. What this says is that the issue of what is a unique entrepreneurial personality is not a simple answer. What we have learned is that what personality and motivational factors that make someone successful as an entrepreneur are the same as those that make one a successful pilot, scientist, or academic (Carsrud and Brännback 2011).

We know from years of psychological research that the characteristics of a successful entrepreneurs in the United States and most of Europe are the same kind of characteristics found in any ambitious persons, whether lawyer, doctor, airline pilot, that is, who are good at their professions. We know that there are high levels of some of the different components of achievement motivation for all of these. What we also know is that pattern may be different in different cultures when it comes to entrepreneurs. One component that seems to be consistent is the desire to work hard. Another is the willingness to learn new and different things. The role of a competitive personality seems to vary by cultural context as does the interaction of these factors with each other. In other words, if you have what it takes to be a good scientist, lawyer, academic, pilot, or other professional, you most likely have what it takes motivationally to be an entrepreneur.

1.12 Entrepreneurial Mindset

We also argue that entrepreneurs and successful entrepreneurs have a different mindset and attitudes (Brännback and Carsrud 2009). Research has found differences in the cognitive styles of entrepreneurs and that successful entrepreneurs have different entrepreneurial leadership styles. Some of these skills can be taught, so entrepreneurial education is not all bad. Because some characteristics are attitudes that can be influenced through education, but some of this is closer to *art*. For an in-depth discussion of various aspects of the entrepreneurial mind, we refer you to our edited volume (Carsrud and Brännback 2009) in which there are 15 chapters dedicated to various topics about the entrepreneurial mind.

Based on research, we strongly believe that any person with a desire to pursue an opportunity and to achieve a goal can be entrepreneurial and can become an entrepreneur if all other factors are equal. While we have to be cautious in defining success—as that is also a matter of kind and degree—it is possible for any entrepreneur to be successful. In Chapter 2 we return to the discussion of what success means. Moreover, for a person to be entrepreneurial does not mean that the person has to start a for-profit company as demonstrated in the preceding example of Dr. Jonas Salk.

To us entrepreneurship is an attitude toward life as much as it is an ability to create and then lead a firm. Having said that, we think it is vital to understand how entrepreneurs think since we also argue that entrepreneurs appear to perceive their reality differently than those who are not entrepreneurs. For example, why do some persons, and not others, decide to become entrepreneurs? Why do some quit a job in a large firm with a good salary and nice benefits and become life-style entrepreneurs by starting a winery or an art gallery? How do some consider such an option desirable and feasible while others do not? While theory maintains that opportunities exist when there is a competitive imperfection, we argue that very few entrepreneurs consider a potential opportunity in those terms.

We believe most potential entrepreneurs will think of a possible idea from the personal perspective of whether it is something one wants to do (desirable) and something one thinks one can do (feasible). This notion is consistent with *the theory of planned behavior*, which posits that a person who finds an opportunity desirable and feasible is likely to create a venture. Absent intention, there is no action, and thus no new venture. For a greater in-depth discussion of this theory, see Carsrud and Brännback (2009) with several chapters that explain aspects of this theory with respect to entrepreneurs.

To make our position clear, this book focuses on *the individual thinking of creating, attempting to, or actually already starting a venture to address an opportunity or need*. Yet, we think it is important to offer some justification to these desires and attempts in a wider perspective. In fact, most societies want entrepreneurs and for these to create ventures. Entrepreneurship is not just associated with Capitalist societies as we find entrepreneurs in avowed Communist countries like Cuba, Vietnam, and China. Most societies, other than North Korea, have realized entrepreneurship is important for national wealth creation. We are sure there are entrepreneurs in North Korea, but this is one place where you can be shot for being one. That ugly reality aside, since the 1980s entrepreneurship has been a mantra for many. It has also become a source of concern when it seems to be in a slow decline as in the United States since 2008. However, entrepreneurship has been around and studied for centuries and we expect it to continue to do so for an unforeseeable future.

Finally, we want to be perfectly clear, *entrepreneurship is for anyone willing to take the time and expend the energy*. Entrepreneurs are men and women. They come in every color of skin and ethnic variety. They are gay, straight, and transgender. They are both young and old. They are geniuses and the not so bright. They may be Olympic athletes and they may have disabilities. You do not have to live in Silicon Valley to become an entrepreneur. We know of plenty of rural entrepreneurs and those in urban centers. You do not have to be rich to be an entrepreneur. We in this book try to give you examples of a wide variety of people who have become entrepreneurs. You can be an entrepreneur regardless of what is thrown at you. We are reminded of a story of a 57-year-old woman whose husband divorced her. She lost everything, including the house, car, and her money. As a parting jab, her ex-husband told her to get a dog. She did, a large English Bull Dog. She started making cards with the dog's picture on them. They sold rapidly, she made more, branched out into other products with the dogs picture. Today, she has the last laugh on her ex-husband as her venture is now a multimillion dollar business. The deciding factor is a mindset.

1.13 Defining Entrepreneurship: It All Depends

While we have used the terms *entrepreneur* and *entrepreneurship* previously, we have not yet defined what these terms mean. To do that, the reader must allow us to digress for another moment into an academic discussion that we feel ultimately will be informative. One reason we think stories about various entrepreneurs have been so intriguing to so many is that these stories reflect a complex set of interrelated phenomena. Trying to frame *entrepreneurship* as a single scholarly domain is nearly impossible. Yet, many have tried as long as entrepreneurship has been recognized or existed as a field of research. Despite plenty of attempts, to date there is no single definition of entrepreneurship. If you have seven entrepreneurship professors in a room, you are likely to have seventeen definitions. Those with psychology backgrounds have one (or two), those coming out of sociology another, economists will have several, and then there are those who come out of finance and management who carry their own bias about the topic. Even accountants are engaged in the field, which is good as too many academics in the field sometimes confuse revenues with profits.

That said, there seems to be a very broad agreement that a commercial entrepreneur (compared to a social entrepreneur) is usually a person who exploits opportunities for the purpose of economic wealth creation. This idea has existed for centuries starting with Cantillion in 1755. Different authors have over the years used different descriptions, implicitly as a risk taker while exploiting opportunities (Cantillon 1755; Knight 1921; and Say 1803), or more explicitly as opportunity creator/innovator (Schumpeter 1934) or as alert seeker of opportunities (Kirzner 1973; Mises 1951). In 1776 Adam Smith actually saw the entrepreneur as a capitalist (Landström 2005). Again, there is still little agreement in the field on how to study how opportunities are formed or exploited.

1.14 Opportunity Recognition

However, there is a common understanding that *an opportunity exists when there are competitive imperfections on a market* (Venkatarman 1997). While Schumpeter (1934) and Kirzer (1973) explicitly recognized that opportunities are at the core of entrepreneurship, they had different views on how opportunities and the entrepreneur were linked. Schumpeter argued that market imperfections (opportunities) were created when the entrepreneur introduced new innovations. Kirzner's (1973) entrepreneur is alert, discovers some imbalance in the market (imperfection), and seeks equilibrium through entrepreneurship. Kirzner's entrepreneur does not have to create anything new but will have to be able to recognize and exploit what is already there. In other words, it is fine to be a copycat.

Put differently, Schumpeter's entrepreneur is on the edge of the production curve and seeks to push the curve outward, thereby creating personal and societal economic wealth. Kirzner's entrepreneur is within the curve and seeks to reach the edge of the production curve by way of entrepreneurship (Landström 2005). We discuss opportunity recognition in greater detail later in this book. What is important here is how stories in the media easily ignore these theoretical differences, but they are there when we look at cutting-edge technology firms and those who are in more traditional industrial sectors.

Academics love to argue in the tradition of which came first, the chicken or the egg. This is played out in academic circles with the ongoing debate of whether opportunities exist out there for everybody to discover and then exploit or whether opportunities are created or formed by the entrepreneur (Alvarez and Barney 2013). In the former case, the existence of opportunities is taken as given and that how opportunities are formed has no impact how an entrepreneur exploits them. The latter is a recent realization that opportunities can be formed in very different ways and that the formation process may actually impact the process by which the opportunities are exploited.

The practical implications of these differences are, however, important. One approach says that anyone can see an opportunity if they are vigilant. The other sees the opportunity as being unique to the individual. It is possible that both are correct but that the opportunities differ. We hope we have not bored you with this academic discourse, but we feel that often the popular press has tended to think that all entrepreneurs are the same and yet the research indicates something far different.

An interesting encounter of attitudes toward life and the pursuit of opportunities is offered by Birch (1987: 91):

> America is a nation of immigrants, but this does not mean we are a cross section of Europe and Africa—and, increasingly, Latin America and the Orient. Rather, this country has always attracted malcontents, who chafed at feudal restrictions in the 18th century and the lack of economic and religious freedom and opportunity in their old countries in the 19th and 20th centuries. Wariness regarding governmental restrictions on these freedoms and opportunities could be seen in colonial unwillingness to follow British imperial policy, which led to the Revolution.

Some have argued this melting pot view of the United States is why Americans are so entrepreneurial vis à vis more homogeneous countries like Japan. Clearly context and culture play a part in how entrepreneurial goals are expressed. In this book we make every effort to show examples of entrepreneurs from around the world we have worked with or are familiar with.

1.15 Entrepreneurial Goals

Some scholars argue that the ultimate goal for entrepreneurship is to create wealth, and if wealth is not created, it is something else than entrepreneurship. This implicitly means that wealth creation is the same as success. This position we have some fundamental difficulty with as wealth may not be the primary or even secondary goal, but just an outgrowth of achieving another goal. Dr. Jonas Salk could have patented his polio vaccine but choice instead to eradicate the disease. To imply you have to be wealthy to be considered an entrepreneur simply is ludicrous.

But, there is another difficulty if you say wealth creation is the only goal of entrepreneurs, because it means that entrepreneurs are entrepreneurs only if they succeed (in wealth creation). That would mean that those who fail are not entrepreneurs. They are something else. The stories of failed entrepreneurs are rarely found in media stories, somehow indicating that failure is less frequent than success. Yet we all know this is not the case. If the twin brothers Francis Edgar Stanley and Freelan Oscar Stanley who founded The Stanley Motor Carriage Company had been successful, we all would be driving steam-driven cars. Failures do occur, some more spectacular than others.

However, even academic researchers have not really looked at failed entrepreneurs. One reason to this is certainly that it is very hard to find entrepreneurs who are willing to talk about their failure. That is simply a very human thing. We rather like to talk about our successes than our failures. It is possible that failure is driven by many of the same factors as success. The reality is that we cannot really understand what drives success without looking at failure. Here is where work done many years ago is informative. There is evidence that entrepreneurs will have as many as seven ventures in a lifetime and yet only one of those will be deemed "a success." The issue is when does that successful try come? Is it at the front of this life-long process or does it happen on the seventh try? Take as another example the bankruptcy statistics to understand the issue is not trying. The real issue is whether society, family, and your attitudes will allow you able to try again. One of our grandfathers once reminded us that you have not really ridden a horse till you have been thrown off and gotten back on again. In many ways entrepreneurship is really like riding a horse, a big bucking one.

1.16 Different Goals for Different Folks

Then there is the fact that an entrepreneur may be in *it* for entirely different reasons than creating wealth. Creating a venture may come from the bare necessity of finding a way of getting food on the table or supporting a family (a necessity entrepreneur), think of our Persian Jews mentioned earlier. Becoming an entrepreneur may be driven by a desire to generate collective wealth—social wealth—the idea of doing well for someone else. In fact, in some cultures individual entrepreneurship is frowned upon as you may be risking the very survival of your family or the community if you fail. Thus, entrepreneurship becomes a community decision and activity.

There is also the reality that for personal reasons, such as increasing ones quality of life (a very subjective definition), an individual may adopt a life style form of entrepreneurship, which is different from those who focus on earning lots of money. Perhaps it is the desire to be able to continue living in one's rural home town, rather than having to move to the big city? Perhaps it is a desire to turn a hobby into a living, for example, a person hooked on surfing or downhill skiing deciding to create a store specializing in surfboards, snow boards, and downhill skis? Perhaps it is a desire to cure a disease, certainly a noble pursuit. The issue is whether the goal set is what really defines success, but is more that is mentioned later in this book. Through this book we give short examples and cases of different types of entrepreneurs to demonstrate that entrepreneurs come in all genders, races, ethnic groups, nationalities, and ages. To us what makes an entrepreneur is *attitude, part of an entrepreneurial mindset.*

1.17 Other Definitional Issues

There is another way to take this definitional issue of entrepreneurship, and that is to try to define what entrepreneurship *is not*. But, that approach is not very helpful either. However, some of our colleagues are on the verge of describing entrepreneurship as something really *exceptional*, that being entrepreneurship is the creation of *high growth firms*. We address the issue of growth in a later chapter of this book . However, for an in-depth discussion on why this is a fool's errand, we refer you to our book *Understanding the Myth of High Growth Firms: The Theory of the Greater Fool* (Brännback et al. 2014).

In the same vein some view second-generation family business owners as not being entrepreneurs, as they did not create the venture but just inherited the firm. If that is the case Ray Kroc was not the entrepreneur at McDonald's nor were the two McDonald brothers Richard and Maurice, but their father Patrick was. This definition would mean that only founders can be entrepreneurs. Just like McDonald's where those who came later would be the acknowledged entrepreneurs, we have plenty of examples of family firms remaining entrepreneurial generation after generation as we can see in firms that reinvent themselves with new products, markets, and organizational structures. Heineken Brewing is another example of a family firm making entrepreneurship happening in terms of new markets and brands under the leadership of Alfred "Freddie" Heineken, the grandson of the founder.

Returning to *Necessity Entrepreneurs*, such as immigrants or oppressed minorities, these individual did not initially discover an opportunity but had to find a way to make a living and therefore had to do something. To say that this is not entrepreneurship is to negate the struggle many of these people have undergone. Interestingly, many necessity-based firms are actually exploiting opportunities and thus the distinction between the types can be fuzzy at best.

There are a few who think that only those with frame-breaking technology can be true entrepreneurs. We totally disagree. These technology entrepreneurs, who are real special cases, face entirely different challenges than many "ordinary" entrepreneurs in established industries or necessity entrepreneurs in trying to survive physically. They need much more initial funding and it takes forever to turn a profit if they ever manage to do so. Biotechnology entrepreneurs are a special case of technology entrepreneurs as that is about developing science first, then technology, and only then figure out whether there is a business opportunity involved there too. Perhaps, the one thing all of the above have in common is hard work and a desire to achieve a goal, which differs for each. If you think being an entrepreneur is easy, this is not the right career choice for you.

1.18 The Self-Employed as Entrepreneurs

Recently, the U.S. Census Bureau estimated the number of domestically based ventures that are ones with no employees expanded by 23 percent in 10 years to a total of more than 23 million firms. Nationally, these *nonemployer* businesses have seen their revenue grow to more than $1.05 trillion. It should be obvious at this point that we take a rather broad and inclusive view of entrepreneurship. We think there are advantages in taking this "big tent" approach to who are entrepreneurs. Take, for example, the creative people or artists who sell their art or craft. In many cases there is little new technology involved in those processes, just paint, clay, metal, and clutter. However, as one will discover, the Internet and digital technology are rapidly changing the visual arts as one can see in the use of *Photoshop* software, or 3D printing. The same can be said for musicians and performance artists who have embraced new technologies in the creation of their art form.

The point is that many self-employed are in fact those who are creating something, not just art, but new technologies like software applications for cell phones. Typically, nonemployer businesses are one-person business, like a freelance graphic designer. We all have people we know who do this on the side as well as friends who blog and sometimes who make an income from on-site advertising. Then there are the YouTube sensations with providing advice on a variety of topics and end up with a huge following. We have seen the same thing happen with Twitter; users who end up making money because of their posts. Sometimes these ventures include family members and friends who aren't paid. These are examples we can all relate to are firms where the venture is entrepreneur's primary source of income. Just think of those real estate agents you know, or even your personal medical doctor. In other cases the single entrepreneur may operate their venture as a *side job*. If you are a parent, you know these people as they provide babysitting and tutoring to your kids.

1.18.1 *The Context for Self-Employed Entrepreneurs*

Cities are often judged on the viability—not just on technology and firms created—based on the quality of life, which include the arts. Where would New Orleans be without music and the culinary entrepreneurs that have made the city as famous for its food as it is for its music and nightlife? Many of those who are self-employed are often considered by the media and policy makers as not requiring attention. Their value has often been ignored. What brought back New Orleans after Hurricane Katrina was the vitality of the art, music, and food scenes. If they had abandoned the city, it would have turned the city into a ghost town with quaint buildings.

However, recently cities like New Orleans and Austin have seen the value in fostering their artists as much as they have their technology firms or oil firms. One only has to look at Austin, Texas billing itself as the "Live Music Capital of the World" and the role music plays in SXSW (South by Southwest) in which technology, music, and film go hand in hand. In Austin alone, for example, one of the fastest growing areas for the self-employed is in the *Arts, entertainment and recreation sector*. In 2003 there were 5,931 such ventures. By 2013 the number of such firms rose to 11,355, an increase of 91 percent with estimated revenues of $271 million in 2013. This is no small part of the economic life of a city like Austin.

One such nonemployee venture in the arts sector is one operated by an Austin area artist, Danny Babineaux (www.dannybabineaux.com). Currently his paintings are focused on animal subjects. He does commissions of people's pets, the ubiquitous Texas longhorn cattle, as well as endangered species such as elephants and rhinos (see Figures 1.3 and 1.4). He has sold his paintings not just in Austin but worldwide; thanks to the Internet that allows him to be independent of traveling to art shows and exhibiting in galleries with their associated overhead costs. By using PayPal, he is able to take credit card payments. The following is an example of some of his arts:

Historically one need only look at artists like Rembrandt Harmenszoon van Rijn, the father of the "selfie," Pablo Picasso, Andy Warhol, George F. Handel, Richard Wagner, or the Beatles collectively, or Lennon and McCartney individually to say that all were successful on a number of dimensions including financially. All had huge impacts on society. Warhol's print runs became immediate production lines. Picasso outsourced his pottery to a family firm to produce. Lennon and McCartney created an entire industry with lasting impact on society and music. One can look at the current success of Taylor Swift. It is clear her current music

Figure 1.3 Texas longhorns (Danny Babineaux, artist).

Figure 1.4 Endangered elephants (Danny Babineaux, artist).

and business skills only hint at what her entrepreneurial talents will produce in the future.

1.19 A False Dichotomy

If you remember earlier we discussed the work of David Birch and discussed the role of small business and entrepreneurs. At this point perhaps we need to delve into these terms in a bit more detail. Many of the early scholars who argued that small business owners are not entrepreneurs (e.g., Carland et al. 1984) had no real understanding of how small firms operate. These researchers fail to appreciate the innovations these firms often create nor how much an entrepreneur's personality impacts their operations (think Donald Trump here). Reading today their definitions of 30 years ago of a small business owner and entrepreneur is rather more confusing than helpful. Consider these (Carland et al. 1984:358):

> A *small business owner* is an individual who establishes and manages a business for the principal purpose of furthering personal goals. The business must be the primary source of income and will consume the majority of one's time and resources. The owner perceives the business as an extension of his or her personality, intricately bound with family needs and desires.

> The *entrepreneur* is an individual who establishes and manages a business for the principal purpose of profit and growth. The entrepreneur is characterized principally by innovative behavior and will employ strategic management practices in the business.

In this same article a small business venture is also distinguished from an entrepreneurial venture (p. 358):

> A *small business venture* is any business that is independently owned and operated, not dominant in the field, and does not engage in any new marketing or innovative practices.

> An *entrepreneurial venture* is one that engages in at least one of the Schumpeter's four categories of behavior: that is, the principal goals of an entrepreneurial venture are profitability and growth and the business is characterized by innovative practices.

Finally, the Carland article presents a summary of a review of the literature between 1848 (Mill) and 1982 (Dunkelberg and Cooper) of characteristics that describe entrepreneurs, but obviously not small business owners. Birth order, gender, or marital status had been excluded (p. 355) ". . . because of the inability of a prospective entrepreneur to alter those variables in order to increase his/her probability of success." These characteristics portraying an entrepreneur included risk bearing, source of formal authority, innovation, desire for responsibility, risk taking, moderate risk taker, need for achievement, ambition, desire for independence, drive, technical knowledge, communication ability, autonomy, aggression, power, recognition, need for power, internal locus of control, personal value orientation, self-confidence, goal orientation, creativity, energetic, positive reaction to setbacks, independence oriented, and craftsman oriented. Implicit was that entrepreneurs were male and Anglo-Saxon in ethnicity.

The Carlands' article is a nice example of how the perception and understanding of who is an entrepreneur, what are entrepreneurial characteristics, and what is entrepreneurship have changed over the course of three decades. Surely the small business owner seeks profitability and growth too. Frankly, the description of small business owners sounds very much like a description of many of today's entrepreneurs as portrayed by the mass media, which makes an entrepreneur essentially a small business owner as well. The preceding list of characteristics would make almost everyone an entrepreneur. These characteristics can also be found in small business owners or anyone else who is *not* an entrepreneur but who is successful in their professions or careers.

1.20 Do Goals Differentiate?

We strongly question the fundamental assumption that the principal goals of an entrepreneurial venture are profitability and growth. We believe these may result from doing something else well and these are consequences of those goals being achieved. For some, wealth may be the primary goal, but not always. If wealth is the only goal, one is reminded of the response of the famous Jesse James of the Wild West of the United States in the 1800s when asked why he robbed banks, his answer being "that is where the money is." We are not suggesting that bank robbery is entrepreneurial, but one can certainly think of it being easier than starting a company and waiting years for revenue or profits to arrive.

If profitability is the goal, this would leave quite a few firms considered entrepreneurial outside the category of entrepreneurial. Most Kirznerian entrepreneurs would be defined as small business owners. If we are to take these definitions and apply them into today's world, we will have problems in defining Jack Dorsey, founder of Twitter as entrepreneurial (although many would certainly view him as one—and a successful one). Consider this quote from an article in *Newsweek*, October 20, 2008:

> . . . consider that Twitter, a "micro-blogging" site launched in 2006, earlier this year raised a reported $15 million in venture funding at an undisclosed valuation—even though the company hasn't made a dime so far and its managers aren't trying to. "We're pre-revenue. We're focused on growth."

Yet, we know that when this founder sold off Twitter, he became a billionaire. The goal was not apparently *firm* profitability, but to drive up valuation so that the owner could exit and create his own wealth, that is, personal profitability. Perhaps this is a legal form of bank robbery.

It should be obvious at this point that it is no easy exercise to define entrepreneurship or define an entrepreneur. It should also be clear that we highly question the requirement of economic wealth creation as the primary goal. For example, Johannisson (2005) has seen the entrepreneur as *existentially* motivated. That is, entrepreneurship is seen as a way of life, involving total commitment by the individual. Perhaps that would explain those entrepreneurs who start seven business ventures in a lifetime. This to our minds points at other possible goals and desires that are involved in entrepreneurship, as we pointed out in Carsrud and Brännback (2011). In other words, goals serve as an important part of entrepreneurial motivation.

1.20.1 A Mini-Case Example

For example of a motivated entrepreneur, let us look at one arts and social entrepreneur in Florida we know well, Patrick Dupre Quigley.

> Patrick was trained as a classical musician at Notre Dame University and later at Yale University. He has worked closely with

Michael Tilson Thomas the famous conductor. Interestingly, he also had worked at various marketing and public relations firms while in school and knew that there had to be a different way to make classical music accessible. He had a clear goal: to create a sustainable classical music group in the South Florida market. Miami, despite having a new and magnificent concert hall and state-of-the-art opera/ballet house, had seen many of its classical music groups struggle and/or fail like the Florida Philharmonic.

It became obvious to Patrick that the cost of such organizations including those of full-time musicians could not be maintained with the traditional model of concert revenues and donations. He also realized that younger audiences were not going to sit through classical concerts that were much over ninety minutes in length. He also knew that there were many excellent free-lance musicians, especially singers, who he could bring in, pay them well for a given concert series and once the concert series was over they would return to their homes or go to their next *gig*. The result of his efforts has been one of the few profitable non-profit arts organizations in Florida, Seraphic Fire and its related orchestra (www.SeraphicFire.org).

We see this example as one where have a clear goal can motivate an entrepreneur, in this case a social entrepreneur in the arts arena. The point is that Patrick saw a need and had a goal to address that need. The result has been pure joy for those of us who have attended his concerts, or bought the CDs, or downloaded the music his groups have performed.

1.21 Opportunity and the Entrepreneur

What most of researchers would agree upon is that regardless of what drives an individual, or regardless of what form entrepreneurship takes, there is a fundamental requirement for an opportunity to exist even if the entrepreneur is doing a business out of necessity. A person intending to become an entrepreneur has to somehow perceive that an opportunity exists. Whether that opportunity is viable as a basis for venture creation is a different issue entirely. Usually, the person who sees an opportunity thinks it is a good one. To reflect this reality, we have for years used a definition of entrepreneurship, which was originally offered by two

Harvard Business School colleagues, Stevenson and Jarillo (1990) that we find most appropriate. This definition also is useful for necessity entrepreneurs (who are forced to find an opportunity). What is more important is that it allows for both Kirzner's and Schumpeter's entrepreneurs to exist. This definition was originally:

> Entrepreneurship is the process by which individuals—either on their own or inside organizations—pursue opportunities without regard to the resources currently control.

While this may not be a great operational definition for scientific research purposes, it allows us to cast a board net over who are entrepreneurs. It allows one to see how stories about entrepreneurs reflect this definition in both new firms, existing family firms, and even in large, multinational corporations.

1.22 Exercises

1.22.1 Look at the following list of names. Who are these individual? What do you know about them? What companies did these start? When? Which are family firms? Still run by the family? Who saw themselves as social entrepreneurs? Which are now owned by large MNCs? Did they have their IPOs? What are their brands?

Jeff Besoz

Chaja Rubinstein (aka Princess Gourielli)

Michael Dell

Cher Wang

Sergey Brin

Don Facundo Bacardi-Masso

Larry Page

Kiichiro Toyoda

Diane Halfin von Fürstenberg Diller

Alfred Sloan

Jacques Defforey and Marcel Fournier

J. K. Rowling

John W. Nordstrom

Arianna Huffington

Jaime Torres

Yang Lan

Erlin Persson

Elon Musk

Dave Thomas

Sara Blakely

1.22.2 Read the article: Carland, J. W., Hoy, F., Boulton, W. R., Carland, J. C. 1984. Differentiating entrepreneurs from small business owners: A conceptualization. *Academy of Management Review*, 9(2): 354–359. How have the views changed over 30 years? Are these conceptualizations still valid in today's business context? Justify your response with real business examples.

1.23 Advanced Exercises

1.23.1 Read the following books and articles. Based on your reading, discuss in class the discovery and creation of opportunity. What are the differences? Think of entrepreneurs whom you know personally. How did they discover or create their opportunity? Did they prepare a business plan or did they have a plan "in mind," which was not written formally. Did they have to revise the plan, how many times, and what were the reasons for revision. Did they consider the possibility of failure? Was there something in the process of creating the firm that they had overlooked? What was the biggest surprise? These articles are not in alphabetical order but in the intended reading order.

1. Shane, S., and S. Venkataraman. 2000. The promise of entrepreneurship as a field of research. *Academy of Management Review* 25:217–226.

2. Shane, S. 2000. Prior knowledge and the discovery of entrepreneurial opportunities. *Organization Science* 11(4): 448–470.

3. Sarasvathy, S. D. 2001. Causation and effectuation: Toward a theoretical shift from economic inevitability to entrepreneurial contingency. *Academy of Management Review* 26(2): 243–263.

4. Eckhardt, J. T., and S. A. Shane. 2003. Opportunities and entrepreneurship. *Journal of Management* 29(3): 333–349.

5. Alvarez, S. A., and J. B. Barney. 2007. Discovery and creation: Alternative theories of entrepreneurial action. *Strategic Entrepreneurship Journal* 1:11–26.

6. Shane, S. 2012. Reflections on the 2010 decade award: Delivering on the promise of entrepreneurship as a field of research. *Academy of Management Review* 37:10–20.

7. Venkataraman, S., S. D. Sarasvathy, N. Dew, and W. R. Forster. 2012. Reflections on the 2010 decade award: Whither the promise? Moving forward with entrepreneurship as a science of the artificial. *Academy of Management Review* 37:21–33.

8. Alvarez, S. A., and J. B. Barney. 2013. Forming and exploiting opportunities: The implications of discovery and creation processes for entrepreneurial and organizational research. *Organization Science* 24:301–317.

9. Alvarez, S. A., and J. B. Barney. 2013. Epistemology, opportunities, and entrepreneurship: Comments on Venkataraman et al. (2012) and Shane (2012). *Academy of Management Review* 38:154–157.

References

Alvarez, S. A., and J. B. Barney. 2013. Forming and exploiting opportunities: The implications of discovery and creation processes for entrepreneurial and organizational research. *Organization Science*, 24:301–317.

Birch, D, 1987. *Job creation in America: How our smallest companies put the most people to work.* New York: Free Press.

Brännback, M., and A. Carsrud. 2009. Cognitive maps in entrepreneurship: Researching sense making and action. In A. Carsrud and M. Brännback (eds.), *Understanding the Entrepreneurial Mind: Opening the black box.* Springer: Heidelberg, 75–96.

Brännback, M., A. L. Carsrud, and N. Kiviluoto. 2014. *Understanding the myth of high growth firms: The theory of the greater fool.* New York: Springer.

Cantillon, R. 1755/1931. *Essai sur la nature du commerce en général.* London: MacMillan.

Carland, J. W., F. Hoy, W. R. Boulton, and J. A. C. Carland. 1984. Differentiating entrepreneurs from small business owners: A conceptualization. *Academy of Management Review*, 9(2): 351–359.

Carsrud, A., and M. Brännback, eds. 2009. *Understanding the entrepreneurial mind: Opening the black box.* Heidelberg: Springer.

Carsrud, A., and M. Brännback. 2011. Reflections on twenty years of research on entrepreneurial motivation: Have we learned anything at all? *Journal of Small Business Management,* 49(1): 9–26.

Dunkelberg, W. C., and A. C. Cooper. 1982. Entrepreneurial typologies. In K. Vesper (ed.) *Frontiers of entrepreneurship research.* Wellesley, MA: Babson College, 1–15.

Gartner, W. B. 1988. "Who is an entrepreneur?" is the wrong question. *American Journal of Small Business,* 12(4): 11–32.

Hoselitz B. F. 1951. The early history of entrepreneurial theory. *Explorations in Entrepreneurial History III,* 3(4): 193–220.

Johannisson, B. 2005. *Entreprenörskapets väsen (The essence of entrepreneurship).* Lund, Sweden: Studentlitteratur.

Kirzner, I. M. 1973. *Competition and entrepreneurship.* Chicago: University of Chicago Press.

Knight, F. H. 1921. *Risk, uncertainty, and profit.* Boston: Hougthon Mifflin.

Koehn, N. F. 2001. *Brand new: How entrepreneurs earned consumers' trust from Wedgwood to Dell.*

Landström, H. 2005. *Pioneers in entrepreneurship and small business research.* Springer, Berlin: Springer.

Mill, J. S. 1848. Principles of political economy with some of their applications to social philosophy. In J. A. Schumpeter (ed.), *History of economic analysis.* New York: Oxford University Press, 1954.

Mises, L. von. 1951. *Planning for freedom.* South Holland, IL: Libertarian Press.

Saxenian, A. 1994. *Regional advantage.* Cambridge: Harvard University Press.

Say, J-B. 1803/2001. *A treatise on political economy.* New Brunswick, NJ: Transaction Publishers.

Schumpeter, J. 1934. *The theory of economic development.* Boston: Harvard University Press.

Stevenson, H. H., and J. C. Jarillo. 1990. A paradigm of entrepreneurship: Entrepreneurial management. *Strategic Management Journal,* 11(5): 17–27.

Venkataraman, S. 1997. The distinctive domain of entrepreneurship research. In J. Katz, (ed.), *Advances in entrepreneurship, firm emergence, and growth,* vol. 3. Greenwich, CT: JAI Press, 119–138.

2

What Is Being Successful:
Well It All Depends

2.0 Why Examine Success?

We hope you see the title of this book, *Fundamentals for becoming a Successful Entrepreneur*, as provocative, or at least challenging. While you may believe you know what *success* means, we are going to argue it is very much dependent on the context in which it occurs. We also think it is very dependent on the individual who is making the determination. Thus, we are going to spend some time looking at the meaning of words *success* and *successful* in general before we focus on these concepts in entrepreneurship. We will try to show that *success* is highly dependent on the specific goals the entrepreneur sets for themselves and their venture. Before we get into that discussion, it may be informative at this point an example of success in an entrepreneurial venture that is not some well-known technology firm from Silicon Valley. We have done this frankly because while the Valley is a Mecca for technology firms, most technology firms in the world are created elsewhere and most new ventures are not in the technology arena.

2.0.1 Case Example from Finland and Sweden

To give you an example of a successful venture, we are going to start by showing how to find a successful opportunity to exploit first. To do this, we are going to tell you about two firms started by Eva Johansson and Petter Karlsson. The first is their initial business at Pensar Syd, in the southwest archipelago of Finland (http://www.pensarsyd.com/en/) and the second is their guesthouse Mullfjället (http://mullfjallet.se/uk/), located in Åre, Sweden (see Figure 2.1).

Figure 2.1 Map of Finland and Sweden, and the locations Pensar Syd and Mullfjället are shown.

Twelve years ago a couple, Eva and Petter, decided to open a small hotel with an attached restaurant on the southern coast of an island called Pensar in the South-West of the Baltic Archipelago in off the coast of Finland. Eva had a background in the tourism industry and Petter had sold off his part of an accounting firm he had founded with two friends almost two decades earlier.

The island on which their business is located only can be accessed by boat. Their season usually runs from early May to end of September during which time they offer recreational retreats to companies, but they also offer a remote place for companies and other groups to organize corporate training sessions or important meetings such as strategy and budget meetings. Their high season is from mid-June to mid-August. This is when families arrive with their private sailing or motorboats. At the start, they thought of the business of as being a year around one where revenues would come from primarily corporate customers during winter season. During the late spring, summer, and early fall their revenues would come from primarily from vacating families arriving by their own boats. After 8 years, it was increasingly obvious that this dream was that, a dream. It was extremely cumbersome to attract winter visitors and their strategy was not a recipe for success.

They realized they badly needed something else to supply additional income during the winter season in order to have a full-time income as well as have resources to grow their business. In 2010 they started to look for ways of extending their business to an all year around one by having another location somewhere else warmer in winter. They thought they would consider something in Portugal. This was not an entirely crazy idea since an increasing number of retired Finns were going to Portugal for the winter months to escape the cold and the snow. They initially looked in Spain, in an area around Marbella, which was already full with retired Finns. They felt there was too much competition there. Thus Portugal rapidly was becoming a viable option for them and for Finnish visitors. They had been looking at various kinds of guesthouses in Portugal for the winter season. However, they had not been overwhelmed by the available options. That was not the only issue. The big issue was the ways business seemingly was done in Portugal. To say the least they were very different from those practiced in Scandinavia and made them uncomfortable.

While tossing around different ideas among themselves, Petter was surfing the Internet one evening. But, this time he was really looking for the opportunity to buy a boat to sail around the islands. He had owned sailing boats before and always sailed during summers in the Finnish archipelago since he was a kid. These kinds of hobby activities tend to become serious habits. He found he had a growing desire to find a sailing boat again. This vision was occupying his mind when he was not active. He did know that a boat was a bit like a hole in the water into which you threw money. Thus, he wanted to buy a new boat, as that would be cheaper he thought. His hope was to be able to sometimes have time to get out and sail, although *Pensar Syd* was more than a full-time job for even two people pretty much during the entire summer. Boats last a long time he thought, so maybe every once in a while he would be able to go on a short trip, or take visitors for a day trip. If that happened, the boat could become a business expense and the trips, a much needed revenue source.

But, you know how it is when you surf the Internet. One tends to be looking for one thing and you end up looking at something entirely different. This was one such time. What he found out of the blue was a listing for the *Guesthouse Mullfjället*. Out of luck in his search for a new sailboat he accidentally stumbled on a guesthouse for sale in Åre, in the northern area of Sweden called Jämtland. Åre is one of the places where the World Cup of downhill skiing competition is organized. The area is a huge winter sports resort complex. He thought "Voilà!" He had found a new opportunity without the issues of Portugal.

From late November to late April this winter resort is full of buzz and lots of customers. Here was this guesthouse for sale, and it came with already booked guests and everything else needed to make the business work. Åre, Sweden is not that far away from south west Finland. You take the night boat over to Stockholm and drive north for about 7 hours. Åre is far more similar to Finland from a cultural and legal perspective than trying to do business in Portugal. Although Portugal would come with sun and warmth and Åre would mean 5 feet of snow and sometimes bloody cold weather, but real winter with lots of snow is actually very good too, especially if you are a ski loving Finn.

Eva and Petter did not have to think too long about this opportunity to grow their business. The couple seized the new opportunity and acquired the Swedish guesthouse, as they saw this as an opportunity to continue their business in the tourism industry, which they thoroughly enjoy and at which they thought they are good. In this perception their paying guests also agreed. They view their expanded operations as running their hospitality business in ". . . the archipelago in South-West of Finland during the summer season and in Åre in the Swedish Alps during the winter." They close operations in Finland by end of September, then relocate to Åre and open up in mid-November when the snow falls there. They then closed in mid-April to reopen in Finland by early May. In 2015 they have just ended their fourth season with year around operations using the two locations and happily, everything is cash positive.

2.2 Defining Success

What the preceding case illustrates is that success (and growth) can, and does, come in various forms and that you have to be observant to see these when they appear. It may not be what you thought it would be. At this point we are now going to look at how the term *success* is defined in a dictionary might be helpful. For example, *success* as defined by any English language dictionary is the <u>accomplishment of an aim or purpose</u>. In other words, success comes from <u>achieving a goal</u>. The above definition perhaps comes closest to our view of success as it is not solely dependent on a monetary measure. This view is consistent with our work on entrepreneurial motivation (Carsrud and Brännback 2011). Some see success as a favorable outcome or a triumph. Certainly, success is seen as the opposite of failure. As our case illustrates previously, sometimes opportunities show up in strange ways and grow out of seeming failures. For example, they can save one from buying a boat, which by all reports from boat owners we know, are really holes in the water for throwing away money.

However, other meanings can be given to success. In most cases when the popular media are discussing *success*, it is defined as the *attainment of popularity*. Some see it as being *profit* and thus synonymous with *prosperity*, *affluence*, *wealth*, *riches*, and even *opulence*, certainly something other than *poverty* or *failure*. It is this latter group of meanings of the term *success* that have tended to dominate the idea of a *successful entrepreneur*, in which there is some monetary attribute. While this aspect of success may well be something a would-be presidential candidate (known for his extravagant excess, alleged wealth, television show, and self-aggrandizement) would embrace, we personally think it is limiting and extremely one faceted. Most entrepreneurs don't have a television show and their name on very tall buildings. But, we must remember that even Trump has had his bankruptcies. We know of no famous entrepreneurs who have not had some failure in their lives.

2.3 Defining Failure

Success also gains meaning from looking at its opposite, failure. The term *failure* is often first defined as the *lack of success*, not really very helpful in some ways. It is seen as nonfulfillment, defeat, or collapse. We personally think that a better way to look at failure is to look at it as synonymous with fiasco, debacle, catastrophe, or disaster. The first attempts to build the Suez and Panama Canals clearly were disasters economically for the French firms who initially tried to build them. The term can be attached to an unsuccessful person, venture, or thing. It can also be reflecting inadequacy, insufficiency, deficiency, scarcity, or shortfall.

Failure can also be seen as a lack of a desirable quality. Failure can be a lack of imagination, or action, including a state of not functioning. Clearly, failure is depressing when you think about it. Every entrepreneur will face their share of depressing moments, so be prepared. We, however, view failure as a learning experience. There is some evidence that an entrepreneur may start up to seven business ventures in a life time and yet only one of those would be deemed a success. It is a bit like learning to ride a horse. You don't really know how to ride a horse until you learn to get back in the saddle after you have been thrown off by the horse. We know that from personal experience with a few of the four-legged creatures. What we are saying is that from failure can come knowledge and ultimate success. Abraham Lincoln failed to be elected three times before he was elected president and saved the Union. Thomas J. Watson, the driving force behind IBM is attributed to have said:

> . . . if you want to succeed, double your failure rate.

What we are saying is that failure can be differentially perceived. It all depends on you. If you are only interested in the final outcome of an activity, anything other than success at every step would consider it to be a failure of outcome. This occurs when the core issue has not been resolved or a core need is not met. A failure can also be a *process failure* even though the activity that was completed was seen as successfully. That is, an individual may be dissatisfied if their performance is perceived to be below an expected standard or benchmark. Given that entrepreneurs are often type A personalities with high levels of personal expectations, this is something every would-be entrepreneur most likely will face at some point.

Failure can also come from failing to anticipate something, failing to perceive something, or failing to carry out a task. These views of failure become critical if one is looking at how entrepreneurs behave and how they learn from failures. That is, they should view failure as information.

They are confident of their abilities and then this information is useful to them in ultimately reaching success. That is, they realize confident individuals are not immune to failure. Instead of failure stopping them, they see failure as merely an information-gathering session. It is a "notch in their belts" a proof that they have at least tried and now have some idea of the direction in which to go. That is confident people embrace the experience for the lessons it has taught and then they course-correct their course of action accordingly. Think of it as falling off the horse.

We are well aware that in many countries and cultures failure can be seen very negatively if not literally fatal. The stories of business owners in Japan who have failed in their business and killed themselves can be found repeated in other countries as well. Culture has a huge impact on how one views both success and failure, but please don't kill yourself if you fail. Take it as a learning experience. That may be one reason why the United States has so many repeat entrepreneurs, even those who have failed in prior ventures.

2.4 Measurement Issues in Defining Success (and Failure)

Pick any field of study, from medical treatment to automobile quality assurance, and there is a paper on how to determine success in that area. What is interesting is that if you look at these articles, they all attempt to have a quantitative measure of success that others can agree to at least in terms of the degree of success using that particular measure. For example, reduction in levels of bad cholesterol would be a measure of success of a given statin drug or a change in your diet. Another example is the reduction in the number of defects in a new car would be a measure of the success of a quality assurance program at a manufacturer.

It should be no surprise that an approach that is applied in the measurement of the success of an entrepreneur would be the obvious quantifiable measure of money. The issue then becomes which monetary measure, revenues, profits, or growth rates in either of these? However, during the dot.com era of the early 2000s the measure was another metric, market share. Politicians seem to be obsessed with growth in employment as a measure of success. When it comes to entrepreneurial studies of success and failure, most empirical work depends on financial measures such as ratio data even though the same studies usually see management issues as being the critical factor.

One of the few articles to really address the difference between success and failure in an entrepreneurial context is a paper by Headd (2003) who looked at fundamentally closing a business versus one that fails. A business that is sold or closed because of the death of the owner is not the same as one that *fails* because of poor management is a distinction that many researchers ignore when looking at various data sets. From a practical standpoint, this is once again an example of when a business ceases to exist, does that mean a failure or reflect another goal that owners may have, like turning the asset into cash. We know several entrepreneurs who have said that when they decided to retire, they are selling their business to their employees and taking the money and moving to the beach in some warm climate.

2.5 Success in the Entrepreneurial Context

Based on what you have read in earlier sections, it should be obvious that we firmly believe that what is perceived as a success depends almost entirely on the perceiver. Perceptions about success are likely to vary from person to person and culture to culture. Thus, success and failure very much are in the eyes of the beholders. We also believe the single most important person to be considered is the entrepreneur and their perceptions of their success. As a helpful hint, your spouse and family will certainly have their opinions as well and we recommend you at least pay attention to their concerns. In this chapter we now build on our discussion of successful entrepreneurs by defining success not solely in a monetary fashion or in terms of what a given society would deem a success. We think it is important to assist you in identifying for yourself what success would be for *you*, regardless of what type of entrepreneurial venture on which you may embark. In this regard we are taking a rather existential approach to this concept. In many ways if success is the result of doing something else, it is an unintended consequence of achieving another goal.

So, to really understand success, one should also understand its opposite, in this case *failure*. Here again, failure must be considered in the eye of the beholder. The entrepreneurial world is full of stories of how some people were perceived as failures. For example, Walt Disney the man behind *Mickey Mouse* and the business empire that now bears his name was considered early in his professional life as a failure and he was fired from his job because the boss claimed he had no imagination. A talking mouse takes a lot of imagination. A teacher once told Thomas A. Edison that he would be hard-pressed to find a job where his minimal skills could be used because he was fundamentally a failure. Well there goes the light bulb.

Then there is Theodor Seuss Geisel, known to most of us as *Dr. Seuss*, the grandest of all storytellers. Yet, he had 27 of his books rejected for publication before success arrived. Today his tales are still loved by children and their parents worldwide. Who can forget the stories of Horton, the Who, the Cat wearing a hat, the strange Lorax, and of course the Grinch. To us, Dr. Seuss was a successful entrepreneur because more than anything he wanted to entertain children with stories.

What these success stories remind us of is something Bill Gross the founder of Idealab found when he looked at the successes and failures in his various portfolio firms. He was hunting for the things that really determined success. What he found:

> The number one thing was timing. Timing accounted for 42 percent of the difference between success and failure. Team and execution came in second, and the idea, the differentiability of the idea, the uniqueness of the idea that actually came in third.

This leads us to discuss how other entrepreneurs view their success and what they saw that drove it.

2.6 How Some Firm Founders See Success

When we hear people say they want to be "successful," our response is often "successful at what?" Recently, a group of entrepreneurs and managers were asked for their personal definitions of success. Some of the responses from these young entrepreneurs are most enlightening:

> I define success as living my true purpose and having a positive impact on the lives of people by uplifting them and inspiring them to think and act in ways that they may not have

considered before.   —Raj Sisodia, co-founder of Conscious Capitalism.

The purpose of our lives is to contribute our unique, God-given gifts to have an extraordinary positive impact on the lives of others and the world.   —David Kidder, CEO of Bionic.

Success, for me, has always been in providing a great quality of life for my family, for those who work for me, and to my community.   —Jeremy Young CEO of Tanga.

My definition of success is knowing that what you are doing is helping you and others lead a better, happier, healthier life. —Kara Goldin, CEO of Hint Water.

To me, success means creating a business that empowers customers, employees, and community in equal measure. We want to add positive value to people's lives, from a personal and professional standpoint.   —Dan Kurzius, co-founder and COO of Mailchimp.

What is interesting in this group of responses from entrepreneurs is that money and wealth are at best only implied and are clearly not at the center of these individuals' perceptions of success. They do support our contention that success is very much dependent on the individual's view. We personally find the following quotation by another entrepreneur to be a wonderful example of a very long-term view of success.

Success is looking back at your life, when you are in your final moments, and possessing a great amount of pride around your creations, accomplishments, and legacy, while possessing little to no regret about what you did not do and missed opportunities (i.e. your family still loves you). If I can die feeling this way, I believe this is success.   —Seth Besmertnik, CEO of Conductor.

2.7 How Entrepreneurship Researchers View Success

At this point a short, and far from comprehensive, review of the entrepreneurship research literature is called for before we go any further. Hornaday and Aboud (1971) defined success as starting a venture. That is certainly a good starting point for an entrepreneur. Merely talking about starting a firm seems a bit incomplete. Theirs is certainly an action-oriented view, and while it implies financial aspects, the researchers saw *starting* as the important goal to be obtained in other to define a successful entrepreneur. Certainly any prospective entrepreneurs should be concerned about the chance of success for their proposed business. As Lussier (1995) has pointed out one of the great desires of any entrepreneur is to be able to predict in advance the success or failure of their proposed business. He believed that a *success versus failure prediction model* would benefit existing entrepreneurs, those who assist, train, and advise them, capital providers, suppliers, and policy makers. Frankly, researchers in the field are still hunting for the magic crystal ball to predict success. We clearly have a lot of work still to do. But in the process we have learned a lot and we hope this book will assist you in that endeavor.

We know that being good with people helps entrepreneurs. We also know that entrepreneurs are good at using their brains (one would hope). In this regard, Baron and Markman (2003) saw that the key to financial success of entrepreneurs was more than just social capital but also social competence. Sternberg (2004) saw successful entrepreneurs as having a mix of analytical, creative, and practical intelligence. But, you do not need to be an Albert Einstein or Leonardo da Vinci to be an entrepreneur. This combination Sternberg called *successful intelligence* and he holds this concept is greater than the sum of the four parts if one wants to achieve entrepreneurial success. Baum and Locke (2004) saw that entrepreneurial skills, traits, and motivation were critical to entrepreneurial success, when measured by subsequent growth of the venture. Crane and Crane (2007) focused on the psychological disposition of *optimism* as being critical for entrepreneurial success. Some might think of this as self-fulfilling prophesy, if you believe you will succeed you will succeed. If you believe you will fail, that will be the result. Now that we have given you a quick ride through the research literature and you still want more go to a more recent review of how researchers look at successful entrepreneurs in terms of their cognitive processes, in Carsrud and Brännback (2009). One factor that still needs work is *awareness*. We think that being *observant* is also one of those critical skills. Being aware of your surroundings seems to be the reason Agatha Christie's detective Hercule Poirot always solved the murder mystery and we also think it may well be how good entrepreneurs recognize and solve problems.

2.8 An Ancient Narrative on Obtaining Success

As one of us has a minor in history and studied church Greek, this is where perhaps a well-known story from antiquity might be illustrative. It involves the term "Eureka" that comes from the ancient Greek word εὕρηκα *heúrēka*, meaning "I have found (it)." It is a transliteration of a word attributed to Archimedes who is reported to have yelled "Eureka!" when he stepped into a bath and noticed that the water level rose. What he had *found* was an understanding that the volume of water displaced in the bath must be equal to the volume of the part of his body he had submerged. This observation by itself was not *success*, as it had to be applied to a problem first for that to occur. It was when he realized that the volume of irregular objects could be measured with precision, a previously intractable problem that one could say he was successful. He is said to have been so eager to share his newly found success that he jumped from his bath and ran through the streets of Syracuse, naked shouting "Eureka." We doubt the population of the city had the same view of success on this occasion.

While this was an insight, the real success was the application to a vexing problem posed to him by the King of Syracuse who wanted to determine the purity a beautiful golden crown he had made by his goldsmith to whom he had given pure gold from which to make the crown. He suspected he had been cheated by the goldsmith who substituted some of the pure gold with the same weight of silver. Equipment for weighing objects existed, and now that Archimedes could also measure volume by placing the crown in water to see whether it displaced the same volume as the weight in pure gold. This ratio would give the object's density, an indicator of the crown's purity.

2.9 Success and Opportunity

The lessons that should be drawn from this story of Archimedes and his bath are twofold. One is that you have to be observant to see an opportunity. This opportunity was based on trying to solve a problem for the King. However, the success was not in seeing the opportunity but applying the observation to a problem. Thus, the success for Archimedes was solving the purity problem. Success for the King was that he caught a thief. For the goldsmith he clearly did not have success in stealing the gold. Thus, someone did fail in this situation.

The second lesson is that success differs for everyone and is usually tied to solving a problem or meeting a need. It is goal based. That is, for anyone attempting to create a venture, it is important to stop and think about what *they* would consider to be successful in this proposed venture and in their particular environmental context. What does success mean to them? Having an idea of what success means for the individual entrepreneurs will offer a sense of direction and a purpose for one's entrepreneurial endeavor. However, we ask you to refrain from running naked through the streets when you have success, unless you are at a nudist resort. What we are trying to make obvious is success comes from observation, anticipation via preparation, and taking action by setting goals. This is what happened in the Finnish/Swedish case at the start of this chapter. Someone was being observant.

2.10 Tying Success to Entrepreneurial Goals

It is important to remember that there are differences between near-term objectives, like renting an office space, and long-term goals, like achieving a 20 percent profit margin. The level of preparation, observation, and action required for each is going to be different in the time required may be significantly different. This suggests that not only are goals different for different individuals, but that for a given entrepreneur their quest to create a venture is really a collection of a set of near-term objectives and long-term goals each of which has their own measure of success be it emotional, intellectual, or financial.

Then there is the reality that for personal reasons, such as increasing ones quality of life (a very subjective definition), an individual may adopt a life-style form of entrepreneurship, which is perfectly appropriate. But, this is different from those whose focus is on earning lots of money. Perhaps it is the desire to be able to continue living in one's rural hometown, rather than having to move to the big city? Perhaps it is a desire to turn a hobby into a living, for example a person hooked on surfing or downhill skiing deciding to create a store specializing in surfboards, snowboards, and downhill skis. Perhaps it is a desire to cure a disease, certainly a noble pursuit. The issue is the goal set is what really defines success.

Each part of a business plan as a series of tasks, completion of each could be considered a success. We discuss planning later in the book. If a task was completed but not to the degree of excellence anticipated, then it might be considered a failure, or more likely a qualified success. The point is that any viable and sustainable venture be it for profit or not for profit is made up of a series of interrelated and sequential tasks that must be completed to some degree for the whole to be considered successful. Our personal view is that writing a plan and then never attempting to launch the firm is a job have done, but that is our opinion, plenty of our students have written plans because the sole purpose of this was to finish a course assignment and graduate. Success in their view, but sometimes a frustration in ours, as some of their ideas were "bloody brilliant" that were never realized.

To reach success, make goals attainable and realize they are steps toward achieving larger goals. Simply saying ". . . my goal is to create a multi-million dollar venture," does not make it an achievable goal. The successful venture is the result of doing a lot of smaller, incremental goals.

2.11 Is Success Wealth?

In Chapter 1 we first said that most entrepreneurship scholars have defined entrepreneurship as a process of exploiting or creating opportunities for the purpose of *economic wealth creation*. Some practitioners tend to define entrepreneurship this way too, expressing it in terms of how to earn lots of money. The public media likes to think in terms of how to become filthy rich, which may also explain their fascination with those who win the jackpot in the lottery. However, as we have shown above with our quotations from various entrepreneurs, everybody does not hold a monetary definition of success. That is, economic wealth creation is *not* at the center of their definition of success. We have known some entrepreneurs who simply saw wealth as an outcome of doing the stuff they really loved doing.

While it is certainly true that for many individuals, wealth is defined as having money and the ability to earn lots of it is a measure of success. However, as we have also shown it is not always so. The alert observer may point out that this definition of entrepreneurship does not say anything about *how much economic wealth* the opportunity should generate nor even if it is for the entrepreneur, it could be for society, for example. What would a cure for a form of cancer be worth? Wealth can be defined in many dimensions, and if success equals wealth, success too can be defined in many ways. Wealth and success are very much like happiness—each person may perceive happiness in a myriad of ways.

2.12 The True Secret to Success: Networking

Regardless of how one defines success personally we have noticed one characteristic that successful entrepreneurs around the world seem to possess. That one fundamental skill is the ability of the entrepreneur to network and interact with a wide variety of individuals, not just family, or friends and not just people in a given geographically area. While those people exist for these successful entrepreneurs, the entrepreneurs have learned how to expand and exploit their existing networks and build new ones beyond their immediate circle of contacts. We are not talking of the pseudo-networks of *LinkedIn*, or even *Facebook*. These Websites are merely tools for maintaining a network. Networks need to be nurtured and are not self-perpetuating. They exist because there is a purpose for the entrepreneur to having them and the linkages between individuals in the network are both physical and sometimes intangible. We have frequently called networking the key to entrepreneurial success (Carsrud and Brännback 2007) and we continue to maintain that is one thing you must do, however, shy you may be.

We like to tell the story of one of our grandfathers, who was a very successful businessman. He often would say "It is not *what* you know that counts, but *who* you know. However, if you don't know the *what*, the *who* will not talk to you." It takes both content knowledge and social skills to be a successful entrepreneur. Both of these can be learned if you are prepared to take the time to learn. Even if you are terribly shy, it is critical you find ways to overcome this fear, as it will inhibit your success. We know people who took up acting classes to learn to get over their "stage fright" of talking to strangers. We think of building networks as value-added behaviors. Networking is more than using Website, having and exchanging business cards, exchanging e-mail addresses or cell phone numbers, or even belonging to a business club.

While going to a given school or joining a professional association may give you access to a potential network, it is not your network until you use it. When one of us was on the faculty at the University of Southern California, we always heard people talk of the *Trojan Family*. Every school has its alumni network and they can be a valuable resource to find people to populate your business network. It is not a *family* unless you use it as such. You need to realize that the real strength of any network are not the people with whom you have direct contact, but those individuals who are known by your direct contacts but which you do not know. This is called the concept of the "strength of weak ties" (Granovetter 1985).

There is recent evidence that the best networks are those where you have a strong core of people and contacts that are supportive, but are not so isolated that they don't interact with other groups of people and networks. In other words, if you have a group that is highly restrictive, you don't have an effective network and if you have such a dispersed network that everyone is in it that too may not be very effective. To use the above comment about the *Trojan Family*, for example, it also helps have friends who went to UCLA or the California Institute of Technology as well.

You have to remember that others in your entrepreneurial network have to perceive you as having the potential to provide, or actually do provide, value to their lives. Networks are a two-way street. You cannot just take, but you must also give; thus the human concept of reciprocity becomes a key part of successful networking. To do this well, you need to know the needs, wants, and fears of those who are our network. You need to be proactive and purposeful in building your entrepreneurial networks. Networking may seem spontaneous, but it is the result of being conscious about what you want the network to do for you and what you can do for others in your network. It will be a time-consuming process and can be overwhelming if you are not prepared for the effort. However, as one entrepreneur said to us several times during the early stages of our work, ". . . you have to be using the concept of over-determinism. That is, when you are networking you have the opportunity in doing multiple tasks associated with the venture. These might include marketing, fund raising, or actually making a sale."

Typical individuals within networks of a successful entrepreneur include suppliers, distributors, subcontractors, attorneys, accountants, government workers, bankers, investors, realtors, engineers, scientists, family members, and hopefully even customers that will refer you to other potential customers. The point here is that your networks need to be broad and as inclusive as possible. You need to belong to trade associations and professional groups as well as social clubs and community organizations. Networks are context based and each organization you join will come with a potential network with which you can become involved. When you are a part of various networks, you will discover various mentors, based on what your particular need is at the time. We know that to be a successful entrepreneur, you are going to need mentors, not just a single mentor. This is quite a bit different than if you are trying to work your way up a corporate career ladder. As you have much to learn and to master, you are going to need different individuals to help you master those. Thus, one benefit of being in networks is that you find those individuals who can mentor you during different situations. This is another reason why you cannot be shy in building networks and meeting people.

2.12.1 Rules for Networking

We are deeply indebted to our colleagues Rein Peterson and Robert Ronstadt for sharing with us how they have taught how to network to entrepreneurs, something we too have taught for years at a number of universities and initially shared in print in Carsrud and Brännback (2007). We remain confident that learning to network remains as valuable as it was a decade or more ago. There are 10 rules and ones we strongly urge you to follow.

First rule, you need to accept as a reality that you will have to meet new people, even individuals that you think would never talk to you like major investor or a marketing guru. Don't be shy but do be diplomatic. The second rule, and related to the first, be proactive in creating a network and think systematically about this process as you are trying to build value-added networks as an entrepreneur. The third rule is to always assess your networks in terms of the venture you are creating. Does the network need new contacts? Are you missing someone who knows a critical part of your business concept? Can your existing network help you meet some of those "weak ties"?

The fourth rule is to locate your venture geographically in the center of your network. This rule is susceptible to the realities of a global economy and the Internet. Some new ventures are more physical like a bed and breakfast establishment in Rome, than say software development firm with programmers outsourced in Thailand. Thus, they need to be where the network can be helpful in a timely fashion. We will admit that the Internet allows for a dispersed network of supporting individuals. But even then face-to-face meetings remain a critical part of any effective network. The fifth rule is simple. You need to use your network to see whether it is useful. The only way you will know whether your network is a good one is to use it.

The sixth rule is related to the role of mentors. Every network has a set of gatekeepers. These sometimes are called secretaries, not just bosses or chair professors. They may be experts in an area, or people who are extremely well connected in an area. You need to keep in contact with these individuals on a regular basis. Nothing is worse in some ways than to learn a gatekeeper has passed away and your access to a network of weak ties has disappeared just when you needed them.

Thus the seventh rule, you need to always assess your network to see that it fits your entrepreneurial venture. You want it to contain individuals in traditional business and industry arenas but also those who may be important to your venture. If you are in technology, this may mean someone familiar with the technology. The eighth rule we have alluded to earlier, you need to contribute to your networks. You need to be available and respond to contacts. Yes, this is time consuming but is part of the price you pay to have a network, remember reciprocity. The tenth rule is one that comes in the form of moderation in everything. Do not become a slave to the networking process. Be passionate about your network but not obsessive compulsive. In the end ". . . it is not *what* you know that counts, but *who* you know. However, if you don't know the *what*, the *who* will not talk to you." Finally, remember that all relationships and networking depend on generosity, be of service to others, and the efforts will come back. That is the theory of reciprocity at work.

2.13 Finally, Success Is Having Fun

For example, we have numerous examples of entrepreneurs who barely manage to make ends meet with their business. They may admit that the business is going so and so. But, they would not change for any money in the world because they get to do what they love and without being bossed around by anyone else but themselves. The fact that they can continue doing this is in their minds a measure of success. Somebody may consider this to be another word for stupid or madness. Somebody else will perceive this entirely differently, like in the quote below from a Chinese proverb, which we have taught in our classes for years:

> Choose a job that you love and you will never have to work a day in your life!

We also know of several entrepreneurs who, again barely making ends meet, are exceptionally happy. It is because their business did not require them to have to move away from their childhood home, which to their minds is next to paradise on Earth. We also know of entrepreneurs who love downhill skiing and started a business selling skis and everything that goes with it, which 6 months of the year is shut down because of the summer season and therefore the *economy* of the business is perhaps not the very best—at least during the low season! Yet, again these get to do what they absolutely love, and the fact that they can continue with is and somehow get by, is to them a measure of success.

We personally cannot stress more our belief that you have to have fun being an entrepreneur. This does not mean you go around laughing all day. This does not mean it is not hard work, or that there are frustrations in the process. What we are saying is choose a job you love and you will never *work* a day in your life. We generally love what we do, except for grading papers, which seems like torture at times. That said, we have found jobs we love. We feel that entrepreneurs are among the lucky folks in the world who have that option of creating their own jobs.

We will now introduce you to some case stories. As you read this book, you may want to think back on these cases and others that we present. These are real, existing small entrepreneurial companies. In some cases we have been asked to de-identify the individuals and the firm, but they are all real.

2.14 Case Example From Italy

Our second case example in this chapter is of Daniele Moroni and Livio Salvatori and how they went from one bed and breakfast (B&B) in Rome to three: *A View of Rome, A Peace of Rome,* and *A Touch of Rome.* (http://www.bbaviewofrome.it/en/).

Passion, passion, passion, passion, . . . it is the word to use to get success in this business! Every travel can be different and can have own experience, now, all travellers think they are already educated and perfect travellers . . . they get it from all internet reviews and they just follow what the other tourist say or write on the web . . . but at the end . . . what makes the difference is the customer service!!! And we are here to offer the best customer service to all our guests! —Daniele Moroni

At the end of 2009, Daniele together with his friend Livio Salvatori decided to start a B&B in the heart of Rome—across the street from the Vatican—A View of Rome. By March 2010 they had become the number 1 B&B according to Trip Advisor and continued to have that position for three consecutive years. Because of this initial success, Daniele and Livio presented the owner of the apartment of A View of Rome with a business plan who decided to finance a second B&B—A Peace of Rome—just a few blocks away. A Peace of Rome opened on July 3, 2010 and listed as number 3 B&B in Rome according to Trip Advisor, for two consecutive years. The owner of the apartment now also became a business partner with Daniele and Livio. On April 1, 2012, they opened their third B&B—A Touch of Rome, situated in the same building as A View of Rome, but overlooking the inner yard (see Figure 2.2). The price point was then and still is a bargain when comparing with package trips and big hotels and with respect to location.

A View of Rome is just across the street from the Vatican on the sixth floor with a magnificent *view*—in fact one could see the window of the Pope's residence and St. Peter's Basilica in its full glimmering glory. Stunning is usually people's response to seeing the building and its dome. As a tourist visiting Rome for the first time with only a few days, the challenge is to make the most of it all. This, of course, Daniele and Livio knew was every visitors' problem, and they were prepared. When in Rome, unless you know your ways, you will be spending most of your time in line with all other tourists, unless somebody knows better. You will also spend lots of money on restaurant bills unless somebody can give you good advice. Yes, there are lots of tourist guides and Trip Advisor, but then there is local knowledge, which trumps it all, and one begins to understand the notion of the *Eternal City*.

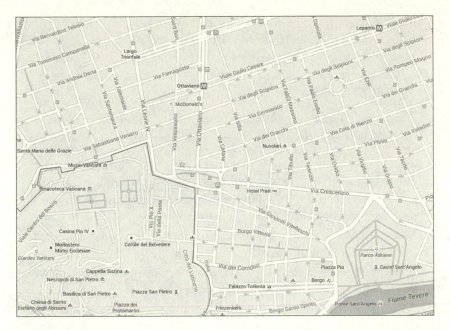

Figure 2.2 Locations of A View of Rome, A Taste of Rome, and A Touch of Rome, indicated with the star. A View of Rome and A Touch of Rome are in the same building.

The changing competitive landscape of Rome has become obvious. After the initial success Daniele and Livio are still passionately in business, but now the competition has changed significantly. When they opened in 2009, there were 1,072 licensed properties on Trip Advisor. In 2015 there are now 3,069 listed properties. To this number you also have to add all unlisted properties that nobody controls, and all holiday apartments that can also be booked online. As of October 2014, www.booking.com, which is the major distributor of these properties decided to list *all* available properties on their site, whether licensed or not. Prior to this date they had only listed the ones, which were licensed with a minimum of six rooms available. From October 2014, anyone can take a picture of their apartment and "rent" it on www .booking.com or on www.homeaway.com. And new dealers emerge, some evidently putting the customer at great risk. *AIRBNB* now offers portion of someone's apartments to tourists, but sometimes the pictures and the reality does not match and Daniele received a message from a desperate customer:

Hello! I have planned a surprise trip for my mama and arrived in Rome today. Unfortunately the airbnb I booked is not at all what the reviews and photos expressed. I am from California and my mom is here from Chicago. I am trying to see if I can find a better quality place to stay :)

Your place looks very clean and welcoming! Hope to hear back from you . . . Best Janet

While Daniele was able to save Janet, it is obvious that this change has created an entirely different challenge to ensure continued success and to survive in the B&B business. The customer has a very hard time determining whether the house/room offered is licensed or not. While price is important, quality is also important as poor quality can destroy a trip even to paradise. As we know nice pictures are sometimes quite far from the reality. The traveling consumer is today wise to read customer reviews very carefully.

2.15 Conclusion

After all of the aforementioned review of definitions, linguistic history, and examples, it should be clear that what we are saying is that the most important person to define what constitutes either success or failure is the entrepreneur themselves. Yes, we admit that banks, families, and society may have their very different views as to what is an appropriate measure of success or failure for them. We remember one wife who told her entrepreneurial husband he could sell everything they had to make the business work except for the house and the kids' college funds. It was only when he started to ask her to sign a mortgage on the house that he realized his family and marriage was more important than the extra money. This forced him to think of a different way to fund the business, which we call bootstrapping. We will have more to say on the issue of bootstrapping later in this volume. Remember, it is the goals that the entrepreneur sets for themselves, which determines whether success has occurred. You need to know yourself first if you are going to go down the rough and rocky road of being an entrepreneur, including just how far you can push your family in the pursuit of your dreams. The biggest roadblock to being an entrepreneur remains personal self-doubt.

2.16 Exercises

2.16.1. From your reading about the Finnish couple, Eva and Petter, operating in different business in different seasons in Finland and Sweden, would you call this couple successful? Are they doing what they love? Is entrepreneurship to them a life style? Are they making lots of money? How do you think they define success? Failure?

2.16.2. Would you consider Daniele and Livio successful? Are they doing what they love? Is entrepreneurship to them a life style or is it opportunistic? Are they making lots of money? What do you think is the key driver of their activity? How do you think they define success? Failure?

2.16.3. How do you define success for you personally? How do you define success in terms of your family life? How do you define success in terms of your professional life? How would you determine whether you had a successful business?

References

Baron, R. A., and G. D. Markman 2003. Be beyond social capital: the role of entrepreneurs' social competence in their financial success. *Journal of Business Venturing*, 18(1): 41–60.

Baum, J., and E. A. Locke 2004. The relationship of entrepreneurial traits, skill, and motivation to subsequent venture growth. *Journal of Applied Psychology*, 89(4): 587–598.

Carsrud A., and M. Brännback 2007. *Entrepreneurship*. West Port, CT: Greenwood publishing.

Carsrud, A., and M. Brännback eds. 2009. *Understanding the entrepreneurial mind: Opening the black box*. Heidelberg: Springer.

Carsrud, A., and M. Brännback 2011. Entrepreneurial Motivations: What do we still need to know? *Journal of Small Business Management*, 49(1): 9–26.

Crane, F. G., and E. C. Crane 2007. Dispositional optimism and entrepreneurial success. *The Psychologist-Manager Journal*, 10(1): 13–25.

Granovetter, M. S. 1985. Economic action and social structure: The problem of embeddedness. *The American Sociological Review*, 91:481–510.

Headd, B. 2003. Redefining business success: Distinguishing between closure and failure. *Small Business Economics*, 21(1): 51–61.

Hornaday, J. A., and J. Aboud 1971. Characteristics of successful entrepreneurs. *Personnel Psychology*, 24:141–153.

Lussier, R. N. 1995. A nonfinancial business success versus failure prediction model for young firms. *Journal of Small Business Management*, 33(1):8–20.

Sternberg, R. J. 2004. Successful intelligence as a basis for entrepreneurship. *Journal of Business Venturing*, 19(2): 189–201.

3

Getting a Good Idea and Making It Work

3.0 Overview

To paraphrase the Bible, "in the beginning . . . there was an idea." All firms, large or small, in every industrial sector, began as an idea that was nurtured by an entrepreneur. That idea comes from being attentive to an opportunity that exists or anticipating an opportunity. As one of us (Carsrud 1989:35) noted several decades ago, all ventures:

> . . . had their beginnings as ideas in entrepreneur's minds. An idea is formed from a number of variables, yet it is not a business concept until it undergoes an active decisional process, a process that has far-flung implications for the ultimate scope and success of the business venture.

3.1 The Idea

In Chapter 2 we discussed how *success* is in the eye of the entrepreneur and highly depends on the goals that individual sets. In this chapter we start the process of setting those goals and critical to that is to take an idea, transform it into a business concept with a business/revenue model that can achieve the goals, and thus achieve the success the entrepreneur desires. It should be noted that ideas are everywhere, you see them constantly, but knowing that there are "bed and breakfast" (B&B) as in our example in Chapter 2. You also know there are techniques to create cell phone apps, or compounds that might treat cancer. However, knowing of something is not the same as turning these ideas into a business concept. These ideas are opportunities, but they may not be opportunities

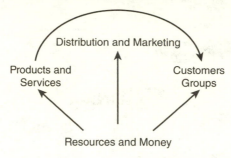

Figure 3.1 The essential elements captured in the business concept.

for you; thus they just remain ideas, perhaps for others to exploit. We discuss opportunity recognition later in this chapter.

However, the following is a simple model of a business concept that we feel captures the ever essence of the factors that make up a viable business concept. Fundamentally, Figure 3.1 illustrates that a business concept is where an idea (product/service) is linked to a customer group by means of both marketing and distribution and that you have to have resources to make that linkage happen. You should be able to describe this process for your concept in two to three sentences as a form of an elevator pitch.

3.2 Idea Generation

To fully grasp our rationale for this chapter, it is worth revealing the roots to idea generation. We believe you should keep this in mind at all times when thinking about business ideas. It is the real reason for the creation of any new venture. Peter Drucker (1974) made a bold statement: "The purpose of a business is to create a customer." It is not to make a profit, which many will claim is the purpose. According to Drucker, profit is a necessary requirement but not the purpose. As we said about *success*, it is the result of doing and achieving something else. Without customers, there is no need to worry about production or shareholder value or even market value. There simply is none of these unless there are people (in other words, a market) who are willing and able to purchase what you are selling at a price you afford to sell at and still make a profit.

The ability to create and please customers is the acid test of the business idea. It is important to remember that price is not the only dimension customers use to judge a product, ask any Apple's iPhone customer. It is important to remember that the resources needed to market and distribute various goods and services depend on the customers being targeted with the venture. Clearly Apple is not looking at price conscious and sensitive customers, at least not yet. It will be interesting to see how the iWatch fairs in the marketplace as its different models have different price points and are aimed at very different markets.

There is a basic rule of thumb within marketing, which serves as a good starting point here too. In its simplest form it means that for a product or a service to have any chance of market, success is that there is a sufficient amount of customers who are willing to buy. For a customer's willingness to buy a product/service, that product or service has to meet a *need* or a *desire to have* held by the customer. The customer must somehow *benefit*, or gain *value*, from buying the product or service, regardless of price. Now, let us turn to a fundamental psychology lesson every entrepreneur needs to undertake.

3.2.1 Concept Benefits: Needs, Wants, and Fears

Here is where being observant and aware of others becomes important. One of the lessons we try to teach every student is that they have to be good at identifying what motivates customers psychologically. Can you identify what *need, want,* or *fear* your business is addressing? It is easy to identify the benefit for a new drug, that is, there is a disease that needs a cure and a customer will certainly benefit from being cured. One can easily go and make an expanded list of benefits for a variety of products. But, not everyone will perceive a benefit as a benefit or something worthy. In other words, *needs, wants, and fears are not universal.* Other than food, water, and air we can think of few other products that are universal. If you are dead, you don't even need these, but you may need a funeral.

For example, not too long ago we were teaching a group of scientists the basics of venture creation and we were touting out this necessity for a benefit, to meet a need or a desire. A young scientist in the audience became annoyed with us. She asked very pointedly what was the benefit of the computer game *Angry Birds*? To her *Angry Birds* and other such internet games were just a massive waste of time and highly non-beneficial. Her level of annoyance increased when we replied that the benefit was *entertainment*. People, lots of people are prepared to pay huge amounts of money for entertainment. Even movies like *50 Shades of Grey* are entertainment to some individuals and a massive waste to others. Hollywood movies, or any Disney amusement park, are created to address this need and desire for a target audience to be entertained. The economies of nations are built on meeting the desires and needs of customers from individuals, to firms, to governments. But we will admit, some do it far better than others. Some people find *NASCAR* to be a form of entertainment others of us think it is just noisy cars going around in a large circle. Then there are the Finns who have wife carrying as a game, which frankly seems a terrible way to take one's wife out for a fun evening. The point is the benefit received is often in the eye of the beholder.

As an entrepreneur you will need to realize that a *need* or a *desire* can be primitive, trivial, and simple much in the same way as it can be immensely complex. We know someone who feels that they cannot live without art museums and art. Others may have no appreciation for that need at all. When speaking of *needs* and *wants and desires*, we caution that you cannot forget customers' *fears*. People are prepared to pay huge amounts for something that will reduce or address their fears, beyond buying a stiff drink. Think about the entire insurance business: it is because of our fear of accidents that we buy insurances. While insurance will not take away the possibility of accidents or death to occur, it is a way to compensate for the loss via insurance. People buy safety equipment because of fears of something nasty to occur, for example, such as bicycle helmets. Others buy helmets as they are legally required and not because they fear injury, but they fear getting a traffic ticket. Some manufacturers of bicycle helmets have realized that these can be turned into fashion gadgets with nice colors or designs and thereby charge a premium price.

For any product or service to have even the elementary potential of commercial success, *demand is a necessary requirement*. Needs, desires, and fears are the sources for *demand*. This is also another way of stating the *opportunity*. Needs, want, and fears are at the heart of the business idea, opportunity, and demand. However, all needs, desires, and fears are not universal. They are situational and individual, which is one reason for some ideas being brilliant in some parts of the world and absolutely ridiculous elsewhere. Do you understand the needs, wants, and fears driving your potential customers? If not, then you need to find out.

3.2.2 Examples of Needs, Wants, and Fears.

Picture yourself living in the inner city of Stockholm and you *need* transportation. You really *want* to go by car, a nice Volvo, but you *fear* getting stuck in the traffic. There are a number of solutions: you can take the metro, which is fast, cheap, and the metro network in Stockholm is reasonably good. But, during rush hour it is really a rather painful experience like in most other larger cities like London, Toronto, Paris, Hong Kong, or New York. For some, the fastest way to get someplace in Stockholm may be riding a bike (with a helmet) especially if the distance is not overwhelming. There are cities now where rent-a-bikes are a growing business, such as Boston and Austin. The point we are making is that sometimes it can be a challenge to figure out whether you are dealing with a *need* or addressing a *fear* or providing for a *want*. But it is an exercise you really need to perform and understand what your concept is addressing.

Recognizing the specific need, or needs, being addressed by your venture concept is important in focusing one's actions toward meeting those needs and in explaining the concept to others, including potential investors and customers who will want to know with minimal effort what it is your venture is doing. We believe you should be able to *quickly and clearly* express what need they are addressing, what desire they are fulfilling, or what fears they are relieving. This ideally should be done in no more than two sentences and with minimal use of jargon. The first sentence is what it is you are doing and the second should answer why this idea is important in terms of the need, want, or fear being addressed. *These taken together express the fundamentals of an entrepreneur's business idea*, and is the first draft of their *elevator pitch*. That is, you should take no more than 2 minutes (ideally less) to get this across to a listener and should not be in technical language, but in simple straight forward sentences. This is important not only to the listener but also to the entrepreneur as it forces you to understand the fundamental basis of your venture.

For example, take parking your car, and fumbling for coins and realizing you do not have any coins. Somebody came up with the idea of paying with a credit card at a kiosk. Another took the idea one additional step by saying it could be done with an app on your mobile phone. Voilà we have two business ideas! The tricky question, which comes a little later, is whether the need to park a car and pay with a mobile phone is big enough to carry a business into revenues and generate profits? We come back to that later in the book when we discuss both feasibility analysis and business plans.

3.2.3 Thinking out of the Box: Not Everything Needs a Hammer

At this juncture, it is worth looking at various contexts that can be the stimulus for generating ideas for new products and services that might support an independent new venture. For example, an especially fruitful place to look for ideas, while perhaps not very pleasant, is when you are experiencing a service "breakdown." Think about a time in your life, perhaps one that occurs frequently, when things go really awry. If you travel frequently (as we do), an occasion might be when you are at the airport. Suddenly your flight is cancelled. Even if you are fuming while standing in the service line to rebook your flight, start observing how the service providers are dealing with the situation (or how they aren't)? How are the people around you in that line behaving? What are they saying (or not saying)? How are you behaving? What are you thinking? These are the building blocks of creating an idea to address this frustration, not just at this one moment, but potentially for the future and for more than just you. This may be translated into a cell phone application or some other product or service.

Some people refer to this process of asking for question is about asking people to "think out of the box." The trouble with this expression is that even if we have one brain, that brain contains a myriad of boxes, so which box should we think outside of? Again, this is why there is a need for asking lots of questions. Basically, we are asking people to question and to challenge "the normal way of doing things." It is about putting oneself beyond our comfort zones of easy and routine, because what is normal, easy, and routine may not be the *best way*. But, once again remember, what is entirely normal in one place may be totally abnormal elsewhere. You also have to avoid thinking that one solution fits all problems.

It is about thinking: "Just because I have a hammer, the world is NOT full with nails. Maybe I should have something else in my tool box in addition to a hammer!" Later when we discuss both feasibility analysis and business plans, we will be asking questions that are there to prompt you to think about the issues being raised by the questions. Part of what we are trying to get you to do is to be able to think of solutions beyond those already available. We do agree with the following quote from a famous psychologist, Erich Fromm sums it up nicely:

> Creativity requires the courage to let go of certainties.

Curiosity and attention are keys to identifying an opportunity and any business idea when moving on to the next stage all entrepreneurs have to start refining the idea, and there are three important things for that: *focus, focus, and focus.* Think of an iceberg where only a very small part is visible most is hidden. More information is critical. It is also important to remember that change is inevitable and you must be willing to change. Sometimes this is called going with the flow. How many of us still use a rotary dial phone? The change to digital brought new opportunities and ideas. Remember when cell phones where the size of bricks and weighed several pounds? Because of the flow of these new technologies into our lives, new opportunities are created to address *different needs, wants, and fears.* However, ideas are not business concepts. That requires linking the product or service to customers. This is what we are trying to get across in our discussion (see Figure 3.1).

3.2.4 *The Role of Creativity*

At this point a brief diversion into the role of creativity in entrepreneurial activity is required. We often hear our students and some clients say they really cannot be entrepreneurs because they are not creative. While we will admit that it is hard to think of a business major in college as creative, the reality is everyone is creative in some why. Creativity is simply connecting things together in unusual ways. Just think of fusion cuisine, for example, where you merge Chinese with French you might get something like Vietnamese cooking, or take Chinese meets Indian and you get Thai. The point we are making is that people have been putting different things together for millennia be it in cuisine, music, and technology. We are firm believers that the really entrepreneurial

---

fun begins where disciplines intersect. Many of the great opportunities today come when fields like biology meet chemistry and digital technology. But these are not the only places. Creativity is in everyone, you just have yet to recognize it in yourself. As the following quote from Apple's co-founder Steve Jobs notes:

> When you ask creative people how they did something, they feel a little guilty because they didn't really do it, they just saw something. It seemed obvious to them after a while. That's because they were able to connect experiences they've had and synthesize new things.

Creativity can be defined for the entrepreneur as the ability to generate or recognize ideas, propose alternatives, or identify possibilities that can solve problems. It requires communicating with others, and even entertaining others by your actions. Think of how the invention of the motion picture has led to being entertained by George Lucas with *Star Wars* films. Yes, Lucas would be considered an entrepreneur by many given the creativity and success of his films, his contributions to the technology of the industry, and his ability to tell a compelling story. What drives creativity is the ability to feel passionate about something. If you don't have passion, it is difficult to withstand the frustration that bringing a product/service to market often brings. As noted by one of the world's great cellist, Yo-Yo Ma:

> Passion is one great force that unleashes creativity, because if you're passionate about something, then you're more willing to take risks.

Many researchers in creativity believe that if you are going to be creative, you have to learn to see things in different ways, or from a new perspective. This is a view many entrepreneurs and researchers in entrepreneurship also see as important to entrepreneurial success. It is one reason we have some trouble in seeing people who purchase a franchise as entrepreneurs. They are usually highly restricted in how creative they can be within the confines of their franchise agreement. They may well be business owners and successful, but the entrepreneur was the one who created that particular franchise concept. In this book we are not focused on the franchisee, but the individual who had the idea that was turned into a franchise-able business concept with all the processes that usually entails.

Let us turn now to being able to see that markets differ. One thing you have to do is realize every location is different, every customer group is different. For example, the United States is not one market, it is hundreds. The north is very different from the south and the east coast is very different from the west coast. Thus, you, as an entrepreneur, need to be able to generate new possibilities or new alternatives as required by your customers' needs, wants, and fears. It is not about how many alternatives you can generate but their uniqueness and ability to meet different needs. The ability to generate alternatives and see unique opportunities do not occur by chance. It is closely tied to thinking, such as flexibility, tolerance of ambiguity or unpredictability, and the enjoyment of learning about the unknown. We discuss this more when we talk about entrepreneurial motivation and the entrepreneurial personality. One personality characteristics or attitude we think every entrepreneur needs to have is the willingness to accept failure. As Edwin Land, the inventor of the Polaroid camera, noted:

> An essential aspect of creativity is not being afraid to fail.

3.3 The Concept

> Creativity is any act, idea, or product that changes an existing domain, or that transforms an existing domain into a new one . . . What counts is whether the novelty he or she produces is accepted for inclusion in the domain.

This quote by the brilliant cognitive psychologist and management professor, Mihaly Csikszentmihalyi, shows the linkage between creativity and a viable business concept. To turn an idea into a viable business concept, the idea has to be something on which a business can be built. A business concept results from linking a customer to a business idea via a distribution/marketing channel and both requires resources and to generate revenues. What this says is that the idea alone is not sufficient, it is the linkages to customers, delivering the product/service, understanding what resources are needed, and finally how to recover value from the process is even more critical. To us, the truly creative part of the process is in creating these linkages in unique ways to create something different, as did our Finnish B&B example in Chapter 2.

Getzels and Czikszentmihalyi (1976) pointed out that only individuals willing to focus on their own goals and rejecting goals set by others have the required motivation to challenge accepted forms of action and thus create new solutions to problems. We are saying that a business concept is a creative process that involves the observation of a problem or need, formulating and reformulating that into a something that can be turned into a business opportunity. Perhaps Einstein et al. (1938:95) said it best:

> The formulation of a problem is often more essential than its solution, which may be merely a matter of mathematical or experimental skills. To raise new questions, new problems, to regard old problems from a new angle, requires imagination and marks real advance in science.

New venture concepts and the ideas that spawn them come from a variety of sources. These include brainstorming, cross-fertilization from others, curiosity, one's current work, by doing marketing research, or from possession proprietary technology. Identifying ideas, opportunities and sources of demand is very much a process of problem solving. In its simplest form, it is really about asking lots of question and the right question rather than having the "right" answers to these questions. The trick is not to find the answer, but to ask the right question. Bet you never thought of Albert Einstein as an entrepreneur, but in many ways he was.

3.3.1 The Conceptual Event

It is critical to *listen* to the many answers that are offered. To us a good way is to ask: "What would my customers want if they knew they could get it?" This question holds an interesting aspect of hidden needs, wants, and fears. That is, what people need, want, or fear is not always obvious, which is why we have to ask lots of questions rather than *one*. We also ask our students to go out and make observations and every time they "stumble" across something where they spontaneously think: "My word, that could be done in a much better way!" Remember, Henry Ford was reported to have said people could have any color car they want as long as it was black. Then along came the CEO at General Motors who realized people did want different colored cars. The realization that cars could be painted different colors, as simple as it sounds, was a conceptual event. At this point an example of how one entrepreneur dealt with a variety of conceptual events to ultimately create his business. For this we will turn to some business history.

3.3.2 A Case Example of the Conceptual Event

How many of you have heard of Amadeo Pietro Giannini? He began his business career selling fruits and vegetables in San Francisco. There he observed an opportunity while working in his father-in-law's savings and loan business.

That opportunity was to service the increasing immigrant Italian population of the Bay Area that lacked a bank. When others did not share his dream, especially the existing banks who thought that immigrants were bad risks. In response he founded the Bank of Italy in San Francisco in 1904 with less than $4000. The bank initially was housed in a converted saloon.

It was Giannini's institution for the "little fellows," those that others forgot or dismissed as not a valuable customer. He saw it as a financial institution for the hardworking immigrants that other banks in California at that time would not serve. He offered those ignored customers both savings accounts and loans. He judged his customers, not by their wealth, but by their character. Some of us think this still ought to be the primary criteria for banks when lending.

Then a fateful event occurred in 1906, the great San Francisco Earthquake and the fire that destroyed most of the city. It was the Bank of Italy that was the first to return to business, long before the more established banks. It was Amadeo Giannini who lent to immigrants following the disaster to rebuild their homes and businesses. Giannini worked from a plank across two barrels in the street, making loans on a handshake to those interested in rebuilding, every loan was repaid as testament to the trust Giannini had in the community. Today, you know this bank by its current name, *Bank of America* one of the world's largest financial institutions.

What you may not know is that Giannini helped nurture the motion picture and wine industries in California. He loaned Walt Disney the funds to produce *Snow White*, the first full-length, animated motion picture to be made in the United States. During the Great Depression, he bought the bonds that financed the construction of the Golden Gate Bridge. During World War II, he bankrolled industrialist Henry Kaiser and his enterprises supporting the war effort. After the war, he visited Italy and arranged for loans to help rebuild the war-torn Fiat factories. Giannini also provided capital to William Hewlett and David Packard to help form Hewlett-Packard.

It is rare today to see a banker who is also an entrepreneur, but they do occur. Generally, banks are a necessary evil to make the economic system work. We will in the chapter on entrepreneurial finance discuss banks and what is bankable in terms of loans for a start-up. Let us simply say we are a long way away from the days of Mr. Giannini and the Bank of Italy except maybe for Grameen Bank and its founder Muhammad Yunus. There will be more we are going to say about Professor Yunus as a social entrepreneur elsewhere.

3.4 The Entrepreneur as a Dreamer

As we have mentioned earlier, dreams are a part of the entrepreneurial experiences, even if they are only day dreams. We had a colleague who always asked one question when he met a budding entrepreneur first time. "Do you have a dream?" It made no difference if this was a person who was thinking of starting a landscaping business, a dot.com, a biotechnology-based firm, a fast-food establishment, or any other kind of a venture in any industrial sector. This question was the essential first step of our colleague in working with anyone.

The question always seemed to surprise the budding entrepreneur. Our colleague's rationale was really quite simple. If the would-be entrepreneur had *no dream whatsoever*, our colleague would not continue talks for very long, because an entrepreneur without a dream would not become an entrepreneur. Underneath an idea for a business, there had to be a dream of creating something however crazy. Try this exercise when you think you have a viable business idea:

- Close your eyes and see your business 3, 5, 7 years from now?

- What does it look like?

- Who are its customers?

- What products/services are you providing?

- Who is working for you?

- Can you see your work environment?

- How is the firm organized, how do people interact?

This is one reason we often tell people to talk about their business in the present tense: it will help them to make the dream more of a real and existing in the current reality. We encourage people to have a name for the firm and if possible a logo. The more you can turn the dream into parts of a reality, the more likely it is that the dream will become real.

Our aged colleague did something else that some investors might find strange and we did as well initially. It was equally puzzling for most budding entrepreneurs who engaged him. Many times people would come to his office, asking for his help in determining what business they ought to start. They would then lay out the various options they have been considering. He would sit either with his eyes closed while listening to the person talking or turn his back and continue typing on his computer as if not paying attention. He asked the person to continue talking. Now, how annoying isn't this? Any hopeful person coming to "make a pitch" would want full attention, right? What was our colleague doing? He would say:

> I am listening. I am listening to their voices and the tone and energy in their voice when talking about an idea or concept. You can hear in their voice if they are really serious and excited about their idea.

He realized that the idea may need a lot of refinement and adjustment before it is ready to be *rolled out*. But, as he would note:

> I need to know if they are excited enough to turn intention into action. I want to make sure their excitement will carry them over all future hurdles that lie ahead. If that excitement is not there initially, the odds of entrepreneurial takeoff are low. I pay attention to the idea with energy, it gets my attention.

What our colleague was doing was completely *nonscientific in some ways*, and clearly not a typical *academic approach*. But it was an *intuitive* test that he had found over many years of experience to be effective, necessary, and informative. He is now past retirement age and not only has had many years of experience, but a lot of gray hair.

3.5 Generating Ideas

We have spent decades working internationally with students, teaching various entrepreneurship courses for undergraduates, M.B.A. students, and Ph.D. candidates as well as firm executives. During our careers there have been numerous occasions where we have been asked questions like: "Where do ideas come from, where do you get ideas (as if you could enter a store and buy them off a shelf)?" The other version we often hear is: "But, we do not have any ideas, none, so ever!"

We tend to think that the creativity and inquisitiveness they had as a child has somehow been beaten out of them as they have been educated. This is where it is important to remember that knowledge is what is left after everything you have been taught has been forgotten. Intuition is often an important part in finding a viable business idea. It is about learning to ask the right questions, once that occurs the answers are easy. This is a view that Einstein likewise held to in his work as we have noted earlier.

At the other extreme we have these *fountains-of-ideas* types of men and women where one idea after another just comes out of their mouths in no particular order of importance, relevance, or feasibility. We have one friend about whom we like to say: "He is so brilliant but disorganized that we would have to lock him in a room with enough space under the door to slide in food and take out the stacks of ideas he has. Our task at that point is to separate the pile into the appropriate idea." He is a bit like James Joyce the Irish writer and his stream of consciousness. We all know individuals who are a bit like an endless run-on sentence. The task is to figure out what statement belongs to what idea. For these individuals one has to apply the listen to the vocal tone process to determine what unconsciously these individuals do not realize: which idea they really want to do. Some say Edison and Tesla both were fountains of ideas.

However, we are not sure which is worse actually, the never-ending stream of ideas or the contending with a desert void of ideas. For those feeling they don't have ideas, we have some exercises later which may help you realize you can create ideas if you free yourself from the restrictions with which you have bound yourself. "I can't and we can't" are self-defeating phrases that lead to self-defeating behaviors. The worst enemy of any entrepreneur is themselves. Money can be found, customers can be found, products/services can be developed, but the drive to make these happen depends on the entrepreneur believing in themselves, even when things seem confusing and ideas for a venture are unclear. As one of our old professors used to say when starting something new "little steps for little feet."

Creating a Viable Business Concept and Business Model

Questions we have often been asked by individuals who seem to have no idea for a business have included:

1. "So, what do I do?"

2. "Are there ways of *creating ideas*?"

3. "How is an idea eventually *conceptualized*?"

4. "How do I create a viable business model?"

These are perfectly acceptable questions to be asking and frankly every would-be entrepreneur should ask themselves even if they think they have a viable business concept. By asking these questions, you will be able to determine whether a new way of doing things is needed. We also believe that it is important to ask yourself the following:

- Can you identify the real issue or need for why something is done the way it is?

- Have you looked for the reasons why are things done the way they are?

- Are these reasons still viable or are they just tradition?

- Are there other reasons why things are done a certain way?

- Are those reasons for doing certain things still legitimate today or are they just historical?

Here is where an example might be helpful. We have an extremely bright colleague who holds several degrees, including a doctorate in food science. He was looking at the lowly potato that has been sliced and fried in oil for decades to make the standard potato chip. As a competitive runner and deeply health conscious, he wondered whether there was another way to make a chip that was both healthier and contained less cholesterol. His answers led to the baked potato chip. However, to make this work commercially required a whole new process for making these type chips including new machinery. While this was a very creative and commercial idea, it was not one that a start-up could have done as the process required major investment in new cooking technology and still required the distribution system of an established packaged food manufacturer.

What this example shows is the value of looking for available information and facts become important (existing products and processes). Are their gaps in information? Are their gaps in technology that can be exploited? It is critical for any would-be entrepreneur to create a way of making systematic observations of their environment. You must keep your eyes wide open to potential alternatives (think baked instead of fried). Sometimes the answer is so obvious that you wonder why no one thought of it before. We are firm believers that one has to let a business concept "bake a bit in the brain" before it is done to the point it is ready to be rolled out.

Another example hits closer to home for us as professors. Because of the trend for online courses to replace sitting in a university classroom, there have been new approaches to the traditional textbook. Some new firms are developing "course apps" for the cell phone, which replace the textbook with interactive software. The development of this approach to publishing and education can allow embedded analytics and other tools designed to enable the monitoring of users. This allows authors to make adjustments, corrections, and clarifications to the application without any additional cost to the consumers. This certainly reflects what we are talking about changing environments and how trends interact to produce change.

Looking for Trends and Counter Trends as Concept Sources

When in doubt, GOOGLE! That seems to be today's *mantra*. Just remember not everything is yet on Google despite the firm's best efforts to download everything into its servers. Likewise, Wikipedia must always be taken with a "grain of salt" as it is not always accurate despite the attempts to make it more accurate. What we are saying is that today, we have the benefit (some think it is a curse) of the Internet. Most information is available for free! One thing we know is that successful entrepreneurs create a systematic way of gathering information and linking that information to create an understanding or knowledge about an opportunity. This linking of information is a way to look for trends, just as one sees "trending" on Twitter or Facebook. However, make sure you are also paying attention to contradictory information. That is, there are counter trends. You may find something you did not expect to find. That is when you want to ask:

- Why did you not expect to find that information?

- In what way were you surprised?

- Are their counter-trends in the information that I am ignoring?

- Are there opportunities that others may be ignoring in these counter-trends?

Here is where an example may again be useful, while fast food continues to be a trend for many, there is the counter trend of slow cooking, using natural ingredients and taking time to enjoy the cooking process. Whole cities like San Francisco have adopted this trend. This is the slow-food movement that has fostered a part of the demand for organic foods and cooking channels on television. The customers for this may be very different in terms of needs that customers who are interested in fast-food options.

We have talked about "understanding" in this section meaning something that is almost a "gut level feeling." Understanding comes from knowing something before you can explain it really well. This is where we suggest you use your intuition. However, remember your prior knowledge, education, and training can be nasty barriers to thinking about new things, new ways to do things, or to understand differences in behavior. It is rarely easy, but you are going to have to learn to deal with uncertainty, and engage yourself and be passionate even in the midst of the uncertainty. We strongly believe that *being an entrepreneur is not for the faint of heart.* Much has been written on passion and motivation, and if you are interested in this topic, we recommend a number of recent book chapters (Carsrud et al. 2009; Drnovsek et al. 2009; Michl et al. 2009). The core of these chapters is that passion and motivation are critical to turning any idea into a viable concept and then into a successful venture. Without that personal drive, the best idea is just that, an idea. How often have you heard someone say "I had an idea for a business like that," but they never pursued the idea. Here again, remember the quote from the musician Yo-Yo Ma:

> Passion is one great force that unleashes creativity, because if you're passionate about something, then you're more willing to take risks.

Brainstorming: The Good and The Ugly

Many organizations use brainstorming for finding new and better ways of doing things. We all have been involved in these processes at some point. Most likely you were divided into groups and asked to come up with new ideas or solutions to a problem. Usually, this kind of group work generates lots of ideas. At the same time a new problem is created; how do you select the best idea? One effective way is to take a break, let the ideas sink in and come back after a while even if you are pressed for time. It is very much the same as what painters do: they walk away, or take a distant view of their painting. The artist comes back and makes the necessary changes to the painting. However, this can be a constant process. It is said Leonardo da Vinci was never really finished with the *Mona Lisa*. He was said to have carried the painting around for decades. In our experience most people and organizations are pressed for time and need to come up with something fast. But, please learn to hurry slowly. One thing we have learned is that in using brainstorming extra time enables the best choice and it is worth every cent of the delay!

3.7 Timing: It Is Not First to Market

One aspect of following trends and knowing when to enter with a new venture is the role of timing. We have always said that if you see your business idea on the front page of the business section of your local newspaper or the *New York Times*, you have probably missed the *window of opportunity*. There is lots of evidence across industries that the firms that are second through ninth in their industry are still around after years. The first firm in an industry is usually dead shortly after starting. We like to say pioneers in an industry are usually shot by other pioneers coming up from behind.

We often hear people discuss an idea and drop it the minute they learn someone else has had the same idea or there is a business built on that idea. There is a myth that one has to be the very first on the market to be successful. This *first-to-the-market* actually is a lot more nuanced than most individuals realize. How many remember the *Osborne Computer*? It was the first "portable" computer although you could have done bench press exercises with it as it weighed more than a desktop does today.

Why most of us don't remember this computer is that while it was the first to the market, no one bought it for a number of reasons including lack of programs and its weight. What we are saying is that it is not first to market that is critical. It is *first to market acceptance* that impacts whether a new technology is successful. Also, don't forget there are new hamburger chains cropping up all over the world although none of them invented the hamburger. In the western United States there is even a chain called *Fat Burger* where the name reflects the burger and customers rave about them on the way to the gym to burn off the calories. Who wants a *slim burger*? It is like fat-free cheese, why bother? But obviously there are people who buy and eat fat-free cheese, but why neither of us can understand. Clearly we are not potential customers, but no concept appeals to everyone, remember that.

What we are saying is that the purpose of any business is to create (and keep) a customer, preferably many. That requires market acceptance even if the name of the venture may seem counterintuitive even if we all know fat tastes good. When thinking about a customer, one should also think of customer groups. In most cases customers are not single individuals today, but form groups of customers.

3.8 Designing a Concept for Profitability and Growth

If you refer to our initial model in this chapter, one of the critical parts is how you make money or get paid by the customer. To us a business concept is fundamentally a statement of your business model. We have already said that the purpose of any business is to create a customer—not profit. But, we also said that *profit is the necessary requirement* to be successful and sustainable as a venture. We also want to add: profitability is a necessary aim from the start. The business model should enable *profitability first then enable growth*. That is the recipe for sustainability and success. We are not suggesting that profit means cheating customers, destroying the environment, or paying slave wages to workers. What we are saying is there has to be a reasonable focus on profit generating concepts. We have more on growth later in this book so stay tuned for that discussion.

A business model is useless unless it also contains a *revenue component*. The revenue component informs us how the firm is going to make money. The rule here is that the amount of incoming money should be higher than outgoing money used to make the product/service, do the marketing, and other operational costs. The positive difference is what we call profit. But, let us go back to Peter Drucker (1974, 2001) once more. Drucker defines profit somewhat differently. To him, profit is *the cost of staying in business*. Again, this helps you focus your business. How much surplus does the business have to create? How much is required for the business to stay in business? What is the revenue model for the venture?

To date we do not know what the revenue model is for *Twitter*. We do understand the revenue model of Facebook, but wonder how sustainable it is based solely on advertising revenues. We will have much more to say on the topic of creating a viable business model in the following chapters, especially the one on entrepreneurial finance. The point here is that a viable revenue model starts with a viable business concept.

3.8.1 *Building a Viable Business Concept*

We are now at the stage for you to take some action either by writing or getting on your word processor. Too many people procrastinate in writing down their business idea and putting it to the test. Once you think you have identified an idea that addresses a need, want, or fear, you immediately have to determine:

- Are these presently not being addressed by someone else?
- If they are being addressed, how well are these others doing that job?

- How stable are these, that is, will they change and how fast are they likely to change?

- How likely is it that someone else introduces a better solution?

- Are there new technologies that can be used as well?

When you then have this information, you can move forward to refine the concept and move into the next stage of developing the idea into a business concept. You need to answer more questions:

- What is the business of your firm?

- What is it really?

- What are you trying to accomplish?

- What do your customers think you are trying to accomplish?

- Are you sure you know what you are doing and where you are going?

- What will your business become?

- Where will this business be in 5 years?

If this sounds repetitive, it is. We think that if you don't get this clear on the front end you are going to lack focus. If you are able to verbalize the answers to questions just previously, you move one step closer to launching your venture, be it a for-profit or a not-for-profit. Even social ventures that are non-profit still have to generate income sufficient to sustain themselves.

Remember our earlier discussion about dreaming about your new venture, this is where you start turning those dreams into reality by putting words to paper. While none of us have a crystal ball and assessing the future is nearly impossible, it is good to try to imagine—here is where the dream can be instrumental! Is it possible to envision the concept and the firm 1 year, 3 years, and 5 years ahead? That is, *what are you trying to do and why would anyone be willing to pay you money for that?* The answer to this question an entrepreneur should be able to answer in plain language in no more than two simple sentences. Conceptualizing the business idea is essentially the process of developing a *business model* of the future firm. The difference is that conceptualizing the business idea occurs *before* the actual firm is created. The business model is for the actual firm and will morph over time. The trick is to not be vague with this process. Simply saying *you are going to be the best firm ever and make money* is neither a viable business concept nor a useful business model. We find evidence that entrepreneurs often use "trial and error learning" when it comes finding a viable business model.

There is some evidence that many new ventures do change the nature of their business model (or models) over time. This seems to be true more for firm working in dynamic environments but less the case in stable industries. For example, being in a rapidly changing area like cell phone apps, the business model with associate revenue sources may see greater change than say a start-up in say the food services industries. Interestingly established firms are more likely to change their business models, because they have more resources. Entrepreneurs with more experience are more likely to make fewer changes in their business model. Newer entrepreneurs sometimes will employ a trial and error approach to finding a viable business model, but again this is restricted by resource constraints of being a new venture. Certainly, having outside investors (angels) or advisors can help through this learning process, but remember investors may push you to adopt a business model that may or may not be consistent with your initial strategic choice of business model.

3.9 More Thoughts on Concept Development

Before you spend money on leasing an office, quitting your job, and selling the family cow to fund your business, you need to get clear what it is that your business is going to be in terms of who are its customers (or customer groups) and what it is that makes your venture unique. Some recent firms that have become all the rage are Warby Parker and Casper. One only has to look at their Websites to know the core business concept for each. The firm Warby Parker that describes itself as an American brand of prescription eyeglasses and sunglasses firm sells its handcrafted glasses starting at a price of $95 with free shipping. You get five pairs for 5 days to try on at home for free. Return what you don't want. It has been called the Netflix of eyewear. Only recently has it opened a limited number of showrooms in the United States.

The second firm is Casper Mattress. Their tag line motto is: *Just the right sink, just the right bounce. Two technologies come together for better nights and brighter days.* These two sentences sum up the U.S.-made mattress that comes in six sizes and shipped in a box. The mattresses are resilient enough to compress-ship and fit through any door. Or as the Website says, *open the box and release your Casper.* It even comes with free shipping and you can try it for 100 days for free. In summary, you can quickly grasp the core business concept of each of these in terms of what they do, who are their customers, and how they get their products to their clients. These almost make you want to get new glasses and a new mattress.

3.10 Some Commentary on Franchises

To be honest we are not great fans of spending money to buy a franchise. We suppose if you are a retired football player with lots of money and having had your brains knocked around, buying a pizza franchise might seem a great idea as an investment, but it does not make the football player an entrepreneur. We are more enthusiasts of those who create concepts that have been developed sufficient to be franchised. Selling a franchise in many areas is a regulated activity much like selling a security. Certainly, this is a way of acquiring a firm that does not require you creating a business concept. It allows an individual to fundamentally purchase an idea and its operations from someone else, a franchisor. If you have lots of money, you can buy a *McDonald's* franchise or a *Starbucks* one. A franchise is a contract relationship that allows an individual to open a location of an existing business with hopefully a proven business concept. Frankly, we do not personally think of the purchaser of the franchise to be an entrepreneur. That distinction goes to the person who created the concept. The franchisee is just acquiring the right to use the same concept.

If you purchase a franchise, the legal agreements allow you to use the business's brand name and logo, sell its products, and to use its methods of production. In addition, the existing company also called the *franchisor* may provide training, accounting, financing, and marketing. The *franchisee* is allowed to operate in a certain geographic area so that he/she does not compete with other franchisees of the same firm. In exchange for these rights, the franchisee typically makes a substantial upfront payment to obtain the franchise rights and then they must make royalty payments, or provide a share of profits after that. The individual making the purchase of a franchise supplies all the capital to equip and operate the franchise. Finally, the franchisee is not allowed to deviate from the standards of the franchisor even if such changes would allow the individual to better serve their market. Fundamentally, you should be paying for a proven business concept.

Typically, individuals who purchase franchises have no experience in that field. However, there are firms that specialize in buying multiple franchises and don't need the management support from the franchisor, but they do want the brand. We will admit that buying a franchise is one way of learning to become a manager and a method to go into an industry. Franchising firms use this method to expand their business quickly with minimal investment. There are risks to purchasing a franchise, which include a number of substantial ones.

First, the franchisor could neglect to be completely honest about the likely success of the franchise or the assistance the franchisee will receive. Yes, there are scams in the franchise arena. Second, the individual franchisee may lack sufficient capital to survive until breakeven. Some franchisors will expect the franchisee to open several outlets within a given time period. This may be great for the franchisor, but it may be beyond the available capital of the franchisee. Besides, consumer trends are always changing and they may move away from the franchisor's core business. This may bequeath the franchisee with sinking sales while maintaining existing high overhead payments to the franchisor. Finally, it should be obvious we don't think that if you have financial resources to put to an entrepreneurial venture that they are well spent instead on buying a franchise.

3.11 The Concept Feasibility Worksheet Exercise

We have over the years used a list of questions as a form of worksheet when teaching entrepreneurship and in some of previous books (Carsrud and Brännback 2007). When we discuss business concepts with entrepreneurs, either those intending to create their first business of those who need to refine their concept we always use this worksheet approach. At one point or the other we will be able to frame the problem. It is a way to create a common understanding of what needs to be done and to identify what one wants to do. You should use these questions not to find the "right answer" but to challenge you to think about what you know and what you still need to discover or uncover from your search for information. To us this is really the development of a feasibility analysis of the proposed venture. In addressing these questions you are showing if the venture is feasible or not. If it is feasible, a full business plan can be developed. Just remember everything is subject to change. So here are the worksheet questions:

1. Can you define the important and distinct functions of the product/service?

2. Is the distinction the product/service or the delivery of the product/service?

3. Can you demonstrate the unique or proprietary aspects of the product/service?

4. Are there existing patents, formula, brand name, copyright, trademark, etc.?

5. Is anything here potentially patentable, copyrighted, or trademarked?

6. Are there any innovative technologies involved with the proposed product/service?

7. Can you show how new or different what you are doing is from what is already out there?

8. Where is this product in an industrial sector? Is it manufacturing, distributor/wholesaler, retailer, etc?

9. Do you know how this sector typically operates and are you suggesting doing something different from how things are normally done?

10. Who is the intended customer or customer group?

11. Who will actually *pay* for the products or services?

12. Who *makes* the buying decision?

13. Who will *use* the products or services?

14. What benefits will be delivered to the customer?

15. What problems are you solving for your customer (i.e., people buy holes, not drill bits)?

16. How will the product/service be sold to the customer? The Internet, retail stores, direct sales, manufacturers representatives, distributors, franchising, through a strategic alliance?

17. Who will make the product or design the service? Subcontractor, in-house, home-base contractors, outsourced, etc.?

18. How will the customer know you exist? How will they become aware of you?

This all sounds very easy, but it is not. The trick is doing it in one to two pages. Get some paper and try to do this for the business you are proposing. Based on years of work and research, we have found it will take approximately thirty (30) versions to get it down to something that is easily understood by *others*. It is not enough that this is clear for you to understand, it has to be understood by others. The value of this exercise is that once it has been done, it is easy to respond to someone in, for example, an elevator when they ask what your business is about or what you do or what you want to do—*the elevator pitch* and be able to answer any follow up questions easily.

3.12 Exercise: Can You Describe the Concept?

The following is a very brief mini-case of some Finnish food artisan entrepreneurs. We think this is a really nice story of how you fight from underneath to make your business work despite the barriers because you have a passion for what you do. See if you can succinctly state what their business concept is. Who are their customers? How are they getting their customers to be aware of their business? What is their product/service? How are they overcoming the barriers to starting their venture?

Three young persons who recently have graduated from trade school as bakers and pastry chefs have decided to open a new business in Åbo (Turku), Finland together. The business they want to open is a bakery; what makes them different is that they want to bake breads and pastries based on sourdough technique. This is one that does not use any yeast at all. Seems there is a trend for this kind of bread making (well known in San Francisco, California) and is all the rage in parts of Europe. In fact, it is *hot as hell* trend at the moment in parts of Scandinavia. However, it is rare to find such bread in Finland. But does this mean there is not a demand, or is there no demand, or is it that the big bakeries have just not realized this trend yet?

Because the leader of the group is young and the business is just starting, no building owner in the center of the city would lease her a retail space with kitchen facilities outlet unless she was able to come up with a deposit guarantee several times the monthly lease payment. Interestingly, at the same time she is unable to find anyone willing to lease to their business there are empty spaces with appropriate facilities in the city center. Many firms are closing and space is clearly available. Property owners don't have paying tenants, but still she could not get herself into a space in the center of the city.

When she asked the real estate agent, all he would say that he and the property owners thought the risk of her business failing was too big. She argued politely that obviously they have no clue vis-a-vis the current trends in the baking industry. She knows this will be a successful venture because this concept is like one she is very familiar with in Stockholm just a boat ride away. She is of the opinion that the leasing agents must think empty places are a recipe for success in the real estate business.

So in frustration she changed her tactic and decided to look elsewhere even though it would not have the walk-by traffic of a center city location. Ultimately she found a place outside of the center of town whose owner was willing to lease them the property. It was an old pizza parlor that she and her partners could quickly convert into a bakery. It is amazing what some fresh paint can do to change the image of a location.

From the very first day they were open, they have had customers and revenues. They are only open Tuesday through Saturday, from 8 am to 4 pm. Since the very first day they have had a line into the street. More importantly they have sold out of their sourdough bread by noon. Frankly, they cannot keep up with demand in their current location and facilities. As she had expected demand for their product, this is going crazy. When asked by a friend what she had done for marketing, she said it was all done using the firm page on Facebook and the rest was viral and word-of-mouth.

As a helpful hint here, use our earlier discussions explaining Figure 3.1 in this chapter.

References

Drucker, P. F. 1974. *Management. Tasks, responsibilities, practices.* London: Heinemann.

Drucker, P. F. 2001. *The essential Drucker.* New York: Harper Collins.

Carsrud, A. 1989. In the beginning: Concept development, feasibility analysis, and value creation. In O. Hagan, C. Rivchun, and D. Sexton (eds.), *Women Business-owners.* Cambridge MA: Ballinger, 35–54.

Carsrud A., and M. Brännback 2007. *Entrepreneurship.* West Port, CT: Greenwood publishing.

Carsrud, A., M. Brännback, J. Elfving, and K. Brandt. 2009. Motivations: The Entrepreneurial Mind and behavior. In A. Carsrud, and M. Brännback (eds.), *Understanding the Entrepreneurial Mind, Opening up the black box.* New York: Springer Verlag, 141–166.

Drnovsek, M., M. S. Cardon, and C. Y. Murnieks. 2009. Collective passion in Entrepreneurial Teams. In A. Carsrud, and M. Brännback, (eds.), *Understanding the Entrepreneurial Mind, Opening up the black box.* New York: Springer Verlag, 191–218.

Einstein, A., L. Infeld, and B. Hoffmann. 1938. "The Gravitational Equations and the Problem of Motion." *Annals of Mathematics.* Second series 39 (1): 65–100.

Getzels, J. W., and M. Csikszentmihalyi. 1976. *The creative vision: A longitudinal study of problem finding in art.* New York: Wiley.

Michl, T., I. M. Welpe, M. Spörrle, and A. Picot. 2009. The Role of Emotions and Cognition in Entrepreneurial Decision-Making. In A. Carsrud, and M. Brännback, (eds.), *Understanding the Entrepreneurial Mind, Opening up the black box.* New York: Springer Verlag, 167–190.

4

The Basics About Marketing
You Have to Know

4.0 An Overview

> I've learned that people will forget what you said, people will
> forget what you did, but people will never forget how you made
> them feel.

This quote from Maya Angelou, the noted activist, actress, prize winning
poet, and professor, describes the desired outcome of effective marketing
in our opinion. For example, it has been reported that in one experi-
mental study, a group of subjects were given unlabeled samples of both
Pepsi and Coke. As might be expected by many of us, not a single individual could differentiate between the two beverages. The interesting
part, for our purposes, comes in a subsequent test in which the subjects
saw the labels attached. Three out of four individuals chose Coke as their
preferred choice. Evidence collected suggested the Coke label activated
parts of the brain associated with the various social cognitive functions,
(memory, self-image, and culture) that the Pepsi label did not invoke.
What this suggests is clearly the idea of how you make people feel about
your product or service that is critical.

Earlier in this book we stated that a critical goal of any business is to create a customer (and hopefully more than just one). Without customers
there are no revenues, no profits, and no firm. We also have said that
demand for one's products/services is critical to any successful new venture. This means that anyone attempting to create a venture has to know
the market they aim to serve in great detail. The more you know your
market, the better your chances of success. This brings to mind someone
most of us would recognize as perhaps the most influential social entrepreneur of his day who made the following quote:

A customer is the most important visitor on our premises, he is not dependent on us. We are dependent on him. He is not an interruption in our work. He is the purpose of it. He is not an outsider in our business. He is part of it. We are not doing him a favor by serving him. He is doing us a favor by giving us an opportunity to do so.   —Mahatma Gandhi

We want to make something very clear. This chapter is not intended to be a discussion on absolutely everything you ought to know about marketing. The field is quite extensive and much of what has been written is aimed at much larger and well-established firms and their marketing strategies. Second, as technology changes so does marketing. We recommend that if you are interested in learning more detail about marketing strategies or conducting marketing research that you refer to various marketing textbooks such as Clow and Baack (2009). Please understand that there are several books on marketing that are focused on specific industries, and as you grow your business, you may well need to find one in your industrial sectors as well. What we are trying to do in this chapter is to look at marketing from the perspective of what every successful entrepreneur should know and how to use marketing in a resource constrained environment like a start-up venture.

4.1 Why Know Your Market?

While understanding who or what is your market is arguably one of the most critical areas for any entrepreneur to know that the reality is many would-be entrepreneurs think this is less critical, they operate like *if they build it they (the market) will come*. This may be true in Kevin Costner's movies like the classic *Field of Dreams*, but in reality thinking that there is an automatic market clamoring at your door is usually the perfect recipe for a disaster. If we ever hear a student answer the question "Who is your market?" with "Everyone," we usually almost instantly know that they don't know who makes up their market. Other than air, water, food, and sex, we know of few things everyone needs and even in that group of four, if you are dead, you don't need any of those, but you may still need a burial. As the old joke goes, funeral directors are the *last to let you down*. Even funeral directors have to market as not everyone needs or wants a burial.

In this chapter we are going to look at why and how you come to understand and know who or what makes up market. This is critical not only in order to develop a marketing strategy and advertising program, but more importantly to designing the products/services you are selling. For the would-be entrepreneur the first question many investors will ask is ". . . do you know your market?" But first, it is important to make sure we are all using the same definitions for terms.

4.2 What Is Marketing?

Marketing has typically been defined as communicating the value of a product/service or brand to customers, for the purpose of selling that product/service, or promoting a brand. One can see marketing as a link between an individual's material requirements (needs, wants, and fears as discussed earlier) and their economic patterns of responses to fulfill those requirements. By making this linkage marketing sets up through the process of exchange and hopefully ends up building long-term relationships between the customer and the firm.

Thus, marketing is a management process through which products/services reach the awareness of the customer. This is often done by telling a story. To us, the following quote sums up our thinking about compelling marketing:

> Marketing is no longer about the stuff that you make, but about the stories you tell.   —Seth Godin

4.2.1 Basic Marketing Terminology

We like to tell any budding entrepreneur that there are essentially five words they need to understand when assessing markets. These are distinct words, but for some reason four of these are often mixed and reduced to one word *the market* and the fifth word is completely forgotten. The four words are *market*, *potential market*, *available market*, and *target market*. The very important fifth word is *demand*. Unless there is demand, there simply is no market!

Let us provide an example here. We have heard entrepreneurs say ". . . China is our market" or ". . . we will enter the U.S. market". This may be true for giant multinational corporations, it is hardly true for a starting entrepreneur. While it is possible that a new firm with a cure for cancer might be a "born global firm," it is important to remember that it is nearly impossible for any firm to capture the entire market of entire country (unless there is a state monopoly present and even then there is the black market). It is simply easier said than done. The likely truth is a particular area or even a particular segment of the market. Not even Wal-Mart has the entire market in Arkansas, its home state, much less the United States. They share that market with small local firms and big ones like *Macy's*.

This is also sometimes called the *Chinese Glove problem*: "if we can only sell one glove to every Chinese, we will make all the money we need, look at the money I would make!" The problem here is that hardly every Chinese can afford the glove or will have the possibility to buy one. A variant on this is that "we only need to capture 1% of the U.S. market." Frankly, a goal to catch only 1% of a market will not impress partners or financers as the reality achieved will most likely be only a fraction of the stated goal. Thus, we think it is very important to understand the meaning of these five words. Think of these as a funnel, where the first term is the largest in size and at the end the smallest and more focused.

4.2.1.1 The Term—Market

Market means the set of *all* actual and potential buyers of a product. This is what often also is called "*the theoretical market size*," which means that the firm catches every single person. For example, there are 5.2 million people living in Finland. The theoretical market—the market—for mobile phones would be 5.2 million, one phone for everyone. In reality it is probably much larger as many people have several phones, and counting the number of phones is not necessarily relevant as you need a subscription to an operator to actually make a phone call. Some people even joke the reindeer in Finland have cell phones [some do as GPS (global positioning system)–tracking devices]. A similar example would be assessing the incidences and prevalence of a disease worldwide, thus assuming that once a cure is found, *every* person with the disease will get a cure. But, again not all diseases are global, which means there will be places where there is *no* market.

4.2.1.2 The Term—Potential Market

Potential market is what most people refer to when they use the word "market." The potential market is the set of customers who profess a sufficient level of interest in the product or service offered. We may think of tourist vacation travels. There are a lot of people who would like to travel to London, Paris, or New York, or spend a week or two in Tuscany in Italy, but may not find the time or the money to actually make the trip. In other words, simply looking at people who may say they like to travel is not then the end of your marketing research efforts if you are serious about selling a trip somewhere.

4.2.1.3 The Term—Available Market

Available market is that set of the customers who have interest, income, and access to a particular product or service being offered. For an example, let us take our tourist, the one who has found the time and money, and has decided to visit Rome, and managed to dine at a really nice restaurant. The service was really superior, the food was excellent, but it is unlikely that this person would become a frequent customer since the trip lasts a week or just a few days and next year the vacation is going to be spent in Paris. There may be several years before our traveler returns to Rome. Availability is not constant but becomes unavailability for our tourist. Thanks to Trip Advisor, our tourist can now recommend the restaurant to everyone who also uses Trip Advisor, and thus they enlarge not just the available market but also the potential market. Another example is how the Website Open Table has expanded both the available and potential market for restaurants in various cities in the United States.

4.2.1.4 The Term—Target Market

Target market is the market the firm decides to enter or capture. To find out just how large this is, firms often segment the market. Trying to serve or please everyone is usually a recipe for failure. Some have said trying to please everyone is a recipe for disaster. Even in Rome, there are non-Italian restaurants as not everyone is into Italian cooking all the time. The target market is quite often much smaller than *market*, *potential market*, and *available market*. The actual size of the target market in turn is determined by the demand.

4.2.1.5 The Term—Market Demand

Market demand is the total volume of a product or service that would be purchased by a *defined* customer group in a *defined* geographical area $Q3$ in a *defined* time period in a *defined* marketing environment under a *defined* marketing program. The demand in turn is determined by the needs, wants, and fears of the customer(s) and the fact that customers are willing to pay the necessary price. There may well be a demand, but the customers may not be willing to pay the set price. If the customers perceive the price too high, they will not buy and consequently there is no demand. Likewise, the price may be high, but the value to the customer does not justify the price, as one sometimes finds in expensive restaurants. At this point we think it is important that you understand how various aspects of your product/service interact. This is often called the four "Ps" of marketing. *Product, price, place, promotion*

While it is important to understand the meanings of the various aforementioned terms, it is equally important to realize that even if one is able to determine the size of these various "markets," all are dynamic and keep changing at what seems an ever-increasing rate. Much in the same way, there are today a myriad of tools to assess the size of anyone of these concepts.

4.2.1.6 The Term—Four "Ps"

The management process of marketing has frequently been called the *4 P's of marketing* (product, price, place, and promotion). At this point some explanation of the 4 P's is necessary:

1. **Product:** The identification, the selection, and development of a product/service (as we have discussed in earlier chapters).

2. **Price:** Determination of its price (can you afford to sell it at a price customers are willing to pay).

3. **Place:** What distribution channels are you going to use to reach the customer?

4. **Promotion:** It is the development and implementation of various promotional strategies that include advertising, social media, etc.

To achieve the four "Ps" today, one must blend art, applied behavioral sciences, and modern information technology. The result of that blending is a marketing strategy or strategies for your venture.

4.2.1.7 Comments on Setting Prices

It may seem a bit odd to discuss price in a marketing section, but increasingly price is becoming a part of how firms market to customers. This creates a bit of a conundrum for the entrepreneur who has to balance the reality of what it costs to make a product or deliver a service and what the customer has determined they are willing to pay. The rise of the Internet has allowed the customer to become very adroit at finding deals, comparing prices and product/service characteristics and determining the price point at which they are willing to make a purchase. Your job is now not just build something, figure out the costs, and then tack on a profit margin. Today, you have to determine whether you can deliver what you are selling at the price point a customer will pay and still make money. What we are saying in as part of your marketing you are going to have to determine your price as a part of that marketing strategy.

4.3 Marketing Research: Doing the Work Upfront

Before one can develop any marketing strategies or materials, it is important to understand how to do marketing research in the context of any new entrepreneurial venture where resources may be constrained. Marketing research as we noted in an earlier chapter is critical in the development of a business concept and as we discuss in later chapters, critical in the process of product and service innovation.

Market research is about finding out who is out there in terms of direct customers and *indirect customers* with which must be dealt. Market research is about assessing the stability or volatility of the market, that is, how likely is it that buying behavior change, how big will a potential change be, and how will the change impact your business or even the survival of your business? Marketing research is also critical in new product and service development. What kinds of features do what kinds of people want included in a product or a service? For example, older people may care less about particular cell phone apps and be more concerned with keyboard size given aging fingers and dexterity. Thus, market research often can and should occur early in the concept development phase of a new venture.

The more data and information you have, the better prepared you are. First of all there is a large amount of readily available data in terms of hard facts and statistics. But, remember that census data, for example, gets dated. Therefore, the U.S. Census provides updates every few years between the 10-year census. Other times information *is* already dated when published (like the number of Italian restaurants in a given area). While this is often the case one can look at data over a longer time period to ascertain and identify possible trends and directions. Some data change more slowly over time, for example, census data. Census data is fundamentally available in every country and is usually extremely detailed in more developed countries, but for some reason it is not often used. Then again, economic disasters like the real estate derivative collapse, which lead to the Great Recession in 2008, are hard to predict. But, we must remember there were voices of warning (that were ignored) raised before it actually happened. Often, these individuals were looking at the same data as other people, but seeing different patterns. Yet, again, we argue the more data and information you have, the better you are going to be in determining the "real market" for what you are selling.

4.3.1 Market Research: Start Personally

Many people take their own experience as a customer as their primary reference point when assessing the market. While personal anecdotes can be a starting place for marketing, it is just that—a starting point. And, of course, we said earlier in the chapter on idea generation that it is good to think of things that you could do better as a potential source of ideas. Therefore, you are a good starting point. Start with taking a good look at oneself in the mirror—it is cheap and informative. Partly one is using ones instinct as well as one's eyes. For example, why are certain things done in a certain order?

Using Google and the Internet are indeed instrumental approaches to get a quick look at a potential market. But these are not enough when the goal is to truly *understand* the market. It is very useful to stop and talk to real customers. From our experience very few entrepreneurs ask ordinary people their opinion, even though this is fairly easy and again does not cost anything. Once again, do not assume you know what a customer wants by just looking at them. Later we will give you an example of a Swiss restaurateur who had miscues about his potential customers and another where a new packaged food firm let the grocery stores (his customer) set his price strategy.

Unless you actually have the necessary experience and knowledge, do not assume you know what customers really want or that it is easy to obtain customers. Over many years we have talked to many of entrepreneurs and have asked them about what was the biggest surprise concerning the difficulties would lay ahead two things stand out. The first and foremost was the complete underestimation of how long it takes and how much effort, money, and time it requires to get the first-paying customer. The second is to set the right price. This is not something to leave to others. Here is where an example in the form of a mini-case may be informative.

Several years ago we had an undergraduate student who started a business selling individually packaged cheesecakes to large grocery store chains. He thought he could easily get stores to purchase his boxed single serving cheesecakes. It took him over 6 months to get his first store and then another 3 months before the chain allowed him access to the rest of its 60-plus stores. He nearly went bankrupt waiting for the first order as he was paying rent and storing tens of thousands of boxes. The stores told him the price they wanted him to sell the cakes for retail. They felt a low introduction price would create sales and demand. The cheesecakes were a premium product and customers knew they were getting a good value.

What he forgot is that it is very hard to raise prices on products once a price point has been set in customers' minds. Worse, he never stopped to think if he could afford to sell them at that price minus the chain's charge for shelf space, costs of ingredients, boxes, labor, and production space. In the end the $1.45 individual box retail price was $.50 below what his fixed costs were. The more he sold, the more money he lost. When he added in marketing (coupons) and distribution costs, he was losing close to a dollar for every box he sold, which averaged 25,000 cakes a month. While he was in 490 stores by the end of the first year and the envy of many start-up food ventures, he was bankrupt by the end of the second year. This is an example of *nothing will kill you deader than success*. His success of being in stores was negated by a poor pricing strategy that did not take into account the true cost of the goods he was selling.

While setting the wrong price may partially explain why it took so long to get the first customer, the primary reason is that the entrepreneur really did not know the market and how it works as well as what his true costs of doing business were. When you are new to the market, adopting a low price strategy is unlikely to be effective as most new start-up firms cannot get their costs low enough to maintain this approach. It is always easier to lower prices and harder to raise them. What the entrepreneur really needs to do is to make the potential customer base aware they exist and that the products/services they provide are value added.

That in terms requires good market research and then effective marketing strategies and tactics, which is dependent on how active the entrepreneur is. Entrepreneurs doing standard marketing approaches will find they are problematic as they can be very expensive and are often ineffective. Sometimes the cheapest way can be the most effective. Public relations and advertising are usually beyond the budget of start-up entrepreneurs, but with today's social media a skilled entrepreneur can be very cost-effective in the use of these as marketing tactics. One of the key issues is to understand who the target audience of all marketing effort is.

Regardless of whether you are a B2B (Business to Business) or B2C (Business to Consumer) new venture, several issues have to be understood. Do you really know the distribution networks or logistics in general and in detail for your particular industry? Again, what does not work in one place may work well elsewhere. It also may mean that one has to overcome barriers in order to reach a targeted market who has demonstrated sufficient demand for a product/service while remaining profitable.

4.3.1.1 You Can Never Know Too Much About Customers

The *basic rule is that there is no such thing as knowing too much about a customer.* The more one knows, the better. Usually, most entrepreneurs know far too little. Therefore, how can an entrepreneur learn to know what the needs, wants, and fears are of customers? In our cheesecake example, our entrepreneur did not know whether the end user would pay a premium for his individual serving cheesecakes. He never asked; he depended on the grocery store chain to tell him. Likewise when picking the flavors for his cheesecakes, our woefully ill prepared entrepreneur made what he liked. When thinking about a product or a service that needs improvement it is important to take the customer's perspective. Their view is informative. Remember you may have more than one customer; in the cheesecake example the stores were a customer but not the end user customer who purchased the cheesecakes from the store.

An entrepreneur is well served if they take a prospective customer's view in when that customer engages the firm step by step. What do customers seek? Or what is it that they do *not* want. What is it that they really do not want to pay for at all? A colleague once said: "I will give you a list of who NOT to hire because of bad service!" Large organizations can afford the luxury of lead user analysis or focus group analysis, but starting entrepreneurs usually cannot.

To successfully launch a new venture, you are going to need a lot of different marketing research information than just looking at yourself. What if you are creating a business, which is not an end consumer business (B2C), but a business-to-business (B2B) venture? Here is where you have to really do some research, both secondary (Google, etc.) and primary (actually asking potential customers).

4.3.1.2 Walking-Around Market Research: Watch and Listen

Understand, we value secondary sources such as census data and other external available data sources as important information resources for the would-be entrepreneur. However, we don't think they are sufficient sources to launch marketing for a new venture. We believe more importantly from a marketing research standpoint you really must be very familiar personally with what is available currently to meet customers' needs. You need to know how you are better at fulfilling those needs, beyond just saying you are better. Remember even businesses have needs and they are looking for firms to fulfill those needs. If you are doing a B2B business, do you personally understand the needs of the firm as a customer? This hands-on knowledge is necessary in understanding your potential market regardless of who, or what, they are.

We strongly advocate *this is not something that can be outsourced to another party*, at least not initially. For every entrepreneur the best marketing research at the early stages of a venture is done by using your own eyes and ears. This kind of market research is invaluable as the evidence is in real time and not provided to you as some abstract number in no real context. This is known as one source of *primary marketing data*.

For example, when we go abroad to conferences, we rarely have the time to read formal economic statistics about a country. We may have some prior knowledge but not the latest update. What we often do is to take a walk, preferably go to a shopping street or mall. We may find something to buy, but it is not really why we go there. We just walk and watch. What is for sale, who is walking with us, do they have shopping bags, are there families, are there kids, is it just old people shopping, are they well dressed, are the stores big or small, what is the price level, are there restaurants, are there just fast-food restaurants, do people seem to live in the inner city, do we see families living in the inner city, are there lots of bikes or cars, or are people using public transport? This list can become very long. What we are doing in this example is known as *ethnographic observation*. Having trained our eyes over many years, we are usually able to get a pretty accurate picture of the current economic situation of the place we are visiting. But, relying on your instinct is not enough. It takes training as the untrained eye is not a good guide as we found out.

4.3.2 *Examples of Walking Around Research*

A few years ago, in 2009 to be precise, we went to a professional conference in Lausanne, Switzerland. A charming and prospering place, we thought, until we took a slightly closer look. We walked several local shopping streets, which were full with people as it was a Saturday. We continued on for several minutes and then said to each other ". . . they have no bags! Nobody seemed to be buying anything at all, even on a Saturday." You could tell that the great economic recession had hit Switzerland too.

Later, in the evening we wanted to go and eat to a nice restaurant on our final evening in town. Since we would all be traveling home, the following day we did not pick the cheapest restaurant (nor the most expensive), but certainly a bit "pricier" than the average for Lausanne.

> We booked a table for six at what was recommended as a multi-star establishment, and arrived as scheduled. We were all dressed in business casual and as a multi-national party spoke in English as the common tongue of the table. At first, everything seemed fine, but then we realized there were two menus. One was available for those who had more money, and one for those who were deemed to not have that much money. It

turned out the proprietor screened each customer when they entered the restaurant. The screening procedure was evidently based on some rather ad-hoc and apparently highly inaccurate criteria. Perhaps we should have spoken French or Russian. We ended up with the menu intended for those with little money. When we requested the second menu we became a part of a highly awkward customer experience. To us the entrepreneur seemed to forget he was in business to make money and to ensure the restaurant was a pleasant customer experience.

We later found out that Oprah Winfried experienced something similar in a Swiss watch store within a week of our visit to Lausanne. That establishment had refused to let her have a closer look at watches as they had determined that she would not be able to afford a Swiss watch given her skin color. From our observation, during the walk we took in Lausanne, we are certain that the Swiss stores and restaurants needed every paying customer! Perhaps the proprietor of the restaurant should have done a bit better job of walking around marketing research.

This case is an example of not only extremely bad customer service but also about poor customer knowledge and an inability to accurately assess customers, which most entrepreneurs cannot afford to do. As we are seeing with firms in the United States refusing service to gay clientele, or African Americans, it is about making judgments and decisions on very bad assumptions. Make sure you have facts when making judgment and decisions. Ask yourself whether you can afford to alienate potential customers. Remember, you can ill afford bad publicity or negative word-of-mouth from customers. In this day of social media coverage and every cell phone being a camera, you are constantly the focus of potential media attention. Make sure it is good attention, not bad.

4.4 Developing Effective Marketing Strategies

To develop an effective marketing strategy requires us being able to answer five very fundamental questions. While this may seem easy, in reality many people find it difficult to clearly articulate and simply the answers to the following five questions:

1. Who is your narrowly defined target customer?

2. In which category or industrial sector does your business exist?

3. What is your unique benefit?

4. Who is your real competition?

5. How are you clearly different from your competitors?

 Marketing techniques used to achieve an effective marketing strategy include choosing target markets through market analysis and market segmentation, as well as understanding consumer behavior. Finally one has to make a customer aware of the value of your product, or service, through advertising. However, advertising is not the same as marketing but merely a part of the marketing process. We will have more to say about advertising for an entrepreneurial venture later in this chapter.

How do customers look at the products or service in comparison to those of the competitors? A survey may reveal some aspects of what customers want. But conducting a few in-depth interviews will be much more informative as these give *voice* to the customer's feelings, revealing opinions, and reasons that most surveys never manage to pick up. From a marketing perspective it is also good to hear the *language* of the customer, that is, most customers do not speak the industry's jargon and sometimes customers use expressions, which can be good to use in, for example, advertising and other means of market communication such as social media, including Facebook, Instagram, and even LinkedIn.

Rigorous market research would be a good insurance policy for most start-up entrepreneurs (and most other businesses too), but since these are expensive, it becomes necessary to learn less expensive ways of getting customer input. The Internet and social media are very nice and good provided you can distinguish between good and bad information. There is a lot of really good data and information out there in space, but there is also very much bad stuff. An entrepreneur ought to know how to find good and relevant customer information from the Internet as well as know how to create, analyze, and interpret market research surveys. If you are incapable, find a good marketing student from a nearby university. However, we believe the entrepreneur needs to talk and act as if they really do understand their various customers and not let others be the sole source of their information about those who purchase their products/services.

4.4.1 Mobile Devices and Marketing

Earlier we defined a number of key marketing terms. Understanding these key marketing concepts is absolutely essential in assessing the market size. Not too long ago there was a sizeable buzz about *apps*; those neat pieces of software that you can install on smart phones. Some apps are free, which you can download onto your smart phone so that you can do something else—usually buy something. Some apps require payment, but usually the sums are perceived small and customers pay the small sum to have the market available. Of course, enough of small drops can become a bucket full or a flood for someone. However, it is unlikely that will happen to all apps—in fact it does not. Despite the hype, most cell phone apps generate little revenue for the developer. However, the cell phone company reaps the benefit of charging you for the use.

Hence, apps can be viewed as tools for making a market available. Phone apps are a part of any modern marketing strategy. While it used to be possible to charge a price for apps, the situation has changed in such a way that most people expect the apps to be for free today. That is, if an entrepreneur wants to sell something, it is almost expected that there is an app making the market available (for free) for the customer. The market for apps has more or less disappeared. For the few apps that people are willing to pay for, the market is not huge and it is highly doubtful that the revenues from the app will be a profitable business anymore. The app has become an "entry-door" to some other market and people are less and less willing to pay admission fees to a store.

4.4.2 The Internet: The Best and Worst for a Venture

We have mentioned observation and walking around, conducting surveys and interviewing and using available statistical data. Statistical data is usually a few years old and in today's world that data can be dated almost the same date it is published. Today we also have the benefit of the Internet but also social media like Facebook and Twitter. Unless you are friends with absolutely everyone, Facebook will probably say more about you than the market (depending on your account specifications). But, Facebook is indeed valuable tool for learning to understand people's preferences and also to learn about new products available somewhere else in the world. It is a highly efficient way to get customer reviews. One only needs to ask whether anyone has any experience with some product and responses are often instantaneous. While Facebook can be restricted to certain groups, Twitter in turn is open to everybody who is on Twitter. Only the "reviews" are restricted to 140 characters, but that may be quite enough. In other words, social media is highly efficient for assessing the market and it is a very efficient way of accessing the market, especially for a starting entrepreneur with a very limited marketing budget. By the way, there are firms that provide regular e-mail and web-based contract with existing customers, such as *Constant Contact*. For some firms this may be an appropriate approach, but we worry about giving control of interaction with one's clients to another group.

4.4.2.1 Examples

For example, during the dot.com boom in the early 2000s, there were a few ideas about selling furniture via the Internet, which at first seems like a nice idea. None of these initial companies survived because they all failed at the very same barrier. None of these companies thought to find out whether the local postal delivery system was prepared to deliver "sofas in a mailbox." It turned out there were size and weight limits for mail orders. It was not that there was no market out there with interested and with potential buyers. It was delivery, which turned out to be the decisive hurdle. Therefore, by solving one problem the companies actually ran into a much larger problem, which they could not easily solve, and thus ended their story.

Only recently has this idea been reborn having found a way to use other means, rather than the post office, to deliver furniture. Some use existing brick and mortar operations as local warehouses for internet orders. Today, Websites like Joss & Main and Wayfair in the United States have demonstrated the Internet can be a way to market housewares, even furniture. Recently, Casper has applied a similar approach in the sale of mattresses. The same issues faced shopping for wine online, the barrier in this case was not distribution, but state and Federal laws governing sale of wine and spirits.

What should be taken away from this section is that ideas that failed a decade ago because of distribution or regulation today may be more viable given changes in both distribution models and regulations. This is where taking a different perspective on the problems can yield very different solutions.

4.4.3 Using the Internet and Cell Phone Apps

Given the preceding discussion, we strongly recommend any new venture have as a part of its launch a functional Website that can be accessed from a mobile device as well as a computer. Today, more and more people use internet search engines to find goods and services and a Website is today's equivalent of having a yellow page add in the old printed telephone directory (which has not yet disappeared). Websites are much easier to achieve today given the large number of web services who will provide you a web address, give you template choices for your web pages, and ensure that it is accessible from mobile devices. With mobile devices accounting for more and more connectivity to the Internet, a firm's Website has to be device friendly. By the way, apps now allow you to take credit cards on your mobile device, which is a huge break-through for the small business owner as much as PayPal was earlier.

It is important to remember that as with any first impression of a firm that your site has no errors, no misspelled word, grammatical errors, that you make navigating the site easy and that users can contact you from the site or app. It is also important to have a page on Facebook as a new venture as a way to maintain contact with customers and be exposed to potentially new ones. There are firms that can help a venture do these, but one does not need to have someone do this if you are willing to learn how to use software. Blogs are likewise a way to keep in touch with potential clients and Twitter can be useful as well. Admittedly, this all takes time and needs to be maintained and updated. There are firms who have readymade templates for Websites. The point is most new ventures will be expected to have a Website.

For example, we earlier in this book looked at an established artist (www .dannybabineaux.com) who is moving into a new genre of paintings and knew to be successful he had to get his paintings in front of potential customers. He knew he had to have a Website ready before launching his new business that focuses on his animal art. He understood clearly in order to sell his art that the Internet was a great marketing tool, but that he had to ensure that the quality of his paintings was obvious on both a computer screen and on a smart phone as well. He realized he had to tell an interesting story about his art, how it was made, and what influenced it. He realized that the quote "you can't sell anything if you can't tell anything" by Beth Comstock was telling him something critically important. Thus, he sees weekly blogs, Facebook postings, and regular updates on the site of all new paintings and commissions becoming part of his regular marketing routine. Responding to comments from these then becomes part of the sales process by encouraging the transformation of interest into a purchase.

4.5 Selling: The Challenge

Selling is one part of the marketing process that often is ignored in university classes or M.B.A. programs. No business can succeed if you don't ask for money in exchange for the product or service you are selling. We are all for the idea of prepayment for goods when possible. We have told students to ask for 50% upfront and if you have done your direct costs correctly you have just broken even with the sale of the item.

Remember that selling is exchanging an item of value for a different item in most cases money. The original item of value being offered may be either tangible or intangible (a cheesecake or an education). The second item, usually money, is frequently seen by the seller as being of equal or greater value than that being offered for sale. However, as our cheesecake example earlier demonstrates, you really need to know the "value" of what you are selling.

4.5.1 Typical Problems in Selling Anything

While one hears stories of the door-to-door salesperson, none has been more famous than the 1949 Pulitzer Prize winning play by Arthur Miller *Death of a Salesman*. While the door-to-door salesman has gone through various variations (Mary Kay Cosmetics and Avon sales ladies, The Fuller Brush man, Tupperware parties, etc.), every entrepreneur has to be able to sell. Even the best entrepreneur has to be careful to avoid believing they can sell anything to anyone. You have to be able to sell your idea to potential investors, employees, distributors, suppliers, and obviously customers.

If you think selling is beneath you and asking for money is demeaning, you are in for a very rough time. Rejection is going to be the name of the game, but remember it is a numbers game. At some point one investor will say yes, a desired employee will sign on, and a customer will hand you their credit card (yes you need to be able to take credit cards and there are apps for that). Speaking of credit cards, there is Squareup, for example, which lets a small business, even a new venture, easily accept credit cards for fees similar to those of established business. PayPal is another example. Remember you want to make it easy for someone to purchase and you want to make selling a lot easier and faster for you as an entrepreneur.

One needs to remember that people very infrequently buy anything on a salesperson's initial pitch. The art may be great, but rare is the person who cannot live without art—no matter how much the artist may say it is a great piece (or for that matter a gallery owner) to build on an earlier example. Potential customers (or clients) have to not just see what you are offering but spend the time to discover for themselves that purchasing what you are offering is the right solution for their need, want, or fear. People, in general, are resistant to being told what they should buy or do. Henry Ford learned that when people discovered they really could have any color car they wanted if they would ask. This may well be preprogrammed into the human brain as even the Chinese Communists have learned that offering choice is economically important.

A much more effective approach is letting potential customers "discover" the benefits of your products/services. This is often done most effectively by asking customers questions about what they need or providing third-party testimonials or stories about the benefits or advantage of what you are selling over the competition. When one sees a real customer talk about a product, potential clients are far more likely to reduce their own resistance to making a purchase than if the salesperson tells them the advantage or even seeing an "actor portrayal" as in many TV ads. You want the customer to own the discovery that your product/service meets their needs. Another example is that the Japanese have learned that provide customers with plenty of written materials on competing electronics for potential purchase. The customer will then do their discovery and make their decision.

However, one needs to be careful. We have seen too many new ventures that are new to the marketplace feel that they have to educate the customer on why they should purchase this new innovation. We have seen more start-up companies, especially technology ones, spend most of the marketing budgets on educating the customer to only see the customer delay long enough that the firm never makes the sale, but the need is met by another company. Education is a very ineffective marketing approach. Remember to ask the potential customer questions, share your materials like the Japanese, and then ask for the purchase.

For more information we recommend you read Khalsa (1999) and Rackham (1988; 1989). We feel that selling is a skill that is needed throughout the entrepreneurial process from obtaining outside investment, to getting your first purchase, and even to exiting the firm.

4.5.2 Selling to the Internet Generation

While normally we consider generational differences a factor, anyone marketing has to address, given the rapid increase in the use of social media (Twitter, Facebook, Google, iPhone with Siri, Instagram, YouTube, Pinterest, Snapchat Periscope, and the list goes on), we think it is important to realize that increasingly people are wanting immediate answers to questions and demanding instant information. "Google that" is a phrase that happens regularly in our households when a question is asked. Given over 400 cable TV changes and news outlets in the hundreds, this information overload has to be screened in some manner. Increasingly, younger consumers rely on the recommendations of their friends and even strangers they encounter on social media.

The day when parents and other authority figures could dominate the influence, mechanisms has gone the way of the dinosaur. Even old well-established firms and brands are having issues commanding attention and respect. These firms, as well as any new venture, has to understand the consumers various interests, activities, and desires if they are going to provide a tailored made product or service to these individuals. Sometimes this means a form of mass customization. People increasingly today want something that is unique to them as we find in showing up in custom tour operators, small boutique shops, and the continued rise of things like craft beers and small wineries.

Increasingly, all consumers, especially those born since 1990, have been consuming information in manners very different from their parents and grandparents, as the decline in the printed newspaper can attest. Instead of having one screen for information, the family TV, today we have any number of digital devices competing for the attention of the would be consumer. Even today the most technology adverse adult in his/her 60s is usually glued to their cell phone or table computer a substantial part of the time. Younger individuals are multiscreen users habituated to consuming a variety of information from multiple sources seemingly all at once. The challenge for the new venture's marketing is to break through this deluge of input. There is some evidence that for younger consumers, they turn to social media as the initial way to learn about new products and services.

Our example of the animal artist has learned that to get their original animal art (that supports wildlife organizations) into a wider audience, they have to use social media. Today, as people only "like" and "follow," ventures that exemplify their values can ultimately influence their decisions to purchase. This is especially true of the younger generations. Those born during the baby boom era of post-World War II are most likely somewhat digitally challenged, but don't underestimate their ability to learn to use social media to communicate especially if that is the way their grandchildren primarily communicate. It is amazing what grandchildren can do to charge the behaviors of their grandparents.

4.5.3 Marketing in the Social Media Age

How many of you get telephone calls asking to sell you something and they cannot even pronounce your name correctly or you get repeated e-mails and/or generic e-mails addressed "Dear Customer"? It turns us off and frankly so do any postal mailings that cannot spell your name correctly, or are trying to sell you something you would never even consider buying, or asking you to donate to cause that is far from your personal concerns as an individual. If this kind of thing turns you off, it turns off others who may well be your customers.

What we are increasingly seeing from successful small firms is that you need to make customers aware of that you see them as individuals and feel that concern is real. One of us has a veterinary clinic to which we bring our pets. After each visit the next day they call to check on the pet by name and ask how they are doing. Frankly, it is not very expensive to make the call, but the personal attention becomes an effective marketing strategy. Remember, today's customer wants to be treated as a unique individual rather than just a name or number on some list, and this even goes for their pets. This vet has also realized that it is cheaper to retain a customer than to find a new one. This brings to mind an interesting quote from Arthur Levitt, the former Chairman of the U.S. Securities and Exchange Commission:

> Firms need to ensure that their ability to provide effective customer service keeps pace with their growth. If you're marketing your firm to new customers, you better be able to provide them service when they do business with you.

You need to remember that increasingly the internet generation and even older generations are using social media to connect with friends and family. It is your task as an entrepreneur to connect with these individuals on a personal level. New ventures that do not use social media most likely will fail to reach a growing part of the consumer market. As we have discussed earlier, when using social media as part of an advertising strategy, remember that it is not a substitute for personal interaction. In many industries, the sale is finally made at the level of an individual interaction. Also remember that you need to test various media platforms to be sure they are actually reaching your target market prior to launching any marketing program. As a start-up you can ill afford a failed marketing effort. Whatever you remember that content is key. It needs to be exciting, it increasingly needs to be visual, it needs to be accurate (no misspelling for example), and you need to respond immediately (certainly within 24 hours) to any contact from a potential customer. Pay attention to your web pages and their ability to be available on a mobile device as that is where increasing information about a firm is viewed and sales are made. Firms like Squarespace and others have taken much of the frustration out of generating a Website and maintaining it.

4.6 Advertising

We remember the rumor that one start-up many years ago spent its entire venture capital funds on a 30-second advertisement at the NFL Super Bowl. True or not, the fact remains that marketing is more than advertising and today social media has become a far more cost-effective method of getting one's message out. We have often taught our students that "word of mouth" is a highly effective marketing tactic and today that is morphed into "word of web" via Facebook, Twitter, and blogs. Advertising is marketing communication used to persuade someone to take some action. While this is traditionally seen as being associated with for-profit ventures, we see it used for non-profits (*Goodwill Industries*, or *Susan G. Komen for the Cure*) as well as the infamous political ads that we all see around election time in the United States. We see this on the side bars of Facebook and increasingly in sponsored pages. Such advertising is paid for by sponsors. You will find this in various formats, including print and mass media (newspaper, magazines, television, radio, outdoor billboards, or direct mail) as well as new media such as blogs, Websites, or text messages.

As with many words in English, advertising comes from the Latin, *ad vertere* that translates "to turn toward." Early on in an entrepreneurial venture internal advertising may also be used to reassure employees or shareholders that a new venture is viable or successful. As a firm matures advertising is used to generate increased consumption of their products/by "branding." We discuss branding later in this chapter. But for now, branding involves associating a name, logo, or image with certain qualities in the customer awareness. Non-profits may rely on free modes, such as a public service announcement (PSA). Regardless of your business sector, you are going to need the public, in particular your customer base, to know you exist.

4.7 Public Relations

Public relations (PR) are widely used by larger firms and can be a useful tool in a new venture's marketing tactic mix. We know of several entrepreneurs who have used this approach. PR is fundamentally the managed spread of information about a venture and the general public including potential customers. PR helps a venture gain exposure to their target markets using topics of public interest and news items that do not require direct payment. This is clearly different from paid advertising as a marketing tool. The goal of PR is to provide information to the public, including prospective customers, investors, partners, employees, and other stakeholders in order to influence them to maintain a particular opinion about the organization, the entrepreneur(s), products, and services. One of the great advantages of working with a PR firm is when disaster hits, or there is a crisis at the firm, the PR professional can assist with messages that can mitigate the fallout from negative media attention. The key here is to be honest and as rapid with a truthful message as is possible. In this day of ever-present social media, the truth as a way of coming out rapidly if a business has problems. Some say it takes 10 good comments about a firm on a social media outlet to match one bad comment.

4.8 Branding

To us a new venture's brand is a "story or image" that is consistent wherever the customer interacts with the firm. It is not what the firm tells the customer; it is what the customers tell each other about the firm. Brands can take years to develop, but it all starts at the founding of the firm. While branding is often associated with a particular product or service, ventures have a brand as one need only think of BMW, Ford, or Mercedes Benz in the automotive industry. The iconic Apple logo is yet another symbol of a brand that is associated with a story of innovation, be it iPhone, iPad, or iPod.

Branding by definition is crafting a name, symbol, or design that identifies and differentiates a venture and its products/services from others. Developing early on a branding strategy can provide a new venture with a competitive edge in competitive markets. A brand is fundamentally a promise to current and potential customers, telling them what they can expect from your firm's products/services. A brand is the consequence of *what your firm is*, *what you want the firm to be*, and *what customers perceive the firm to be*. Here is where you need to be able to answer the following questions:

1. Is your venture innovative or is it imitative?

2. Are you experienced in the area?

3. Are your products/services reliable

4. Are your products/service high-cost, high-quality, or the low-cost, high-value? Remember you cannot be all things to everyone.

5. Who are your target customers?

6. What do they need and want your firm to be?

The answers to these will give you some insights into developing the identity of the firm. Now use these insights into creating your venture's image. Fundamental to a new firm's brand are your name and your logo. Websites, packaging, advertising, and PR should communicate what you stand for, your brand. Thus a branding strategy includes how, what, where, when, and to whom you are delivering your venture's messages. Even your distribution channels are a part of your firm's branding. What you communicate visually and verbally is important also. We encourage new firms to design templates and create standards for all marketing materials. Consistent color schemes, logo placement, are critical. You don't need to be innovative, just consistent. Think of how consistent Apple, Ford, and Coca-Cola look like in everything that they present to the public.

4.9 Exercises

Try your hand now at developing a name for your new venture. Does it reflect the firm and what you want it to be? See whether this name is being used by others? Can you obtain the web domain with this name?

Sketch five logos for your business? Do they evoke the "feeling" of your venture? Now ask friends who are familiar with your business to tell you which one they feel best reflect their understanding or your business. What colors fit the image of your business? How well does the logo look in black and white?

Devise a twofold (three-panel) brochure of your firm and what it does? Can you translate this into three web pages?

References

Clow, K. E., and D. Baack 2009. *Marketing management*, 10th ed. Sage Publications.

Khalsa, M. 1999. *Let's get real or let's not play*. Salt Lake City, UT: Franklin-Covey/White Water Press.

Rackham, N. 1988. *SPIN selling*. New York: McGraw-Hill.

Rackham, N. 1989. *Major account sales strategy*. New York: McGraw-Hill.

5

It Is All About Building a Better Mousetrap: Product and Service Development

5.0 Overview

> A thinker sees his own actions as experiments and questions— as attempts to find out something. Success and failure are for him answers above all.

Perhaps no quote captures the critical task of developing a viable product or service better than this one by the great German philosopher, Friedrich Nietzsche. Every product or service will evolve as you refine them. Sometimes the change will be an improvement worth keeping and others may be too expensive to commercialize or they may be just not useful to the end user. There is an old adage that many engineers overbuild. We wonder how many of us who use Microsoft's PowerPoint or Word regularly use all of their features. Most likely very few of us do. Thus in this chapter on the fundamentals to being a successful entrepreneur, we look more deeply at one component of the business concept: the development of the product or service that you are potentially selling. We believe this is often underappreciated by entrepreneurs until they learn that what they are selling breaks down or fails frequently.

While most people would think this is something only useful to technology-based firms, we believe the same processes are important to any new venture from restaurants to retail firms. We remember one biotechnology firm we had worked with, which had a potential cure for glaucoma. However, it required injecting the patient's eyeball with a needle several times over a period of time. While maintaining one's eyesight is certainly desirable, the delivery mechanism gave many individuals considerable pause to wonder if the cure was worse than the disease. We still shutter when we think of this.

You might think medicine is best when it is in pill form, which has its own issues of absorption and survival through the gastrointestinal track. The point here is that what the market wants can be translated into a variety of characteristics or features of a new product or service. In the case of medicine, characteristics are not just the active ingredients but also the delivery mechanisms. Culture plays a role; for example Americans prefer things to be in oral pill form rather than injections. The French, on the other hand, seem to prefer suppositories for some reason. Each approach has different issues of getting into the bloodstream as well as cultural preference.

For a more enjoyable example, we have spent time with some of the leading chefs in New Orleans and have found they will spend weeks, if not months, to develop a new dish for their menus and specialty drinks for their bartenders to serve. Here is where creativity intersects product/service development in a very personal way, especially if you love haute cuisine that is a fusion of Cajun and Creole dishes. The time taken to do this right has huge implications for the success of the restaurant venture. We have heard plenty of these chefs comment on failed recipes and fallen soufflés that tasted wonderful but looked like large thick hockey pucks. The point here is that there is a balancing act between different product characteristics that both biotechnologist and chefs have to negotiate to bring a successful product to the customer.

We have previously discussed the role that marketing information in terms of customers' needs, wants, and fears can play in the development of a firm's business concept. While not all products are "new and totally" innovative, even a new "hamburger joint" will put its own unique twist on the classic ground meat patty between two slices of a bun. Some of these "innovations" could cause a heart attack (like meat patties with cheese between two donuts with a calorie count of 3,000 and more fat than two sticks of butter). Interestingly, there seems to be a market for these "killers" at least in some Las Vegas casino hotels. We wonder if the related fatal service innovation is that the wait-staff are cardiovascular nurses?

5.1 Product/Service Innovation

At this point perhaps it may be useful to define what makes up a product (or service) innovation. To us it is the creation and introduction of a product/service that is either new, or an improved versions of previously available products and/or services. The critical part of this process is to have products/services that are practical and sustainable (although the preceding hamburger example could indicate the need to constantly replace customers who have suffered fatal heart attacks). All joking aside, the ability to develop *viable* products and services is critical to venture success. To be blunt: if there are no sales, there is no business. If there are no customers, there are no sales.

When we speak of a *viable* product or service, we explicitly mean one Q^1 that it is actually sold and can generate *enough* revenues. There are plenty of products and services on the market that generate some sales, but not enough to cover costs (think of our example in Chapter 4 about the cheesecake company whose retail price could not even cover costs of the goods much less indirect costs). Revenues must cover costs as well as return sufficient profit to continue operations. Remember, there have been plenty of products and services out there, which at first seemed like really nice ideas, but which failed to address a real need, want, or fear.

For example, we have a former colleague who worked on developing the equipment that allows spacecraft to dock with the international space station. The key to the innovation was that depth perception in humans partially depends on shadows that only occur where there is an atmosphere. While the resulting innovation was highly useful to those attempting such a docking procedure, the market for this equipment remains rather small. He always joked that he *sold five to the Americans and one to the Russians*. It is not like this has mass market appeal and everyone has one in their car trunk. While product and service development in turn may involve innovation, it is not a necessary requirement. As we will see, innovation is a very complex concept and what actually *is* an innovation is often in the eyes of the beholder. Therefore, we start this chapter with a discussion of what, in our minds, is an innovation and if the entrepreneur is an innovator as well.

5.1.1 Entrepreneurs Versus Inventors

You must recognize that not all entrepreneurs are inventors. We do think that entrepreneurs can be innovative in how they approach their business. In fact, a product innovator usually would define an already established manufacturer of an existing product. If we look at innovations from the perspective of functional sources of innovation, we begin to see that there are a lot of innovators out there that are neither the entrepreneur nor even the manufacturer. For example, if the benefit of an innovation comes from using the product or service, the innovators are the users.

Innovation process that used to be *closed* to outsiders is now opened up for various actors. Innovation increasingly has become *open innovation.* This is demonstrated recently by Elon Musk sharing his patents for battery technology with other electric car producers. Ford Motors is doing the same thing. Musk's view is that it will help create a bigger market for electric vehicles, including the Tesla. One of the reasons for embarking on open innovation is to reduce the risk of failure. This is important as it is estimated that 80 percent of innovations fail to ever enter the market. The reason some innovations never reaching the market is that they don't work, work badly, or frankly have been invented before. We think you should love your product/service but not to the point you cannot see its weaknesses or flaws. The following sums up this nicely:

> If you're not prepared to be wrong, you'll never come up with anything original.   —Ken Robinson

5.1.2 Stage-Gate Model of Product Development

Most engineering schools and technology firms practice some form of the stage-gate model of product development, a model we have used in teaching in a number of institutions. The process is sometimes long and very frustrating, especially for students and inventors who think their initial idea is "perfect" just as it is. We certainly agree that to get through this model, one has to be passionate about at least solving a problem. As the design genius, entrepreneur, and co-founder of Apple, Steve Jobs pointed out:

> You have to be burning with an idea, or a problem, or a wrong that you want to right. If you're not passionate enough from the start, you'll never stick it out.

This quote also points out an important reality you have to endure a lot of dead-end approaches and product failures to find ultimate success. The very first Apple computers where all recalled with only a few escaping destruction. To try to address these potential wrong turns, one of the most common procedures for product development remains (regardless of whether it is a closed or open process) and that is the stage-gate model. This procedure has been shown to reduce time and costs associated with failure and increase the probability of success. Another important factor that will increase the probability of success is to integrate technology development, design, and marketing expertise from the start. Building a product and then throwing it to the marketing people to then sell is often a very bad strategy. We believe someone representing marketing should be a part of the product development team.

For the entrepreneur it is important to learn to deal with ambiguity and to be willing to transform an idea into a real product or service that is:

- *Superior* to existing ones

- *Well researched*

- *Market-driven*, based on identified needs, wants, and fears

- *Well launched*, on time as promised

- *Well designed*, without flaws

- *Existing demand*

- *Well supported*, with necessary service and maintenance offered

We think this is true for almost any product or service be it a high-technology product for computing, or a new cocktail.

There are fundamentally five stages in the development of a new product or service. Some can be moved through rapidly, others may take some time to complete, but they all build on each other. These stages are best defined as follows:

1. **Stage 1:** Initial investigation of the project, is it feasible.

2. **Stage 2:** Detailed investigation of the project including developing a business case in which this stage defines the products/services to be delivered and a plan for moving forward if justified.

3. **Stage 3:** Is what we call advanced design in which detailed plans are made for manufacture and operations. These include marketing launch and additional planning.

4. **Stage 4:** Is where testing and validation occurs. Does the product or service do what you expect them to do and more planning on marketing and production are made.

5. **Stage 5:** Is the launch and commercialization of the product/ service including ongoing marketing and selling.

Stages 3 and 4 are often the ones that take the longest to investigate, but if your idea requires modification, you may well go through these stages multiple times before your product/service is at the point to be launched. Better to clean up issues at this stage than wait to find them once they are on the market.

5.1.3 Using Stage-Gate Model

At this point we think it would be informative to the reader to walk through those parts of the stage-gate process we consider absolutely critical to the entrepreneurial process. We believe that if the entrepreneur follows this process early in the new venture's development, it will save a great deal of headaches and trauma of the launch process. The following are some of the steps one should use in approaching product development. Many of these steps depend on an understanding of your customer's needs based on marketing research. Designing any new product requires you really understand what customers need. For example, what characteristics or attributes does a handheld can opener for a senior citizen with arthritis have to possess? Do you really want a needle in your eye? Just remember:

> Design is the intermediary between information and understanding.   —Hans Hofmann

5.1.3.1 Preliminary and Detailed Assessments

As you are reading this section, you will notice that it relies on a lot of the information we discussed in the earlier chapter on marketing. From our experience, the first stage is probably the most important. Also, from our experience this is the one with which many innovators and entrepreneurs spend the least time. It is at this stage where it should be possible to get a good indication of whether the entire idea is actually a poor one—and move to the next product/service idea.

During the preliminary assessment stage, it should be possible to determine whether there actually is a market for your product/service or not. Information on market size and market growth is very often available (if you dig into the numbers) to determine whether there truly is a potential for your service or product. At this stage information should be found on what kinds of market segments there are available to you. This information should include the size of the market and their buying habits, as well as whether there is a real demand and potential competition.

We have often heard the phrase *there is no competition*. To this we offer two answers: *Either you have not looked* or *there is no market*. Most likely there is at least a substitute product or service available, which may well be inferior, but it *is* out there. What we are saying once again is that markets (with their associated needs, wants, and fears) should early on have an impact on the ongoing development of products and services.

As we have noted in earlier chapters, there is a huge amount of data and information to offer initial answers to these issues that are available for free. Census data usually does not dramatically change from year to year. Census data is available for free, and is highly detailed in most countries. Most countries offer statistical reports on just about anything. Industry and trade associations also offer statistical data. Patent data is public information. Of course, do not forget this is where using Google or another search engine is valuable tool.

We recommend that if you are developing a new product that you spend time looking at existing patents. Both the United States and the European Union have Websites on which one can search concerning existing patents and in some cases patents pending. Nothing will kill a new venture faster than a patent law suit. The same is true on copyrights for names, logos, etc. as these can be legal barriers you are going to have to address. With the advent of Websites like Legal Zoom and others, you have little excuse to do your homework. However, remember you will still need to have specialized lawyers in your network to call upon when necessary.

In addition, if you are planning on launching your venture and your product internationally, you will have other issues. For example, if you choose what seems like a catchy name in your native language, please check for its potential meaning in the language spoken in any intended international market. Just remember a catchy name may have a less catchy meaning in some other language. Also, please check if the name is already taken or if there already is a web address with such a name. This can be done in a few seconds and save your venture from potential disaster. Be aware of slang and how, in some countries, words carry different meanings.

At this stage it is also necessary to consider additional risks, which are not limited to legal and technological risks, but also include *moral, ethical*, and *environmental* risks. It is also necessary to make rough financial assessments of the product or service; sales, costs, and necessary investments to make the product (including return on investment). This means also being aware of those risks not just in your home market, but if you outsource production the risks in the location of that activity. The last thing you need is a social media campaign who has found out you are using child labor, or you have killed off the last of the bamboo that a panda eats to make your chopsticks.

5.1.3.2 Advanced Development Stage

This stage involves prototyping and testing, partnering, if deemed necessary. This is when pricing considerations should be determined. *Prototyping* is important whether we are considering new food, a new cocktail, new web-based service, or even sewing a new dress. Thank heaven for 3D software that makes some forms of prototyping products easier. Having some kind of a testable product or process should take place *well before* launching the business. Learning on the spot during launch is not a recommendable approach at all. No restaurant would open the first day without testing the menu for several weeks (if not months) on friends, employees, and family before opening day. These *soft launches* are critical to test-drive the menu. It may not be possible to get a second chance to fix the initial mistakes with a dish if the local press is there to do a review on opening night. Don't forget the power of *word-of-mouth* and now *word-of-web* to spread the good and bad about a new venture. Even if there has been adequate prototyping before the launch, it is most likely going still to be a learning process, for everyone involved. The aim is for it to be a *pleasant* one.

As noted, earlier product and service development is rarely carried out in locked and restricted facilities far away from everybody else, unless you are designing the newest stealth bomber for the Air Force. To get traction with a new product sometimes means sharing your innovation or working with other firms who are sharing their innovations. While *alliances and strategic partnerships* first became common in marketing and distribution, we now have open innovation, joint development with partners or through alliances as a standard procedure. For example both Tesla and Ford have opened their battery technology patents for others to use. Linux operating system is another example of an open system that encourages users to add and participate.

Another area we have frequently seen start-up firms have major trouble grabbling is *pricing*. We feel that the price of a product/service should be determined *before* launch and examined in terms of its impact on cash flow (which we discuss in chapter 7). We encourage you to do this early and not let this be determined by external groups like distributors who have their own pricing agenda. Certainly, you need to be aware of the margins for distributors and the price sensitivity of customers and end users. Remember, customers will ultimately determine whether the price is right. If they are not willing to pay the price you have determined, you have a huge problem. They do not perceive the value.

First and foremost, price should be based on *value* not *cost*. The price you set has to cover for the costs, but above all it has to reflect the *perceived value* of the product or service. If you cannot cover the costs, a redesign of the product/service will be necessary to achieve a proper balance between cost and value in which value is sufficient to cover costs. Think here of our previous discussion about the cheesecake company. If the product adds value, by ultimately providing the customer with a compelling reason to buy, the price will not be the most decisive criterion leading up to the choice to buy. Some may argue that pricing is not an issue for product/service development, but we think it is very important to consider *price*, *cost*, and *value* as part of the product development process.

There are numerous examples of expensive products adding very little value and therein not justifying the requested high price. For example, how many times have you gone to an expensive restaurant and after paying the bill said the meal was not worth the price you paid? Then think of the time you went to what some might consider a cheap diner or a food wagon. You may have concluded after paying the bill at this lowly eatery that you had received a superb meal, easily worth double the price. This is an example of exceeding expectations, which is critical in the hospitality industry. For example, there are actually walk-up food-wagons and BBQ joints like Austin's Franklin BBQ now on the James Beard Award list of top places to eat and with a PBS TV show.

As the preceding examples illustrate, if the customer is not attracted to return because of a poor product/service, ultimately both the product/service and the firm will fail because of the inability to recoup the direct and indirect costs of the business. Similarly, there are many examples of the misconception that a low price will make any product an easy sell. A product, which possesses significant added value with a low price is potentially only leaving a lot of "money on the table." It is important to understand that it is always easier to drop a price than it is to raise it.

Likewise, it is important to understand what role the price has in a customer's decision-making criteria. Is it the most important, or somewhat important, or not at all important? Once it is understood what role price has, it is possible to choose a pricing strategy. We are reminded of a member of one of our families who was famous for saying "I am too poor to buy cheap." She recognized early on that what is cheapest may need to be replaced more often or will break more easily and in the end cost more. This is something we think every entrepreneur needs to understand. How many times have your bought a product and have it break down right after the warranty has expired.

5.2 Types of Innovation

There are in fact many forms of innovation. Most entrepreneurs think about those related to product or process innovations. These are known typically as technological innovations. Think here of the iPhone or solar cell production of electricity or even frying potatoes with hot air and not in grease. However, there are additional forms of innovation that are related to the creation of new markets, new business models, new processes, new forms of organizations, and new sources of supply. We have found that often individuals will mistake innovation and innovation processes with continuous improvement and processes. They are very different things.

To us an innovation must have a significant and major impact on pricing structure, market share, and a venture's revenue, especially profitability.

Once again think of the roles iPod, iPad, and of course iPhone played in Apple's growth. You contrast that with continuous improvements, which usually do not create competitive advantages over any period of time, but are associated with *maintaining the competitiveness* of existing products/services in terms of cost. It is this continuous improvement that Wal-Mart expects its suppliers to adopt in order to drive the retail prices lower. By the way, this is another reason we never recommend a new venture to look at Wal-Mart as an outlet for their goods, new firms are rarely able to be the low cost leader.

5.2.1 Focus Innovation

Innovation can be classified in terms of their foci and their impact. When thinking of focus you can think of product/service innovation. Some of these comprise changes in product characteristics including how the product or service is noticed by consumers. One only need remember of how GM painted cars different colors when Henry Ford told customers they could *have any color they wanted as long as it was black.*

Not too long ago product development was "the secret resource" of many large companies. It was something carried out in secret, in-house, away from publicity until the day of launch. Companies were fully integrated product or service developers. Then some three decades ago, the idea of outsourcing parts of product development or the entire process started to emerge. Ventures specializing on certain parts of a development process were created. For example, within the pharmaceutical industry, small drug development companies were started. Some of these small companies became giants, like Genentech or Amgen, but a lot of them failed. The idea was for these firms to develop a drug to a specific phase within the three-phase clinical trial process and hope that a large pharmaceutical company would take the development further and on to the market. What these early-stage drug development firms were doing was essentially to develop the science. Since the science was not proven, a lot of these embryos remained only that, and the firm did not last. Other examples of firms that emerged, where *contract research organizations* (CRO), which were firms that specializing in some specific part of the R&D process. By the way, if you use an outside group to develop your product or software, make sure you are the one who owns the intellectual property generated, especially software code. We have seen way too many firms who forgot to take this simple step of protecting the products/services they have paid to be created.

5.2.1.1 Process Innovation

Another focus is on process innovation. This is where continuous improvement becomes a part of the confusion. Process innovation comes from changes regarding the production process. It usually does not impact the product, but produces efficiencies in the production process, thereby increasing productivity and reducing costs. The role of robots in manufacturing is a classic example. Some new ventures have been built on a process innovation but often this kind of innovation is more likely found in established firms. Certainly some new ventures can use a change in process to achieve some cost savings. Thus, we are not saying that process innovation is not important to a new venture, merely that we have rarely seen a new venture built on this kind of innovation alone.

5.2.1.2 Business Model Innovation

Now we are going to turn to an innovation that frankly is one where new ventures have made a difference. In fact, this form of innovation often is associated with entrepreneurial ventures (think Amazon or eBay) and happens when there are changes in the manner a product and/or service is proffered to the target market. There may be no changes in the product/service or production, but in the manner in which it is brought to the market's attention or delivered. Another example is where manufacturers go directly to customers, cutting out the "middle men." We see this in how Elon Musk is offering the Tesla electric cars directly to the customer without the mark up of a dealership. Such innovations are often great disruptors of the market place. The same can be said for how music is now distributed (think iTunes here). Casper has provided innovation in the sale of mattresses in the United States. It remains to be seen if existing firms can do something similar.

Innovation in business models is a place where new ventures have a competitive advantage as they are starting from scratch and are not necessarily bound by the traditional way of doing business in an industrial sector. We think every company needs to know the business models in their industrial sector and to be willing to challenge those models with new ones. We have long encouraged our students to *think of another way to do their business* and not copy existing models in their industrial segment. In other words, *think out of the box.*

5.2.2 Innovation Impact

Innovation can also be classified in terms of its impact. One form of innovation impact is incremental. Once again, this is often confused with continuous improvement as it reflects small but perceptible improvements in products or services. It represents small improvements in benefits that can be noticed by the customer, but it usually does not significantly modify the business model or the way a product or service is consumed. Think here of the DVD versus Blu-ray.

Then there is *radical innovation* that happens when there is a major change in the way something is consumed, be it a product or a service. Such radical innovation often brings a new way money is made; that is, the business model changes or brings a new paradigm to the market segment that modifies the existing business model. Once again, think of iTunes, iMusic, or iPod. Remember people want something that is simple to understand, which is a "not so-secret" aspect of Apple's products. American males only read the instruction books when they have no other choice and most instruction books for new products are thicker that the device or are confusing instructions on a Website. With Apple the view is how to operate their products is intuitive. With any innovation, be it service or product, we are reminded of the following quote from the man who gave us $E = MC^2$:

> Everything must be made as simple as possible. But not simpler.   —Albert Einstein

5.3 To Innovate or Not: That Is the Big Question

> Anxiety is the handmaiden of creativity.   —T.S. Eliot

This quote by the noted English playwright and essayist reminds us that it is perfectly acceptable as an entrepreneur to be nervous and to wonder if they have to be creative themselves to be an entrepreneur. To many, innovation is one defining dimension of entrepreneurship. There are those who will argue at great length that entrepreneurship and innovation are one and the same. To them an entrepreneur who does not innovate is not an entrepreneur. We can partially agree with this, but only to a certain degree. We have already argued and given multiple examples in earlier chapters of entrepreneurs who have not innovated anything, but who we consider as entrepreneurs—take our couple in the Finnish archipelago. We argue that many, if not most, entrepreneurs are essentially *copycats*. They create a business selling an existing product or offering an existing service. The following from lengthy quote from an American independent film director and entertainment entrepreneur about making a movie fits nicely:

> Nothing is original. Steal from anywhere that resonates with inspiration or fuels your imagination. Devour old films, new films, music, books, paintings, photographs, poems, dreams, random conversations, architecture, bridges, street signs, trees, clouds, bodies of water, light and shadows. Select only things to steal from that speak directly to your soul. If you do this, your work (and theft) will be authentic. Authenticity is invaluable; originality is non-existent. And don't bother concealing your thievery-celebrate it if you feel like it. In any case, always remember what Jean-Luc Godard said: **"It's not where you take things from—it's where you take them to."**   —Jim Jarmusch

As an aside, yes we consider every movie a business venture that is a standalone business with its own market and entrepreneurial team.

Remember the greatest new technology is built upon the shoulders of older or existing technology. A new venture that copies parts of a prior business can still be successful if that product/service being offering is somehow different (and better) than what is already offered on the market, or that there is still an unmet need, want, fear, and therefore a demand. That is, the market is not yet saturated with potential solutions. We believe it is perfectly fine to create a business around an existing product and/or service, or even an existing story like Shakespeare' *Romeo and Juliet* that has morphed into any variety of movies, including *West Side Story*. In fact, many of the cases we have shown you earlier (local B&Bs) are one examples of "a familiar plot line told in a new context."

It is important to remember that just because the product/service is better or different does not mean that it is also an innovation. To further complicate matters, we also argue that innovation is not the same as new technology. It can be but is not necessarily always the case. This is where our earlier discussion on types of innovation above needs to be recalled. What you should have gathered from all of the preceding lengthy discussions is that what is important is what you do with the innovation you have at hand. Can you commercialize that innovation?

5.3.1 Commercialization Is Key

Just because the product is *new*, what many like to call an innovation does not mean it is a real innovation let alone that it will sell and generate revenues. One *defining characteristic of an innovation is that it can actually be commercialized*, not just has a potential to be sold. This means that we can define something as an innovation only *after* it has proven itself on the market. Commercializing a product/service requires effort where marketing becomes absolutely essential. While there used to be a time in history when new products, often new technology, would sell by themselves, those days are long gone. As much as believing in "luck" is a bad new product strategy, so is the "build it, they will come" approach, which only comes in movies about baseball with Kevin Costner as the star.

As we have mentioned earlier, innovation can be a product or a service. It can also be a process; a new way of manufacturing or delivering a product or a service. It can also be new material. While innovation often these days involves technology, it does not have to be technology. An innovation can also be a new business concept—a new way of doing business. The key word here is *new*. However, we have to define new.

5.3.2 Defining New: In the Eye of the Beholder

To us "new" is not the same as an "innovation." Frankly, we believe that there are varying degrees of newness. Are we speaking of these distinctions:

1. New to the world, something based on a break through scientific discovery

2. New to the market, which can be an existing product first time presented to a particular market, which can be a country, region, or a market segment

3. New to the company or the entrepreneur

4. Really not new at all

If we conceptualize newness this way, we will at the same time get an understanding of *how long it will take before the product/service is likely to generate revenues*. The time can range from 1 day to 18 months to 18 *years*. Obviously, the time delay really depends on the nature of the business, its revenue model, the amount of preparation, and marketing prior to launching the venture, and even if there is a customer waiting for the business that might have actually provided the start-up capital. A service-based business has the potential to generate cash flow (does not mean it is yet positive cash flow) from the first day of operations. That initial income depends on whether there is a customer who has already been identified and is waiting for that service that shows a degree of preparation prior to the launch of the business.

What we know from experience and data is that it usually takes 18 months for a typical firm, regardless of being a product- or service-based venture, to generate a positive cash flow. Understand, revenues will have started sooner, but they may not cover ongoing expenses. Notice here we are talking *positive cash flow*. That is inflow in revenues is greater than outflow of money to cover expense. If, however, the company is developing their products, which is based on a scientific breakthrough, like a biotechnology company, it could well be 18 years before any revenues are seen and years longer before positive cash flow. That is the time it takes before passing through all phases of clinical trials and final approvals with the authorities. How does a company stay afloat for almost two decades with negative cash flow? We will have much more to say about cash flow in chapter 7, but to us this is a concept that impacts new product/service developing even prior to the launch of a new venture.

In the case of such a biotechnology firm, innovation based on scientific breakthrough is fundamentally *not* about product *development* in the beginning of the *research* process. It is about getting the science right. Early-stage biotechnology firms are more about *R* as in *Research*, than *D* as in *Development*. Therefore, many of these kinds of firms depend on research grants from both public and private sources during these years. Many things can go wrong along the way, which will result in an innovation not being commercialized. Strictly speaking, if such a product

---

development eventually fails the product is not an innovation but only an idea or an invention that failed to be commercialized. Remember that it is a defining characteristic of an innovation that it can actually be commercialized—put on the market and sold. One only needs to look at newspaper reports over the last 60 years to see various R&D firms that said they were about to have the cure to cancer only to find it was not the case.

5.4 Building on the Past

Please recall our earlier discussion on types of innovation. It should be clear that not all technology is based on scientific breakthrough, but on technological improvements that have occurred. Take, for example, the development of a new car. Even if there is some technological innovation in the engine, which may lead to lower fuel consumption or something similar, the basic product is an old one. This process is much more about development than research, as we already know how to build cars and car engines. An innovation in this context is about some improvement that enables a *significant improvement* on some other dimension—fuel efficiency. You may think that the electric car is a new idea, but actually it is an old one, dating back to the age of Henry Ford. The reason for the success today of Tesla is really in the battery storage of energy.

5.4.1 *Reinventing an Industry's Products: Examples*

A similar example would come from the music industry. Some of us still remember Long Playing records (a lot of us may have them in our homes) made in vinyl. In fact, vinyl records are still being made, and to some audiophiles, they remain superior to digital recordings. That said, they are now just a small fraction of the output as they were replaced by a new format, the compact disk (CD). Even if there was only one good song on the LP-record or CD-disc (a hit), the consumer had to buy 17 other songs that were on the record. A measure of success was that if a record sold *gold* or *platinum*, which usually meant that there were a few more other good songs on the record. Consumers were lining up at the store on release days to get their hands on some of these treasures. The reality was that often it was only one song that typically drove the sales of a given album.

Today, music is bought and delivered by the song via Spotify or iTunes or some other internet or cell phone app. The consumer now buys just the song one wants to listen too, or in case of Spotify, pays a subscription fee, making it possible to listen to just particular songs. The delivery of music has clearly been innovated—significantly improved from the consumers' perspectives. Whether it is equally good for the artists or the record companies is an area of much discussion and debate. What is not debated is that the rate the change in the delivery of audio content has certainly changed the earnings logic; that is, how revenues are generated in the music business. It has also forced a change in the revenue model of how musicians make money. Many now see their primary revenue sources being tour ticket sales for a concert, not record sales. Some recording artists actually release their music for free on the Internet to drive interest in their tours. Others like Taylor Swift have taken all of their music off *Spotify*.

5.4.2 E-Commerce: Using Innovation in Marketing and Distribution

We all know how shopping has changed dramatically for the past two decades for most of us in the developed economies. First, we had the big super malls killing off small local stores, but now we see developments that threaten the existence of super malls. One of these has been the return of the "shop local" movement, which is an example of trends and counter trends. However, a bigger change has been brought with the advent of the internet. The savvy small business entrepreneur has taken advantage of this trend via eBay and Etsy the e-commerce sites as well as using payment options like PayPal or Squareup.com. Artists have learned the value of these innovations to reach customers that would never have been available to them in the past and take payment from them easier than ever before. We tell any new entrepreneur, especially artisan entrepreneurs, that they should explore these as a part of their marketing and payment tools, but also as a form of innovation in their particular market.

While mail order has been around for decades, e-commerce has basically globalized retailing and, as discussed previously, localized it as well. We know people who have taken advantage of Black Friday sales in the United States from Finland by using the Internet. Levi's was selling at 75 percent off the U.S. price and the U.S. Dollar was 35 percent cheaper than the Euro at that time. A pair of regular Levi's 501 cost €100 in Finland from a brick and mortar store. This huge difference meant it was possible to buy four pairs of Levi's 501 for the price of one. Finding the right size was no issue since an inch is an inch any place in the world. Even counting in mailing to Europe, the savings were substantial.

Another example we know comes from an American art collector we know who adores and collects contemporary Cuban surrealist art. With the existing U.S. embargo on trade with Cuba, obtaining such art by visiting Cuba would be nearly impossible. However, via eBay he has been able to locate a small gallery in Canada (www.cubanartbeat.com) co-founded by Richard Wiebe. This gallery specializes in such art, and thus a small business in Canada now has a major new customer in the United States via eBay. Of equal importance is that several new artists in Cuba now have their works in collections around the world. Clearly once the embargo is fully lifted, the relationship may well shift again with collectors dealing directly with the artist. The point here is that one technology has impacted the ability of several entrepreneurial businesses (the gallery and the artists) to reach new customers.

An additional example can be found in traveling where the Internet is significantly changing the business of tourism and hospitality. Not only are trips booked and purchased online (as well as flight check-in), but customers post reviews of restaurants and hotels online through for example Trip Advisor. Through www.booking.com the customer can find hotels, but also rooms to rent or apartments to rent as viable alternatives to hotels with various numbers of stars. Needless to say these rooms and apartments range in quality from excellent and good to bad and just awful too, as noted by this poor customer (recall the quote from Chapter 2, which we repeat here) arriving in Rome, and desperately trying to save herself from what seems like a total disaster.

> Hello! I have planned a surprise trip for my mama and arrived in Rome today. Unfortunately the AIRBNB I booked is not at all what the reviews and photos expressed. I am from California and my mom is here from Chicago. I am trying to see if I can find a better quality place to stay :).
>
> Your place looks very clean and welcoming! Hope to hear back from you. . . . Best Janet

These rooms, whether hotels or independent ones are as such no innovation, but clearly the delivery process and the sales process has been innovated through the use of the World Wide Web—a technological innovation only 25 years old. What we are saying quite simply is that you have to have a web presence in most cases for a new or existing venture.

5.5 Industry Change as Opportunity for Product/ Development

Some say change is inevitable and we could not agree more. If you only saw your business as a railroad, you will never see the airplane coming. That example brings to mind the following quote from the ancient Chinese philosopher Lao Tzu:

> Life is a series of natural and spontaneous changes. Don't resist them; that only creates sorrow. Let reality be reality. Let things flow naturally forward in whatever way they like.

For an entrepreneur it is essential to learning to identify early signals of potential change that could impact their new venture. This also holds for anyone who has the intentions to become an entrepreneur in the future. While such signals can be threatening, they also are important sources of opportunities. We have discussed this previously in an earlier chapter, but we believe it is important to repeat this message. The ability to identify signals of change offers possibilities to anticipate either potential successful opportunities or potential down falls. Important questions are as follows:

- What developments will matter the most?
- What customer groups should be especially watched?
- Are there contextual factors that influence change and innovation?
- Are the changes global, national, or just regional?

5.5.1 Examples of Industrial Change Fostering New Models

Here is where some examples we are all familiar with may be useful to examine. Take for this exercise the media industry, specifically printed newspapers and magazines. During the last dot.com era when e-commerce took off only to crash-land a few years later, change was in the air despite the dot.com bubble at the start of the new millennium in the

2000. Already then, there were predictions that people would soon be reading newspapers from the Internet and the traditional papers would not exist very much longer. Yet, to make this change happen, some additional technology was needed to allow for portability.

Sometimes major change requires several innovations to have occurred, which, taken together, produce unintended consequences and thus new opportunities. The real change in this direction within the print media did not occur until smart phones and tablets were launched. These allowed for significant improvements in delivery and legibility of digital content, especially portability given cell phone and WiFi technology. Initially, many in the newspaper industry did not take threats of significant changes in consumers' media consumption seriously until it was too late for many. Many newspapers saw it as a good idea to offer their papers for free on the web, which in turn allowed consumers to get used to this. To introduce fees for readership or so-called pay walls was not an easy procedure. A few, like the *New York Times* seemingly have been successful in making that transition. Many newspapers offer a free weekly digital subscription if the buyer purchases a weekend printed subscription.

However, it was not only consumers who changed their consumption behavior. Perhaps the really decisive factor to hit mass media was that advertisers moved away from newspapers (and major TV networks) to place their ad dollars on other more effective and targeted channels. The hard fact is that all through the history of newspaper industry's existence, *news* has never been a source of profit. Advertising has been the real business of newspapers. As anyone who watches the major national TV networks in the United States, both local stations and the networks had the same revenue model and have been hit with a similar problem given the plethora of cable and satellite channels (400+) vying for ad dollars. Interestingly, the typical American only watches 17 of these channels, and the tricky part is that those are spread over the 400 and vary by customer. By the way, we don't recommend a new venture to do TV advertising and one would do far better using a local community weekly newspaper closer to your customer base (if they are located in a given geographical area), than to advertise in a major newspaper.

Perhaps the most classic example of how changes in technology can change an entire industry comes from the development of hard disk drive industry. The size of the disk drives went from 14-inch diameter

---

disks in the mid-1970s to 1.8 inches in the 1990s. Storage was measured in megabytes that soon became gigabytes. Today smart phones store gigabytes and computers (tablets and laptops) store data in clouds. At this point it seems that most mobile phones were really sold as cameras rather than traditional voice devices. All evidence points to mobile devices being the leading mechanism for accessing the Internet as we mentioned Chapter 4.

5.6 Spotting New Trends for New Products/Services

When seeking to identify weak signals of change, one should look at the behavior of *non-consumers* (Christensen et al. 2004). The second group of consumers to observe is *existing consumers*, who are prepared to pay a premium price for higher performing products. The third group you should track includes those individuals we call *overshot customers*. These are the people who will say something costs too much, or a product is too complicated. This is where it is very hard to earn premium prices for any improvement on any dimension of a product or service. This is also when a product/service has become a commodity. That is, everybody has it and the market is about to become saturated. It is essential for entrepreneurs to look for changes in their industry and to understand how those changes will impact their business success or potential failure. These potential changes pose opportunities for new, or improved, product and service development as much as they represent serious threats to firm success. Also don't forget that the entrepreneur themselves are change agents. Remember the quote from the famous American anthropologist, Margaret Mead:

> Never doubt that a small group of thoughtful, committed, citizens can change the world. Indeed, it is the only thing that ever has.

Here is where a mini-case may be illustrative as to the importance of innovation in design and the importance of having patents to protect those innovations:

One day while dealing with one of her children in a messy bathtub in her home in Arizona, Rebecca Finell has an idea for a new product, the Frog Pod. This almost sounds like a repeat of a Eureka moment.

To capitalize on these innovatively designed product and other design ideas she had, she formed Boon, Inc. with her business partner. At Boon, she held several posts simultaneously (president, principal designer, and chief brand strategist). Today it has become a leading firm in the area of innovative baby products, including a highchair that was all the rage at various product fairs. Rebecca holds nearly two dozen patents on her various products including the highchair. While at Boon she found a knockoff of the highchair being sold and she sued the manufacturer who had just signed a deal with Wal-Mart, a firm Rebecca had wisely avoided as a retailer. The resolution to the patent infringement was that the manufacturer kept Wal-Mart as a customer, but Rebecca received a substantial royalty on every chair sold. She got the benefit of the outlet without the headache as she likes to say. Being a serial entrepreneur, Rebecca decided she wanted to turn her considerable talents in design to more "upscale" consumer goods. This meant forming a new company with a very different focus "neo luxe."

Rebecca then launched *FINELL* (www.finell.co) (yes "co" not "com") in January of 2013 and based her new business in Austin, Texas. In two short years the firm and her designs have received international acclaim. The firm's products are to be found in Barney's of New York, Bergdorf Goodman, and gift shops in major art museums. In addition, its products can be found nearly two dozen countries. The firm defines itself as a designer and manufacturer of neo luxe housewares and fashion accessories, "Great design is what drives every part of the *FINELL* brand" explains Rebecca. She sees her competitive advantage as being "simplicity and smart design." She does this by ignoring conventional views of modern design to create new utilities and exciting products while having the finest craftsmanship and quality. The firm's products are made from an unexpected mix of luxury materials, which Rebecca sees as "progressive aesthetic and innovative feature." She wants products that are as unique and refined as the customer who appreciates them.

5.7 Basic Conditions for Successful Products and Services

We have partially addressed these earlier in the book when discussing developing a viable business concept, but these deserve repeating in this context. In general, there are four economic conditions that successful products and services appear to share. They are usually based on systematic and rational thoughts. We do not believe, as often portrayed in popular press, that they are the result of randomly and accidentally emerging ideas that people stumble upon. Luck and serendipity may occasionally be involved, but not as a rule. These conditions are as follows:

- **Buyer utility:** answer to needs, wants, and fears

- **Strategic pricing:** fit with what enough people are willing to pay

- **Business model:** is this profitable

- **Adoption hurdles:** why would customers, employees, partners, or even society accept the product or service

It is worth noting again at this point that utility and technological advancement are not the same. While it is often portrayed in popular press, that technology is key, we argue that buyer utility—*needs, wants, and fears*—is the key driver of success. Another way of expressing buyer utility is *usability* or *user friendliness*, which is dependent on the following:

- Customer productivity that allows the customer to do something better

- Simplicity

- Convenience

- Risk mitigation

- Fun and image

- Environmental friendliness

For some customer groups, and even in some countries, *environmental friendliness* is becoming extremely important. If there is no clear ecological utility, the product or the service has no chance of succeeding. An increasing number of customers are willing to pay a premium price for ecological utility!

5.8 Case Study of New Product Development in a New Venture

The following case is real. We have only de-identified the individual and the city at the request of the entrepreneur. We see this case as a good example of how to develop a viable new venture in a very traditional industry that is heavily regulated. We also see it as a good example of how to develop *new* products, and *rediscover old* ones which are new to the current market. The result was very innovative within the liquor beverage industry. Here is her story:

It was 2010 and Ann was about to have her 45th birthday. She had just quit her well-paying position in a high technology in California. She had an engineering degree and enough money saved from stock options and investments to start a new venture without needing outside investment. She wanted to build a venture for which she had a burning passion. The business concept was one built from her experience traveling for her job in telecommunications. She had spent a lot of time in Europe and the East Coast of the United States and had seen this as a growing trend among young professionals that attracted those who wanted a unique experience like an upscale wine bar, but focused instead on high-end, designer cocktails.

What she wanted to start was a small, intimate, and neighborhood cocktail bar while informal would still be seen as sophisticated and upscale. She had seen this concept work in London, Berlin, New York City, Boston, and Washington DC. The city she chose would hopefully not have such an establishment but might have restaurants that served such cocktails. She knew that what she had in mind was not just any typical bar in a city with a large university population and a vibrant club scene. She knew there was a market for upscale wine bars and for intimate cocktail lounges if she could find a city that was underserved with this kind of establishment. She wanted a small bar, targeting not the undergraduate college crowd, or convention tourists, but local cocktail lounge aimed at established young professionals and couples living within a five mile radius looking for a unique experience in terms of cocktails and ambiance. She also wanted to be sure she could find a location with sufficient space for parking as well as with easy access for residential neighbors to walk to the lounge, which she named *Lioness*.

During Ann's travels she found a city, with a growing population, highly educated, increasingly known for its food scene and growing taste for expensive restaurants and fine cuisine. She also discovered that while the city had a vibrant bar scene because of a large number of university students and young professionals, there was still an opportunity for the kind of business she wanted to start. Given the city and state she chose, one of the hurdles to clear was whether she could get a full liquor license from the state's Alcohol Control Board (ACB). Obtaining the license depended on the location as she did not intend to serve food and a stand-alone bar license was far harder and more expensive to obtain than one where food service would account for at least 50 percent of the revenues. Such an establishment, in this city and state, could not be near schools or churches and had to be in an area designated for retail businesses. Very few of these licenses were granted in a given area and thus served as a barrier to entry for competitors.

The location she chose was in an up and coming gentrified neighborhood of older cottage style and bungalow homes that were very popular with younger well-paid technology and medical professionals who had sufficient income to afford more than a dollar beer night at some local bar full of noisy and drunk college students. She found a small retail space that could house an establishment selling just alcoholic beverages, a process that took 2 months. She could not start the ACB process till she had a location, but it had to be an acceptable location to the ACB, a bit like a catch-22 she often thought.

Then she went about the task of obtaining the liquor license, a process that took more than the normal 6 months. By the time the ACB approved the license, it was 12 months since she started the process and nearly 10 months of paying rent on the retail space with no revenues coming in during that entire time. Ann, being a detail planner had foreseen the process might take longer than the normal "6" months and had even doubled the delay time in figuring her cash flow requirements.

Despite the license delay, Ann acquired an antique art-deco bar and seating for the *Lioness*, sufficient to seat 25 only. She also set about searching every local antiques and junk shop in the city for unique cocktail glasses to be consistent with the image she had for the *Lioness*. At the end of the process she had 10 dozen including unique highball, martini, flutes, and other glasses in which to serve her beverages.

The only remodeling she did during this time was painting in a vibrant but tasteful burgundy color with golden brown trim, which was part of her "branding," and a new floor that were covered as a part of her rental agreement with the landlord. A friend designed the Lioness logo that was painted on the windows to the Lounge and included in all the printed materials and web page. Now Ann turned to the most important part of what would make the Lioness unique—the cocktails.

During this time Ann designed her cocktail menu, including weekly specials. To keep the customers coming back, Ann learned from talking to potential customers that there needed to be changes in the entire cocktail menu every month. She also learned that customers preferred a single price for every cocktail. She discovered that most of the customers she wanted to attract were interested in small craft beers brewed locally as well as a few locally grown prize winning wines.

To achieve her unique drinks, she first turned to a book collection she had been acquiring over the last 10 years. It contained recipe books for cocktails, some dating back to the early 1900s in a variety of languages, including English, German, French, and Spanish. Many of these dated to the "Roaring 20s" and to the period after WWII when cocktail lounges were a part of every major hotel and the Rainbow Room of Rockefeller Center was the place to be seen having dinner and cocktails before dancing. Taking many of these mixed drinks as a basis, Ann proceeded to develop new versions of some of these drinks. She reworked the traditional *Sazerac* made with rye whiskey and *Death in the Afternoon*, which is absinthe and champagne. One of our favorites was the *Hummingbird*, made with locally produced gin, tonic, lime juice, and homemade *Limoncello*. Another great cocktail was the *Desert Sand Tequila Sunrise Cocktail* and then there was the *Bee's Knees* with gin, honey water, orange juice, and lavender bitters. Always in a new product development mode, Ann infuses gin or vodka with a variety of herbs and spices as well as brandies infused with different fruits that she would then use as the base for various cocktails.

What is important to note is that she tested each of this cocktails on numerous potential customers prior to opening the *Lioness*. Of potentially interest is the fact that each drink she sold was priced at $7.50 each and she only offered a dozen different cocktails on any one day. This reduced waste and issues with keeping a variety of liquors for mixing to a minimum at any one time. She did not offer traditional cocktails like a gin and tonic or even the standards. She saw the cocktails as a unique experience that would have customers coming back to see what was new the next week. By not having beer and wine, she differentiated her establishment from wine bars and the other competition in the area.

5.9 Patents, Trade Secrets, and Copyrights

While this may be the last section of this chapter, it is not the least important. It is important to remember that some innovations are capable of being patented (certainly in the area of technology) and numerous things can be copyrighted like music and works of art. Today the Internet allows individuals to look at currently issued patents not just in the United States but also in Europe. Often, technological innovations build on existing patented inventions so it is imperative that as an entrepreneur you are not infringing on the use of others' patents. We strongly recommend that if you are of the opinion that you might have a work that can be patented, you check with a patent attorney who works in that particular technology. Provisional patents are easy to file as you work through the process. What is critical is that you have patents filed or applied for before you offer your product to the general public. Otherwise you may lose your ability to protect your devise or process. Once again, given Websites like Legal Zoom, you have no excuse not to protect your intellectual property where possible. In closing, our discussion on legal matters is not a substitute for a good attorney, which can be money well spent if you have done your homework and done it early. No attorney likes to clean up a mess and mistakes that did not need to have happened.

Trade secrets are things you don't want the public to know about. When you file a patent, those "secrets" must be divulged as a part of the patent process. However, trade secrets can be effective. Perhaps the best known trade secret is the recipe for Coca Cola. Just remember that today many things can be reversed engineered and Pepsi has come pretty close to copying the recipe. Likewise, it is important that you observe copyrights with care, in terms of the use of others creative endeavors. Likewise, if you are creating logos, works of art, etc. that you register those with the appropriate authorities in your country, for example copyrights for music are registered with the Library of Congress.

5.10 Exercise

Following the stage-gate model try to create a new product or service that you can include in your new venture.

Reference

Christensen, C. M., S. D. Anthony, and E. A. Roth. 2004. *Seeing what is next. Using theories of innovation to predict industry change.* Boston: Harvard Business School Press.

6

Finding Team Members and Building an Entrepreneurial Organization

6.0 Overview

> When you're in a start-up, the first ten people will determine whether the company succeeds or not. Each is 10 percent of the company. So why wouldn't you take as much time as necessary to find all the A players? If three were not so great, why would you want a company where 30 percent of your people are not so great? A small company depends on great people much more than a big company does. —Steve Jobs

We know few quotes from famous technology entrepreneurs that capture the critical importance of the first hires of a new venture like this one from the co-founder of Apple. In this chapter we discuss some of the critical steps in finding the right people and building the right organization to grow a sustainable new venture. This is a topic that most entrepreneurship books largely ignore and human resource management books assume that start-up firms are mini-versions of large corporations with similar resources. Having been in charge of hiring for one of the fastest growing ventures in the airline industry, one of us familiar with the challenge of hiring in large numbers and we both have had to guide new firms through the process of finding both start-up team members as well as building procedures in a new venture for finding and hiring the right employees. Let us say from the start that we strongly believe in sharing the potential upside of the new venture with those who have made it happen, the employees and entrepreneurial team. Thus we encourage you strongly to take the time to hire the right people and build the right organization.

6.1 Building the Venture One Person at a Time

A very critical part of venture creation is the process of finding partners, building a start-up team, hiring employees, and developing an organizational structure. All of these are what contribute to the *culture and values* of the firm from the very beginning of the venture. That is, it is the entrepreneur and the start-up team who creates the culture of the venture that often outlasts their tenure with the venture. To us these tasks are among the most important that a new venture undertakes, and yet are often given short shrift. Those early hires are the people who will formulate and execute the initial strategy of the firm, produce the products and services, undertake the marketing, interact with customers, and in the end determine the success or failure of the new venture. Make sure your business concept is one that will engage your potential employees as well as investors if you want them to be entrepreneurial leaders of the firm. It all starts in the beginning with the *entrepreneurial team*. It is very rare that one person can do everything needed to create a viable new venture.

6.1.1 The Entrepreneurial Team

It should be obvious that a firm is only as good as the first people who work in it. Gathering these persons into the firm (the founding entrepreneurial team) is often an underappreciated and haphazard task. Yet, these are the individuals most likely will be the total staffing for a long time. Thus, they have an enormous impact on the success of the firm. The ability of an entrepreneur to build a strong team is reflected in the following quote by one of the greatest German literary, scientific, and philosophical figures of the 18th and 19th centuries, Johann Wolfgang Von Goethe:

> A great person attracts great people and knows how to hold them together.

Some people even say you should always find people better than you are to work in your venture, a view with which we strongly agree. One way entrepreneurs attract others to their dreams is by sharing their vision for the firms and their business plan with others. Here we have observed an interesting paradox. When reading business plans, we typically find projections in logarithmic growth of number of employees or even higher growth rates, such as two persons the first year, then 8, 16, 32 in each of the subsequent years, but a closer look at projected revenue growth rates does not justify that level of firm size. What may be equally bad is projecting growth rate in sales with no increase in personnel to service that growth. Those points made, we think the really important objectives here are to be both realistic in the numbers of people you need and find individuals who share your vision for the firm and can contribute to the success of the firm.

When we look into national data of almost any country, we find that 98 percent of the companies do not employ more than 10 persons. In fact, 93 percent do not employ more than 5. And, when we ask entrepreneurs about this, they all say they do not want to hire lots of people. In fact, we have yet to meet the entrepreneur who says: I created this company in order to hire lots of people. That is, what we read in business plans and the reality are worlds apart. It takes people to make money and you have to have revenues sufficient to justify hiring new people. It is a bit of a "catch 22" situation. Later in this chapter we discuss more about how to build entrepreneurial teams.

We suspect that when the firm is up and running, a nasty reality suddenly dawns: while you may need people, you learn that people cost money. People usually cost more than just the salary that is paid to them (think payroll taxes, benefits, retirement, etc.). But, do not get us wrong here. While people cost money, they are also necessary resources and we believe that should actually be seen as an asset. Their input should positively impact revenue and profits. It then becomes an issue of balancing personnel cost with revenue income, which is more complicated than just balancing one to one.

In fact, there is a general rule of thumb, which states that for every new person added to the company, it is necessary to increase revenues threefold. This, of course, will vary across industries and countries. Simply paying less is often a poor choice as pay is a reinforcement for work done, and if that is perceived as less than the effort, either effort will decrease or individuals will leave. We strongly urge you pay a living wage to any employee if you want to have their undivided attention at work. For example, employee turnover is much higher at Wal-Mart than it is at Costco for the very simple reason that Costco pays more and have been rewarded with higher per-employee productivity. In other words, treating your employees well has a positive payoff even in a new venture.

There is a lot of evidence that when employees are worried about how they are going to make enough to put food on the table, you are not going to have an engaged employee. If you worry about labor unions, we know one entrepreneur who famously said "I have never seen a firm with a labor union it did not deserve."

6.1.2 Other Issues to Consider

Two of the reasons for the variation in industries and countries are labor laws and labor unions regulating salaries for various employees. If there are only founders and owners working in the company, it is usually up to them to determine how much salary they decide to pay to themselves. In fact, they can refrain from taking any salary. We frankly don't recommend the founding team not take a salary. The firm has to ultimately be able to support such an expense and one does not need the start-up team "moonlighting" to pay the bills.

But, as soon as the company decides to hire someone, it is a different ball game. In many European countries, especially in the Nordic countries, up to 90 percent of the qualified workforce are members of their respective labor unions—in certain industries it concerns 100 percent. Even if unions are not so pervasive, when unemployment rates decline to under 6 percent, there is a sellers' market and the sellers in this case are the would-be employee. Remember salary is only one part of the equation for compensation that could include benefit packages for health, educational benefits, vacation, retirement packages, and even equity in the venture.

Here an example may be informative. In most of Europe if you want to hire an electrician, the company has to pay at minimum according to the industry-wide labor union agreements, not what the company thinks would be suitable for the financial situation of the firm. They are free to pay more, but not less. Firms also have to follow all the other employment laws, which regulate vacation, maternity leave, sick leave, health and retirement insurance fees, lay-offs, etc. Again, these all vary across countries, but in general such labor laws exist in most of the developed world and you need to be familiar with them. In the United States, there are Federal, State, and local ordinance that can govern employees and it is your responsibility to know these. Firms like NOLO Press put out books on labor laws for different states (Steingold 2013). Here is where potentially outsourcing payroll to a firm that specializes in that can be useful and can reduce the headaches of doing payroll and paying payroll taxes.

What we are trying to say is that all these regulations incur costs that are significantly higher than the actual salary paid to the employee, but which the entrepreneur has to pay for, and everyone begins to realize that the rule of thumb of the ratio of revenue to costs is pretty close to reality and why the initial logarithmic projection of employee growth becomes just wishful thinking. Having said this, we think it is now rather obvious that hiring the right people becomes a critical issue, but also considerations of whether *it is at all necessary to hire anyone* becomes equally critical.

6.1.3 Outsourcing

Needed skills can be "bought" as services from another entrepreneur or already establish firm that specializes in those services. Some work tasks can be outsourced and others, that are a critical part of the competitive advantage of the firm, most likely should not be outsourced. Part of the decision to outsource is both financial and operational. For example, if you are a new bakery, you most likely will outsource the maintenance of the ovens and delivery trucks to other businesses. The reasons are simple. The gourmet baker is an in-house expense whose expertise is a competitive advantage. However, who maintains the ovens is one skill that can be outsourced along with the added labor costs including fees, licenses, taxes that have to be paid becomes the headache of another entrepreneur. It is therefore sometimes both necessary and smart to out-source certain functions of an organization, especially when it is a start-up company, which still lacks a steady and positive revenue stream, or the time and expertise to perform those tasks well.

Remember, if the skills are the key competitive advantage you have, think twice before outsourcing them. In fact, think about the downsides of outsourcing three or four times. If your firm's business is involved in writing computer code and you outsource that task, be sure your firm owns the code and the copyright to it; otherwise you may find you have no control over your key asset.

6.2 Finding New Employees

One of the neglected topics in most books on entrepreneurship is how the entrepreneur(s) or start-up team find individuals to get them join in their new venture. We know that even in established firms, finding the right people and getting them to join the firm is sometimes a difficult, potentially expensive, and lengthy process. One of the challenges for the entrepreneur is to have new employees share their vision for the firm. Here again, the great German writer Johann Wolfgang von Goethe has summed it up well:

> Dream no small dreams for they have no power to move the hearts of men.

As an entrepreneur it is your responsibility to create an organization made up of individuals working as a cohesive team. This requires finding talented people to join the venture, a task, while seemingly mundane, is perhaps one of the hardest for most new ventures to do well. As mentioned earlier, one of the authors of this book was involved in the start-up of People Express Airlines in the late 1970s following airline deregulation in the United States. In this firm every employee owned stock. His job was to do the psychological evaluations of every potential employee (over 250,000) following an initial screening by the human resource teams of the firm. Given the importance of finding the right person to fly a crewed commercial aircraft carrying hundreds of passengers, the cabin crew was likewise critical to the safety of those passengers and their flight experiences. In this company, one had to interview over 100 people to find one employee who met the standards. Spending the time to find the right people to fly a crewed commercial aircraft is literally a life or death decision if you pick incorrectly.

What we are trying to drive home is that taking time when bringing on new partners as a start-up and hiring your first employees are efforts well worth taking. Taking on a partner who does not fit the context of an entrepreneurial venture is asking for problems from the very beginning. It is literally easier to divorce a spouse in many places than it is to get rid of an undesirable employee. Hiring the wrong person, especially in a new venture, can be costly, not just in terms of salaries and lost time, but in potentially losing business or failing to develop a new product/service in a timely fashion. Then there is the loss of time and energy on training the individual as well as the negative effects of having to fire someone including the potential negative effects on other employees. This is summed up nicely in the following quote from one of that well-known co-founder of Apple, Steve Jobs:

> Recruiting is hard. It's just finding the needles in the haystack. You can't know enough in a one-hour interview. So, in the end, it's ultimately based on your gut. How do I feel about this person? What are they like when they're challenged? I ask everybody that: "Why are you here?" The answers themselves are not what you're looking for. It's the meta-data.

The last thing a new firm needs is a high turnover rate in their employees. In the case of People Express before a pilot could fly the plane, he had to go through several months of flight training even if he was already licensed as a commercial pilot and flight crews had to likewise go through a month training prior to being allowed to crew an aircraft. Thus the airline had to invest heavily in its employees (easily over $50,000 in the case of pilots) before these individuals could fly and thus positively impact the revenues of the firm. Staff turnover, therefore, was something to be kept low especially when the airline was new and finding crews to keep a plane operational was a critical task. Hiring a pilot who is unsuitable for the job can be fatal, literally. Hiring the wrong person for your new venture could be fatal to your firm.

6.2.1 Big Hiring Errors

One of the biggest errors we have discovered over the years of working with entrepreneurs in the early stages of their business is the mistake of hiring the first person who ". . . can fog a mirror." The only thing worse may be to hire that relative of yours who can never seem to hold a job, but they are available now. That is, we have seen entrepreneurs who hire the first person they find or interview who is even marginally functional. While you don't have to interview 100 people to make a decision on hiring one, it is critical to avoid just interviewing one person, even if you have previously worked with that individual or they are a relative in need of a job. Remember, someone who has worked in a large bureaucratic organization may not be the best choice for a new small firm where the most appropriate line on the job description is ". . . and all other tasks assigned."

Some human resource (HR) consultants will say you should interview at least three people for a position; we personally feel that the more you interview, the greater your choices for that position and finding the right person. We strongly believe this approach is even more critical if you are hiring a member of your own family. We have often seen people either under- or overestimate the abilities of a family member. We are not saying you should avoid hiring family; rather what we are saying is that you hold them to the same standard you would use for any hire.

6.2.1.1 Using a Buy-Sell Agreement

We also recommend that when starting a new venture with partners that you from the very start have a buy-sell agreement between the partners for the evitable time when someone wants to leave the firm. While these agreements may not state the value of the firm and the share owned by the departing partner, it is critical that you state how the value will be determined and to whom the departing partner's shares can be sold. We also see this as important as well when there are spouses, as divorces, and deaths do occur. Think of this as a prenuptial for the firm. No one wants to admit problems might occur, but having such a document, signed by all parties, will save a lot of headaches in the future. We have seen a lot of potentially good firms break apart at an early stage simply because one person wanted to leave and there was no system in place to guide the separation process.

6.2.2 *Characteristics of a Good Hire*

What we have learned is that not only does the entrepreneur have to be a "jack of all trades and a master of a half dozen." We have also learned that the same must be true of the early start-up team and those first employees. One of the characteristics of a good entrepreneur is the ability to cooperate with others and we feel this is a critical skill for any new employee. Thus, the more the potential hire is seen by others in different settings, the better you will be able to determine whether they will fit within the existing organization and can work with different people in the firm. Potential hires are usually on their best behavior during the first interview, but if it is just an acting job that can often be determined after subsequent interviews and interactions. However, as our own research (Helmreich et al. 1986) has demonstrated there is often a honeymoon effect when it comes to hiring, one does not know the true level of achievement motivation of an employee or even an early partner until 6 months after they are hired. Here another quote comes to mind:

> If you can hire people whose passion intersects with the job, they won't require any supervision at all. They will manage themselves better than anyone could ever manage them. Their fire comes from within, not from without. Their motivation is internal, not external.   —Stephen Covey

This quote reflects what we believe based on years of work in the area of entrepreneurial motivation (Carsrud and Brännback 2011) that you want to hire people who are not just "smart" but are masters in their skill sets. Employees of an entrepreneurial venture need to be able to learn new and different skills as well. That is, they have to have a belief in their mastery capability to learn new things. It is not just getting people who fit the organization today, but who are capable of adding to the venture and making it better. These people tend to be highly productive. You want to find people who have a passion for what they do and a passion for learning.

You also want someone who will work hard, as that has been shown to actually predict job success. If someone is not willing to work hard, don't assume that by hiring them their behavior is going to change. We all know that at least in the United States that a 40-hour work week is not reality; this is especially the case for the entrepreneur trying to create a new venture. You better find people to love what they are doing as a new venture is not a 9 to 5 job; it is more like a 24/7 one. You want to find individuals who not only want to work with you but can show why they are the best person for the job at hand. You want someone who sees working for a new venture as an opportunity to perform well and add to the firm. Thus, they should see themselves as team players who are able to get along with others. This is especially the case in the early days of a new venture when the culture of the firm is forming. You want to make sure their values and those of the newly emerging venture are aligned and that they can work with customers. As you grow, the firm gets others to be involved in the interview process. This helps cement the culture of the new venture.

One example of finding self-motivated employees and building that into your organizational structure and culture is Zappos—the online shoe retailer. Starting in 2015 they instituted a self-governing model. They abolished managers and adopted what some have called a "holacracy." This is a system of self-governance in which employees and even the entrepreneur are evaluated and rewarded by peers, instead of by a manager. Frankly for some entrepreneurs and firms, this is what essentially what happens in the early stages of the venture. To embed this into the organization as a permanent approach really requires finding a very unique set of employees that have a real dedication to the firm. We have seen this before in firms like People Express. One advantage is that you get rid of middle management totally. This may not be for every firm, but for some it may be an alternative.

6.2.3 A Mini-Case Example

When hiring employees, it becomes absolutely critical to considering what skills are really needed. To make this point clearer, please consider the following real-life example.

Heikki founded a company that creates software for hospitals. Today, the company employs 35 persons and is highly successful, but that success nearly turned into failure due to two near fatal hiring decisions.

In 2006, Heikki's company was a start-up in its third year. The company had two employees in addition to the two founders. The employees were all programmers. One of the founders, and the president, had spent three decades working in large multinational corporations. Pekka, other founder and CEO, was a university dropout. The company was planning for international growth. They believed they needed an experienced international marketing manager and an experienced chief technology officer (CTO). This is how they stated their needs that ultimately framed their solution options. To anyone listening they sounded like they were going to look for two rather pricy individuals in terms of compensation. This is the option that they did. In reality what they needed was a very good sales person and an IT specialist with some managerial competencies.

They ended up hiring a marketing and brand manager, who spoke seven languages fluently, from a large pharmaceutical company, who had no sales experience and not a very good understanding of what it is to work in a small start-up company as compared to large multinational company, and a CTO who had been working in London's financial district with good experiences in information technology (IT), but who was really interested in pursuing an academic career, which meant completing a Ph.D. dissertation. Both persons came with a large price-tag in terms of total compensation packages. Frankly, the financial situation of the start-up really could not carry the burden. Within a year both of these persons had left the company, fortunately for Heikki and Pekka.

What this example shows is that this company had not carefully thought about what skills they really needed. Moreover, it seems the president was "hiring" with the lenses of a multinational corporation. Moreover, the economy was booming, so salaries were high. Three years later, in 2008 after the start of the Great Recession and the resulting increase in layoffs, salaries had come down 30 to 50 percent on the IT sector and skilled people had been laid-off and were looking for work. This venture eventually found a very good sales person, with a successful sales career in a jeans and t-shirt store. He was one of these rare natural-born salespersons.

The lesson to learn here is that as an entrepreneur you need to think like one, don't get caught up in the false context of a large firm mentality. As one of our old mentors use to say "little steps for little feet." A new venture is simply not a mini-version of a large firm. He also meant that you have to start small and learn before you try to play with the big boys. Even a human embryo grows from two cells to a stage where it looks like a fish and then suddenly 18 years later you have a college student. This process takes time and you have to be very conscious of the context of being in a small firm where being cross-functional is critical and people will grow into their jobs.

6.3 Whom to Hire or Not, Whom to Fire or Not

To us there are four important decisions every entrepreneur has to make. The first two are around do you hire someone, yes or no? The second is do you have to let someone go from the firm, yes or no? Frankly the lesser time you spend on the hiring decision, the more time you will spend in the firing process. If you have never had to let someone go from employment, you don't understand how painful it is for you as well as for the person being laid off. The best way to avoid firing is hiring right in the first place. Remember that there are labor regulations that govern the kinds of questions you can ask and regulations governing discrimination.

One thing we believe in is that diversity is an asset to be encouraged. Women and men bring different dynamics to a firm as well as different ethnic groups bring a level of sensitivity to certain markets that a new firm may well need. These all will help you avoid group-think and it will provide you with viewpoints you may not realize are there and critical to success. In the next sections we are going to discuss the two downside tasks that are as important as the discussion earlier on how to select new employees and entrepreneurial team members.

In many countries you can hire a person for a test-period, sometimes called a probationary period. That can last up to 4 to 6 months. This allows you to release an employee without explanation or reason. This also allows the person to leave without any reason as well. Once this period is over, all labor laws apply about firing an employee. If such an option is available to you, we advise you use it as it will benefit all concerned.

6.3.1 Saying "No" to an Applicant

We also recommend that you treat all applicants with respect and let them know the outcome of your decision even if they are not chosen. Remember those individuals rejected for employment have the power of "word of mouth" and you want them to be as positive about your venture as possible, even if they did not get employment. You need to think of every interaction with another person as dealing with a potential customer. You never know when you are going to interact with that individual again, potentially as a customer or as a competitor. Think of it as one application of the "Golden Rule: Do unto others as you would have them do unto you."

6.3.2 Firing an Employee

We also believe that the "Golden Rule" of treating others as you would like to be treated holds as well when firing someone. To us the most expensive and painful part of starting a firm is firing an employee. We firmly believe that if you hire right in the first place, this will be a rare occurrence. It is better to take the time to hire well than to fire poorly. We are reminded of something once said by Thomas Watson, Jr. who followed his father as the second CEO of IBM when asked if he was going to fire an employee who cost the company $600,000, his answer was:

> . . . No . . . I just spent $600,000 training him, Why would I want
> to fire someone to his experience?   —Thomas J. Watson, Jr.

Sometimes you keep an employee who has cost the firm dearly because they know not to do that again. For an entrepreneur firing is hard, but telling the employee they have been fired is the hard part. Don't do this via e-mail or Facebook post. Almost every good manager will tell you that firing an employee face to face is a most difficult task, and a sad one. In some ways it is also a measure of the performance of management. A good manager (all entrepreneurs are managers as well) should be there to make sure no member of the team gets to the point they have to be let go. The entrepreneur themselves have to be prepared to leave if that is what is best for the firm.

Data clearly shows that how you handle a termination in large part determines whether you end up in a wrongful termination lawsuit. Only thing worse than that even in today's political climate is a sexual harassment law suit, especially in the United States. The best general rule to abide by is to be professional at all times, even in the informal setting of a start-up venture. It is fine to consider the start-up team to be like family and for everyone to be friends, but remember this is a business first and foremost. Thus, a professional demeanor will always serve the firm well.

We remember one entrepreneurial firm where a very talented woman started a public relations (PR) firm. As the business grew, she needed to add new employees to service her customers. One day her youngest son, who had just graduated from college, asked whether he could come to work for her. After some negotiation and planning, she agreed. What was interesting whenever they were in a work situation, he either called her by her first name, "Jane" or "Mrs. Smith." However, the minute they were at home, or in a family gathering, it was always "Mom" or "David." This leads us to the following discussion every new venture may face if started by two or more family members or if a family member wishes to join the start-up team.

6.4 To Be a Family Firm or Not to Be

You probably think that few entrepreneurs, especially when they create the venture, think that they are creating a family firm. The reality is that you have one from the start if your spouse is a business partner. If you have the children as employees, and/or your parents invested their life savings in your venture, you are a *family business*. Often, family members become the first involved with a new venture simply because they are close at hand and may be *cheap labor*. Here a discussion on what is a family firm may be useful in helping you make a decision to employee family members or take them as partners or investors.

Many people when they hear the term *family business* think a small *mom and pop* operation, which is certainly one form; however, some of the world's largest firms are family owned, such as BMW and Wal-Mart to name a few. Most people when thinking of a family firm see it as a business, which is passed on to the next generation. This often means that firms are *family owned and managed*. This assumes that at least some people in management are family members and thus have been hired to assume these roles. This is a common notion of what constitutes a family firm. However, there are those who will argue that a company is not a family firm before there has been at least one succession having taken place. We believe if there is a strong emotional bonding between members of the start-up team, they usually act as if they are "family."

6.4.1 What Is Firm Owning Family?

What this conceptualization of family does is to challenge the notion of a family as the one we like to call the core family: mom, dad, and two kids. However, that is *not* what most families look like these days and increasingly what families look like in all countries all over the world.

Today, we have ex-spouses, in-laws, ex–in-laws, grandparents, cousins, and children from different spouses working in what they perceive as family firms. Increasingly, we are seeing firms started by same-sex couples who have children. The issue is that what constitutes a family is more fluid than at any time in the past. While the nuclear family may now be smaller in the United States and Western Europe, the reality is that in many regions, such as in Latin America or in Asia, families are huge networks of relatives that may all be part of a single family firm, or who may manage multiple family firms that are tied together by shared ownership.

To us, a family firm is also one run by two first-generation siblings, or even cousins. That said, it is important to realize that many family firms are among of the largest and oldest firms in some countries and they are frequently publicly listed on the stock exchange. Some estimates put 60 percent or more of the New York Stock Exchange firms as "closely held firm" meaning a few individuals have controlling interest.

Because family firms are sometimes less willing to take financial risks, this sometimes implies that they are not very good at renewal even when it is absolutely vital for the continued existence of the firm. However, there is evidence that family firms can be very innovative and are prepared to take the time to see that innovation take hold when a publicly traded firm might not make that long-term investment. All we are suggesting is that you be aware of the potential upsides and downsides of working with family and be objective in that awareness.

6.4.2 Family Goals Impact Hiring

However, family firms differ in many respects from nonfamily firms. These firms usually have dual goals: one is to run and sustain a company and the other is to run and maintain a family. This becomes particularly visible in family firms that are several generations old. There is a saying that the first generation creates the firm, the second grows the firm, and the third ruins it. There is probably some truth to this saying, but there are many firms that have been in the control of one family for several hundred years, some wineries and breweries have been in the same family for over a thousand years and there are hospitality-based family firms that are over 500 years old. In our experience the dualistic goal of family firms tends to make family firms more solid and sustainable because it is about preserving two important institutions: the family and the firm. Family firms tend therefore to be less prone to take risks; however, they are also known for innovation as well. Perhaps one important reason for this stability is that many family firms carry the name of the family owner/managers and few persons want their name to be associated with bad publicity and failure.

6.4.3 Long-Term Impact of Hiring Family Members

The really important issue when hiring a family member into a family firm becomes obvious when the issue of leadership succession arises. Succession and managing the succession process becomes critical, and experience shows that this is usually not handled well or at all. It is not only a question about finding someone in the family who is *willing and capable* to take over the firm. It requires that the one who is to hand over the company is willing to *surrender control* to the one who is willing and most capable. In-depth discussions of this and other topics, such as divorce in a family firm, can be found in our research volume on family business (Carsrud and Brännback 2012) and detailed cases looking at these topics can be found in Brännback and Carsrud (2012).

More often than not in today's business environment succession crises are the result of a mismatch between generations that often reflects changes in culture and role expectations. For example, in many cultures it is assumed that the oldest male or only sons should take over the firm, while the best candidate might be a daughter or there may not be any sons in the family in the first place. Or there may not be any children at all who want to work in the family firm. Increasingly, families are facing the issue of how to attract family members into the business and with the reality that it may be the daughter that is most capable of taking the firm over. When this does not occur, the choice is then to shut down the company, or sell it to a nonfamily member, or sell it to another firm. It is still rather rare that family firms take in CEOs that are not part of the family, but it does increasingly occur. Usually, an outside CEO can mean there are unresolved issues in the firm or family members lack the capability to be the firm's leader. Hiring a nonfamily member to be CEO of a family business requires spending a lot of time defining what their role will be and to determine whether they have the skills necessary to deal with the family shareholders as well as the external business environment.

6.5 Compensation, Benefits, and Stock Options

At this point let us turn to the issue of paying the start-up team and employees for a new venture. Many books exist that discuss developing compensation strategies for existing firms, such as Berger and Berger (2008), yet few address starting from scratch a compensation system.

When we talk about compensation, most people assume it is what someone is paid. While this is correct, to some degree, it is only one part of a complex set of procedures, policies, and activities that compensate an individual for participation in the new venture. These can be direct and indirect rewards of which a salary is only part of the package.

We urge any new venture to early on develop a compensation program to reward performance by individuals and teams in the firm. This will include a mixture of salaries, benefits (gym memberships, insurance packages, educational opportunities, etc.), and rewards (vacation trips, recognition awards, etc.). As a start-up venture these are often hard to provide given the lack of financial resources. However, we know that new ventures can be creative in this area. We had one new firm whose employees could well be considered "nerds." The firm operated on a 24/7 schedule, which meant that some people worked the "grave yard shift." This firm decided that putting video games in the break room and having a well-stocked refrigerator that included craft beers as well as regular deliveries of pizza were something they could do to help them be competitive in the labor market for technological skills and thus reduce staff turnover to help them retain their staff.

Compensation includes all rewards given in return for labor. These include *direct financial* rewards like wages, salaries, stock, and other bonuses. Indirect financial rewards such as various types of leave, retirement plans, stock options, education, and other services are a part of the employment contract. Nonfinancial reinforcement could include career development opportunities, recognition, and obviously working conditions like a refrigerator full of beer, or even "casual Fridays." We know from evidence that while new employees clearly focus on financial compensation, nonfinancial factors have a huge impact on retention of employees. As an entrepreneur who is most likely short on cash to pay salaries, get creative in compensation, it could be something as simple as letting the start-up team bring their kids or dogs to work that could make all the difference in their attitude toward the position you are offering.

Any new entrepreneur and their start-up team need to be aware of various legal issues that will impact their hiring and operations. These are things that by law you are required to provide or meet. These are very much determined by local, state, and national laws, and a review of all would take more space than we have available here. Some of these laws included exceptions for certain types of employees, such as managers and professionals. Areas you need to be aware of as they will ultimately impact the cost of any employee that includes, minimum wage, number of work hours per week, minimum age of employees, overtime, various leaves (like vacation, sickness, and maternity), grievance mechanisms, and employee termination.

As a final word on compensation, remember that what you are trying to achieve is the individual's commitment to the new venture and that their performance is the best possible. You want them dedicated to the new venture. It has been well shown that when individuals in a new venture are engaged, they are more productive, content, and dedicated to the venture. You want those in the new firm to feel satisfied, safe, and able to work to their fullest ability, which will reduce turnover.

6.6 Building an Entrepreneurial Team Structure

Whenever an entrepreneur has two or more people in the firm, the issue of command and control begins. Even if you embraced the "holacracy" system of self-governance like Zappos, you still have to have some form of command and control, even if it is peers. Yet, too often the idea of building an organizational structure is resisted by the entrepreneur. We have frequently heard entrepreneurs say "I will never have a firm like the one I left" or "I never want to have a bureaucratic firm as that is one reason I am starting this new venture." Ultimately the entrepreneur (or start-up team) has to decide what kind of organization they are going to have, a formal one or one that is more team oriented and relatively informal. Most people are well aware of the formal organization in which there is an organizational chart and form job descriptions. The results are that relationships between people are usually defined and with them come formal titles for each position.

We are strong believers in the admonition of "form follows function," and thus an entrepreneurial firm needs an entrepreneurial team structure that fits what the firm wants to achieve and how it wants to achieve it. Before we proceed to discuss what we feel are potentially useful organizational characteristics for a new venture, let us briefly review some of the types of structures that many adopt. It is important to realize that any organizational structure will evolve over time and that no one type will define a firm forever. However, as with a firm's culture, the structural relationship between people becomes harder to change over time, and thus it is important that this be a conscious decision by the start-up team.

If you look at any book on organization design and behavior, you will discover that there are fundamentally nine types of organizational structure formats from which to choose. There are eight formal ones and the fallback position of *informal or no formal structure*. The informal structure exists in every organization, but especially in the early stage one. Briefly the eight formal types are listed as follows:

1. Line

2. Staff or functional authority

3. Line and staff

4. Committee

5. Divisional

6. Project

7. Matrix

8. Hybrid

Of these, only a few are really seen in early-stage firms and only three of them are really appropriate for a new venture. Now we look at the three more useable forms for an entrepreneurial new venture.

6.6.1 A Line Structure for Entrepreneurial Teams

The one most frequently seen structures is also one with which most of us are familiar. The line form is where there are only direct (usually vertical) relationships between different levels in a firm. A big set of assumptions with this form is that there are sufficient people to staff each level and that you can afford specialization at an early stage such as departments of marketing and another for production. We are reminded of a recent advertisement for a logistics firm who showed a lone entrepreneur in his garage answering the phone and being asked to forward the call to the sales department. He puts the phone on hold and then picks it up again and in another voice answers "Sales department, how can I help you?" While this may have the advantage of making the new venture appear bigger than it is, it shows that this approach can make an individual a bit schizophrenic in behavior.

In a line structure authority follows the chain of command. This simplifies authority, responsibility, and accountability. However, it neglects planning and can overload key persons as our previous example demonstrates if taken to extreme. A line form also does not encourage a team approach, which we see as critical in an entrepreneurial venture. If you take an entrepreneurial approach to a line structure, it can foster fast and flexibility decision making, especially when the firm is small and everyone in the firm has greater closeness. The downside is that as the firm grows, the process can become ineffective, and while spend and flexibility are desired, it may not offset the need for specialized knowledge. While we jokingly say "entrepreneurs are a jack of all trades and a master of a half dozen," it becomes at some point impossible for any individual to be an expert in everything. It also makes the firm too dependent on a few key people who can do numerous jobs.

One idea we strongly recommend for an entrepreneur adopting a line approach is to avoid having too many levels in the structure. Increasingly we are seeing organizations with only two to three levels. If you want to make everyone in the firm feel as if they are empowered, we also strongly recommend everyone in an entrepreneurial team has a *manager* title. When one of us was at People Express Airlines (PEXP), the other airlines of the time had nearly a dozen layers of management with very few holding any manager title. At PEXP we had Managing Officers (C suite level), Flight Managers (pilots), Customer Service Managers (flight attendants), and Maintenance Managers (the teams that kept the airplanes flight worthy). We also made sure that in any given set Flight Managers and Customer Service Managers flew together frequently so they became a cohesive work team. This was done to improve effective performance and improved safety. Thus each aircraft was like a small business with two levels of management in the aircraft and two on the ground. Thus what we had created was a project team, where the project was flying a crewed commercial aircraft. Each plane was thus manned with a team and the airline was in effect a firm comprising many teams.

6.6.2 Project Approach to an Entrepreneurial Team Structure

While the various line type structures facilitate the formation of clear control relationships, most new ventures are more like a collection of projects that have to be accomplished. For many of these early-stage projects (e.g., those entailing of a number of interdependent and independent activities) information, work, and control may flow horizontally, diagonally, upward, and downward. This is often the case in some technology-based firms and in those dependent on a high level of creativity. The direction of these flows depends on the distribution of talents and abilities in the new venture and the need to apply them to the problem that exists.

A project structure assumes that there are at least some individuals in the new venture with functional expertise, such as marketing or finance or product development. It is usually a temporary group designed to achieve specific results by specialists from different functional areas. The project team then concentrates its resources on the project. Once completed, the members go back to their previous positions or move on to a new project. This approach works best when there is a project defined by a specific goal and target date for completion, as in launching a new firm, a new service, or a new product. It also works well when the project is unique or unfamiliar to firm, or when it is complex and where independent activities and specialized skills are necessary, where it is critical because of potential gains or losses, and where the work required is not repetitive. Open communication is essential among those working on the project as it is with any new venture.

6.6.3 Informal Structure: Key to a Successful Entrepreneurial Team

An informal organizational structure best reflects the reality of a new venture with its constantly evolving relationships and patterns of human interaction as new members are added to the firm. This form can and does exist alongside more formal structures, like line, but in many new ventures it is often the only structure that exists for quite some time, given the early stage of the firm. It consists of informal relationships created by the new venture's members at every level. You cannot avoid these informal relationships as they reflect individuals joining together to satisfy their personal needs as well as providing some sense of stability in the continuously changing and dynamic context of the new venture.

The informal structure cuts across all levels of any formal structures adopted. It is also heavily impacted by outside and prior relationships. If you keep these facts in mind, you can see why the initial individuals in the new venture are usually friends, family, and personal contacts from previous employment. Because of this, some individuals are ascribed greater standing than others in informal group; thus it has its own chain of command and control. The benefits of this informal organization are that work is accomplished faster and overcomes any weakness in any existing formal structure. It can affect the span of control to even those outside the firm and improves management of tasks. It provides additional channels of communication if a key person in the formal structure is unavailable.

However, it can be a potential problem as well for the new venture by the risk of the informal structure working against the purpose of the firm, something frequently seen in family-owned and -managed firms in which the family structure can be in conflict with the formal structure of the firm. Informal structures can reduce control by management and may impact the number of alternatives reviewed in making management decisions. Finally when dealing with people's personal emotions and relationships, the informal structure can increase the time spent so that individual feelings are dealt with as a part of the process. Regardless, we believe that an entrepreneurial team is well served by exploiting the informal structures that friendships bring for the effectiveness and success of a new venture. We urge entrepreneurs to avoid becoming too bureaucratic as this will often stifle the creativity in a new venture as well as a sense of commitment to the firm.

6.7 New Firm Governance

Typically the entrepreneur and/or the entrepreneurial team of managers are also those who govern the firm and serve as the final word in strategy and hiring. However, depending on the legal structure you chose for your firm and/or if you have outside investors, you may be required to have a formal board to oversee the firm and serve as the final arbitrators in decisions. We have long advocated that family firms that are well established need both a board of directors and a board to govern the family, also known as a *family council*.

The reality is that most new ventures do not have any formal firm governance even if required by law. The legality is simply dealt with by often a "nod and wink" at legal protocol. However, if you are going to be serious about growing your business, we urge you to start firms with an outside board of advisors. We don't mean your lawyer and accountant, but people not associated with the day-to-day operations but to whom you feel free enough to discuss issues and whose advice you trust. We have some evidence that being active in a trade association and other business organization can provide some support to a new venture in finding out good governance practices and individuals to serve as advisors. If you have dreams of being a publicly traded company at some point, you need to be prepared to have an outside board and know how to effectively use them.

Deciding what kind of an organization and its governance will also impact issues concerned with leadership and ownership. In very small companies the same person or persons may well carry out these two functions. Usually this is also the case in family firms. However, as the company grows, and depending on what legal form the company has, the governance, leadership, and ownership are likely to be separated.

6.8 Legal Structure Decisions

When a budding entrepreneur has finally reached the decision that creating a new venture is the right thing to do, another question arises. *What kind of company is necessary* for the firm to exist or is it necessary to create a *formal company at all*? We are not going to go through the various types of legal forms of businesses in the various nations of the world, but we have found after years of working with new ventures in most of the developed world that similar legal forms exist across all of them. They vary in specific detail, but each gives the firm what is considered "legal personhood." That is, they are an entity that must be protected by management and shareholders. This also usually provides the individuals in the firm some form of protection from lawsuits that may be directed that the firm. This protection is often called the "corporate veil" that does not exist if you are a sole proprietor.

In most countries, the very act of filling out the paper work and paying business licenses is not an extremely complicated thing and at best it may take a couple of hours. However, we are aware that in many countries actually getting the legal entity of a business can take months, if not years, and can take hundreds of steps as well as fees, licenses, and even bribes. This level of complexity explains why many in these countries are part of the "informal economy" often avoiding taxes, but also lacking the legal protections that often come from a formal legal structure.

Deciding what kind of an organization may be somewhat more complicated. The legal regulations and tax regulations of different forms of formal companies vary across countries and therefore it makes little sense for us to firmly give specific piece of advice on what legal form is best for you. Should it be *sole trader or proprietor*, a *limited partnership*, *limited company or incorporated* or even a *cooperative*? There are differences between these with respect to ownership, risk, and taxation, which vary between countries; therefore one form might be more preferred to others in some countries. In the United States we are seeing more use of *limited liability companies* (LLC) and *Subchapter S corporations* that are taxed at an individual tax rates, but have the *corporate veil* protections of regular corporations. Those individuals who are professionals in the United States like doctors, lawyers, and accountants often have a *professional corporation* designation that operates much like an LLC.

Even if an entrepreneur decides to start as a sole trader or proprietor, the company can later become a limited company or even a cooperative for instance. The legal form a firm's start does not mean it will always have to remain in that form. Therefore, our advice here is to, for that purpose, consult the expertise of your attorney, local business incubators, regional development organizations, or other public agencies offering these services usually for free or for a very agreeable fee. In the United States, this can also be done using Websites like *Legal Zoom*. While legal Websites are quite useful and can be cost-effective, the more complex your business, the more you need to seriously consider finding an attorney familiar with your industry, and this is especially the case when dealing with patent attorneys.

Even when you are creating a venture just for yourself, to employ yourself, there are situations when an LLC is more preferable to creating a venture as a sole trader/proprietor. Moreover, it does not mean that a sole trader cannot have employees and a self-employed can very well create a limited company. The choice is usually driven by how to handle risk (debt and loss) and taxation (personal vs. corporate tax laws).

Because of these issues, we have artists, who on face value are individuals, who decide it is better to have a company for handling financial transactions, to separate the really private from the artistic. But whether that company then has to be a limited company or not is a different issue. A limited company will need a certain amount of initial capital. How much, is regulated differently in different countries. In countries where there is a value-added tax (VAT), payments are connected to turnover (revenues) and in some countries there is a base limit; that is, if turnover does not exceed a certain sum, the firm will not pay VAT. That limit again varies between countries (e.g., there is a significant difference in that limit between Finland and Sweden). In the United States, different states have different tax schemes that affect a new venture depending on how it is legally structured. Once again, we recommend you talk to both your lawyer and your accountant on the implications these forms may have for your business.

Likewise, there are big differences between countries on how corporations are taxed. Therefore, it may become an issue to decide in what country the company should be registered. The difference is significant, for example, between Finland and Estonia. For an entrepreneur it is more favorable to register the company in Tallinn, Estonia, than in Helsinki Finland, and it only takes 4 hours by boat over the Gulf of Finland or 30 minutes by plane. The difference is significant to such a degree that this is currently actually taking place at a growing rate. There are also differences in employment laws, which is also necessary to consider when deciding where to register the firm. While many large firms that are public in the United States are registered in Delaware, for a smaller firm whatever advantages there are can be minimal to nonexistent.

6.9 Final Thoughts on Entrepreneurial Management

As you grow, your venture you will be presented with many new opportunities, which can be very good, or potentially dangerous. Understand that growing a business encourages you to learn new skills. Those new skills will allow you to address opportunities that were previously unavailable to you. You will learn to cooperate with other firms while competing with them at the same time. Being a successful entrepreneurial manager means increasing the firm's competencies as to not only exploit existing opportunities but to explore potential new opportunities as they become available. As your new venture grows more established, you will find your methods of operating morph into new ones.

As you establish your venture, you will find yourself networked with potential competitors that you may need to call upon if you get an order you cannot satisfy. As you grow, you will add organizational structures, processes, and controls that create needed policies and procedures. You as an entrepreneur will need to curtail non-income–generating middle-level management. We have found that too often these kinds of structures as they inhibit innovation. You must adopt an entrepreneurial leadership style that instills entrepreneurial thinking in the people you hire. You will want to foster an innovative and entrepreneurial environment within your venture. Realize that you will have to constantly invigorate the venture and reawaken innovation and entrepreneurial thinking. Being an entrepreneurial leader is not a job taken lightly if you want to avoid unnecessary bureaucracy or compliancy.

6.10 Exercises

Make a list of every company or venture that you have worked for in the past. Under each of those have two columns. In one column place everything you disliked about the organizational structure of your former employer. In the second column place everything you liked about that firm's structure. Repeat this for each firm. Do you see a pattern in either list?

Do the same exercise about each firm's compensation package, fringe benefits, etc. Once again, do you see any pattern? This can now be a blueprint for what you do and do not want to have your new venture's structure to look like.

References

Berger, L., and D. Berger. 2008. *The compensation handbook*, 5th ed. New York: McGraw-Hill .

Brännback, M., and A. L. Carsrud, eds. 2012. *Family firms: case studies on the management of growth, decline, and transition.* New York: Springer.

Carsrud, A., and M. Brännback. 2011. Reflections on twenty years of research on entrepreneurial motivation: have we learned anything at all? *Journal of Small Business Management,* 49(1): 9–26.

Carsrud, A., and M. Brännback, eds. 2012. *Understanding family business: undiscovered approaches, unique perspectives, and neglected topics.* Heidelberg, Germany: Springer.

Helmreich, R. L., L. L. Sawin, and A. L. Carsrud. 1986. The honeymoon effect in job performance: temporal increases in the predictive power of achievement motivation. *Journal of Applied Psychology,* 71(2): 185–188.

Steingold, F. S. 2013. *The employer's legal handbook: manage your employees & workplace effectively,* 11th ed. Berkeley, CA: NOLO Press.

7

Everything You Really Need to Know About Entrepreneurial Finance

---

7.0 Entrepreneurial Finance: An Introduction

Before we discuss money and capital perhaps, it would be nice to remember the origins of these words. As one of the authors grew up in a family ranching business, it is nice to know that cattle and other livestock were the first form of money, and in some parts of Africa are still considered a form of wealth where each head of cattle was called a *caput*, which is Latin for "head." Thus an individual with a herd of cattle had a lot of *caput* or *capital*, a term we use today to describe wealth. Everything from Yap disks of stone to bird claws and bear teeth have been used as money. The ancient Romans forged their coins in the temple of Juno Moneta, the goddess of marriage and women. From *Moneta*, we get the English words *mint* and *money*. But is money the goal for an entrepreneur?

> Starting out to make money is the greatest mistake in life. Do what you feel you have a flair for doing, and if you are good enough at it, the money will come.

This quote by the legendary Hollywood actress Greer Garson reflects what we think is important about any revenue model for any business. If you are not good at something and not passionate about it, it is going to be a lot harder to generate revenues, much less gain profits from that endeavor. With that as our guiding assumption, in this chapter we discuss various issues of financing including building a sustainable revenue model for your new venture. We have seen too many would-be entrepreneurs waste their energies by believing in a "big money" approach to starting a firm. They waste time and what money they have trying to attract investors instead of using their brains and energy getting their venture started.

This entrepreneurial process is more critical than simply having some money and spending it. It is important that you understand how your venture makes money; where it makes money; when it makes money; when you spend money; how you spend money; and where you spend money. Every entrepreneur needs to understand that there is a money cycle. That is, you have to spend money (which time and effort) to make money. The real trick is to spend less than you make from the process and to do that as quickly as possible. We think that the following quote from one of America's great entrepreneurs, experts in affairs of state, scientists, and diplomats, Benjamin Franklin, sums this up quite well:

> Your net worth to the world is usually determined by what remains after your bad habits are subtracted from your good ones.

What "Old Ben" was saying is your good business decisions have to outweigh your bad ones. The only way to know that is by managing your cash flow. We feel that many traditional finance books fail to discuss the importance of cash-flow management especially in the early stages of the new venture. This is absolutely critical to a new venture that is both resource and asset poor. Thank heaven for the advent of Quickbooks and other accounting software programs that make at least the bookkeeping side of a new venture manageable. With the advent of this technology, an entrepreneur can now spend more time dealing with the strategies associated with the finance of their new venture.

7.1 Building an Entrepreneurial Financial Strategy

We believe it is critical that whatever the financial strategy that an entrepreneur adopts must be harmonious with total strategy of the new firm, including marketing strategy, production, and human resource. The business concept and the opportunity it addresses determines the overall strategy of the venture and ultimately creates value. What we are saying is that the overall business strategy determines what is required financially, especially operational needs and any asset necessities. To do this adequately means you have to have a solid grasp of the day-to-day internal activities of the venture. The resulting financial requirements to address these activities determine which sources of financing will be used, such as equity, debt, grants, or even bootstrapping. Taken together, this determines the entrepreneurial financial strategy for the new venture. Once a strategy is chosen, there are going to be limits to how much freedom the entrepreneurial team will have in the future to modify or change their strategic approach. These limit possible future sources for funding, changes in risk and reward, and finally the control issues the entrepreneur versus those of investors. In other words, once you start down the road to having external investors or financial partners, they start to want to exert the influence in the direction of the firm and who will provide future funding options, *it is a bit like letting the fox into the hen house. Once in, the hens are hostage.*

We have found that there are some fundamental standards to have a successful start-up. The first is to get operational fast. The second is to achieve a quick break-even. The next is to focus on cash-generating projects. Another goal is to offer high-value products or services that can support personal selling to clients. Interestingly the next key behavior is don't spend excessive time trying to hire the perfect start-up team, but find one that believes in the business and can get the key tasks done. The next principle is one we firmly believe in, which is *keeping growth in check by focusing on cash flow*. Finally, start cultivating banks early before you need them. Keep in mind that change and uncertainty is the contexts for a start-up. Think of change as part of the reward for success. As your ventures starts, grows, and ages, it will require you to take a fresh look at everything again: roles, organization, finance, even the very policies that got the new venture up and running. All of these will be reflected in a changing financial strategy.

7.1.1 Entrepreneurial Finance: Not Just Venture Capital and IPO

Rarely do finance books talk about the financial realities of starting a venture: lack of bankable assets, lack of a track record, and no revenue among other things. Most finance and accounting books all seem to assume that the business is operational. We acknowledge that there is a large amount that has been written on venture capital (VC) as a part of entrepreneurial finance. This work is aimed at looking at an extremely small portion of the total number of new firms, which assumes the firm is going to have double-digit growth rates with a rapid cash burn rate and that their ultimate goal is an *initial public offering* (IPO) or a *merger and acquisition* (M&A) with a larger firm. The reality is that these options are in fact the exception, rather than the rule for most new ventures. We have seen way too many entrepreneurs who spend all of their time chasing after the next investor. To this group we this quote from Tim O'Reilly, a media entrepreneur is one that may help them focus on what is really important:

> Money is like gasoline during a road trip. You don't want to run out of gas on your trip, but you're not doing a tour of gas stations.

There are around a half million new ventures a year in the United States, fewer than 2,000 will obtain funding from a venture capitalist (usually after they are already well established), and perhaps 100 will ultimately see an IPO event in a typical year (at this point they are most likely several years old). While we will discuss VC, outside angel investors, and exiting the venture, we are going to concentrate in this chapter on what we feel every new venture needs to know about venture financing and most likely will use at some point in their business venture's life span. The key among the things every entrepreneur must know is their cash-flow requirements.

7.1.2 Building a Sustainable Revenue Model

While a lot of people will say that money is one of the biggest headaches of an entrepreneur, it should be obvious by now that we do not quite agree. Money *is* important, but it does not trump the entire business idea and the business model. The model tells us how the company will make money and why money is needed. We want to emphasize that a *business model* that does not have a *revenue model* is not a functioning business model. At worst, it is a disaster waiting to happen. At best, it is a documentation of some nice intentions. The *revenue model* for a venture informs us what is going to be done and where more money is going to be made through sales. Money is the gasoline of the car. It is what makes the world of the entrepreneur go around. No money, the world will not go around. The business model has to generate money, if it only uses money, then sooner or later it is going to be the *end of that world*. Usually, a smaller world will need less money than a larger one. Remember, we are firm believers in the adage of *little steps for little feet*. Unless you are Elon Musk with a great track record, don't attempt to develop a firm like SpaceX for space travel. Remember, Musk has sunk a lot of his own money into this venture as well as into Tesla.

The WiFi space is likewise an area where there are firms that exist because investors are willing to keep pouring money into them. It is important you realize that Spotify is growing by leaps and bounds, but is still not profitable. *Selling memberships has not proved to be a viable revenue model and an advertising revenue model has not proved to be viable either.* Bragging that you will make it up on volume of people and locations has not turned Spotify profitable, nor will it. We have seen this before in various early Websites in 2000 that sold $10 bags of dog food for $5 with free shipping and who swore they would make it up on volume. Suffice it to say, those sites and their firms don't exist anymore. Build a revenue model that works from the start is sometimes what every entrepreneur needs to do. One way to force you to think of a viable revenue model is to understand your firm's cash-flow needs.

Another good example of a revenue model where the product (a bed in a box) is sold via a Website is Casper. It does have VC funding, but its product is of very high quality; you purchase off the Website and it is delivered by the USPS or FedEx. Its products are cheaper than buying from a retail establishment without the pressure of salespersons. You are limited to choice of size with no frames or box-spring base. These savings are passed on to the customer. It makes its revenues off the purchase price. Most of its marketing is by word of mouth and internet search. The point here is that it has a revenue model not unlike that of the eyeglass frame Website Warby Parker. Both Casper and Warby Parker have created business models that are unique and are reportedly profitable. It should be pointed out that both have or will have competition as the models are replicable.

You, as an individual, need to comprehend fully your financial projects and how you got to those numbers. Many failed entrepreneurs have had someone else develop their financials. When pressed on their projections, they have no idea what the numbers mean. You need to understand how your financial model ties to the various aspects of your new venture like operations, human resources, and marketing, the key drivers of the venture's success or failure. If you manufacture something, you should be able to tell someone what is generated (units, revenues) by any given production process you are using. If you are in the magazine business, it might be expected you know the renewal rates. Distribution approaches is key in software business. Today, internet downloads are all the rage, but here it is critical to know how you get paid for the download. Regardless, you need to be able to address what is the break-even point. Remember break-even refers to the level of sales (and how many units) when the venture begin to make a profit.

7.1.3 Cash Flow: A Numerical Scorecard

We have waited to this point in the book to discuss financial issue because cash flows, profit and loss statements are a numerical representation of decisions you already have made in terms of strategy, marketing, human resources, and product/service development. Financial statements are numerical score cards on your past behaviors as a manager. The ability to build financial statements in particularly monthly cash-flow statements is something we feel every business should do. It will tell you where you are and how well you are doing. We have said in another of our books (Carsrud and Brännback 2007) there are no *conservative cash-flows* projections, as they *all* are always a dream. Many investors will say ". . . I don't ever believe in a firm's financial forecast as they are never realistic. We have to believe in the people running the firm."

Cash-flow projections are your dreams for the future. We should note that we have never seen a cash-flow projection that was negative, but we have seen a lot of those dreams that turn into nightmares. The reason simply being they did not know accurately what was coming in and what was going out in terms of money. As we said earlier in this chapter:

- Know how your venture makes money

- Where it makes money

- When it makes money

- When do you spend money

- How do you spend money

- Where do you spend money

This information will help you manage your firm through rough times. We are very firm believers in good cash-flow management. Do not do what one young entrepreneur we know who very honestly said ". . . I have checks in the checkbook, I must have money in the bank."

While in some ways the need for start-up funds are critical, the reality is that while people feel they need lots of money to start, there are plenty of businesses that begin with little or no money from external sources. If you have a good handle on your cash-flow needs and income stream(s), you may find you need little outside investment. The most often used form of financing as an entrepreneur is called *bootstrapping*. That is, doing the most with the least amount of money possible, often only with the hard work of the entrepreneur and the entrepreneurial team.

7.1.4 Determining Cash-Flow Needs

To us the most important part of any entrepreneurial financial strategy very simply is determining the cash needs of the new venture. That is, you need to understand how much money (including hard assets like buildings, equipment) it is going to require to start the new venture and to keep it running until the firm is capable of generating sufficient positive cash-flow from sales. We are not saying this is going to be easy. It is a bit like *looking into a foggy crystal ball with finger prints all over it*. That is, it is never easy and rarely an accurate procedure. But it is one you need to undertake as it may point out how little you really know about income and outflow. For example, a frequent issue we have seen is the often outlandish estimates of how long something will take to turn cash positive (earning more than you spend) or how much money it will take to achieve the development of the first product/service. These are usually very dissimilar from what actually occurs.

Some experts recommend the use of benchmarking against other firms based on public information. This usually means benchmarking against established larger firms. If you are attempting to benchmark against other start-ups or smaller firms that information is quite difficult to find as what one hears is often highly filtered information. No one wants to admit that it took more money or time than they expected, although that is usually what it does for most. How many of us remember the very first Apple computers where all recalled and scrapped? We bet that was not in the cash-flow projections. What we are saying is that as a start-up it is very hard to know what is going to impact your own operations much less what is going on inside your direct competition, even if you previously worked at a competing firm. Cash-flow needs are best done as thoroughly as you can and tied as closely as possible to other internal activities you should have thought through.

In one of our earlier books in new venture creation (Carsrud and Brännback 2007), we wrote on the various steps that any entrepreneur should take in order to assess the cash needs of their new venture. The very first step is to understand the various processes and activities in your firm, and how they all interact with each other. In other words, what are the key tasks that the firm has to make in order to make its product or deliver its service? This may well include several tasks done by many people over a period of time. The number of people and the length of time and sequence of activities all have impact on cash needs obviously. Some have defined being profitable as the price for staying in business. To us the real job of a firm is to find a paying customer. *But you have to be able to cover the costs of acquiring that customer and staying in business.*

To understand your cash requirements, you need to understand the value of what you do in order to charge appropriately for what you have created. This is the same value we discussed when talking about pricing. Are you the only part of the value chain like a painter of portraits? Or is your firm one, which makes a nut and bolt that then is used in, say, a new automobile? This is where pricing strategy comes in play. An artist has a different price ceiling to determine while the nut and bolt manufacturer has a very different one. Each has to deal with potential substitutes if the price is excessive. Remember, you want to recoup as much of the value as possible while still letting the customer feel good about the purchase.

In today's internet world, a potential customer can hunt for a substitute and determine the typical price for something rather easily, and all over the world or literarily space. Remember, price has to cover costs, so don't get into the *lost leader* where you think you can sell something below your costs and folks will then decide to buy more expensive products or services you also sell, and that is how you will make up for the loss. Grocery stores often use milk as a lost leader to get customers in the store to shop. That worked fine till milk prices rose and the stores could not take the hit to the bottom line. This includes giving things away to get people in the store. As another example, we know of one bar in Los Angeles where the owner gave away drinks to get people in the bar for cocktail hour. The first two nights he was open he was busy. He made $3,000 on drinks he sold, and he gave away $11,000 worth of alcohol. To say the least, he did not stay in business very long with that pricing strategy.

7.1.5 Timing and Cash Flow

An area we have seen many entrepreneurial firms fail to understand is the amount of time it takes for their venture to turn investment cash into revenue cash. It rarely is instantly, in the case of a biotechnology firm it might be 18 years. Many businesses are subject to seasonal factors (for many retail stores the bulk of all sales are at Christmas, or many beach-related businesses only make money during the summer months). Timing of your opening is critical then you don't want to miss the money months. Here too, it is important that you know how rapidly you can acquire new customers or have repeat customers.

- What it is going to cost you to get that new customer?

- Would you do better going for repeat customers as they are *cheaper to acquire*.

Remember, time can be monetized!

A critical part of cash-flow management is to match the cost of operations with revenues from your sales forecast, which ought to be part of your strategic marketing plan. We know that these estimates are going to be wildly hopeful if not overly enthusiastic. However, you must learn to control any excessive confidence in your cash-flow projections as frankly they rarely turn out as expected. That said, there is some research evidence that on average new firms will need 25 percent more investment than they initially have estimated.

We typically tell students to *take their revenue numbers and divide it by two, take their cost factors, and double those and then triple the time it would take to make a sale*. This approach may give you a more accurate idea of the money you will ultimately make and when you will make it. What we are saying is that people vastly underestimate costs and time and overestimate revenues. This is true for any business from consulting, self-employed artists, to biotechnology firms and not-for-profits. *Unless you are being paid upfront, you are carrying costs, remember that from the start*. One reason to do sales forecasts is to help determine when you are going to need to spend more money to meet those new sales. Here is where care and attention to detail is needed.

We strongly recommend, as a part of your financial planning process, that you expand your sales forecast and establish what new capital expenditures will be required to meet projected new sales figures in years two through five. We have rarely seen any business plan that says it is going to consume money for as long as they actually do. It is rare to see any business not lose money for the first 18 months. The term used to describe this turn is often known as the *hockey stick*. That is, you lose funds till revenues finally start to kick in and losses are reduced. When you finally get there, it is called *the break-even point*.

7.1.5.1 Break-Even and Sensitivity Analyses

We believe you need to know your numbers and this requires doing sensitivity analyses about your cash-flow projections, but you also need to do a break-even analysis. This will give you a "reality check" concerning if you can *afford* to do this project and is it a *feasible* and *viable* business. It will also give you some ideas as to how to turn a business idea into a profitable one. Here is what you have to do:

1. Determine any and all fixed cost. These are not just costs associated with start-up. For example, rent, utilities, and equipment leases including; are these paid daily, weekly, monthly, or annually. Estimate variable costs expressed on a per unit basis.

2. Calculate your break-even with its associated market share.

3. Ascertain whether this market share is both possible and probable.

Make a list of your fixed costs (FC) (these could be daily, weekly, monthly, or annual) associated with your providing product or service. These should include any capital necessities for the new venture counting training, leases, licenses, taxes, equipment, required deposits, and any setup charges. Then sum all of these costs. Now, make a similar roster of all the variable costs (VC) connected with your product/service. Sum all of these expenses. Now, determine the break-even using the formula:

$$\frac{FC}{(Price - VC)}$$

Next, you determine the size of the market for the product or service (preferably in units, not dollars). You can now calculate *break-even market share*. The big question concerns this market share. *Can you reasonably attain this share given the marketing strategy you have developed for the firm*?

Then we recommend you do some analyses to see what happens if sales *do not* meet expectations or the costs are higher than foreseen. In business school speak this is called *sensitivity analyses*. Build in a contingency factor, as the unexpected does occur quite frequently. Few would have predicted the 9/11 disaster in 2001, or oil price increases of over 100 percent in 2006, or the great recession of 2008, or the 60 percent drop in oil prices in 2015. In other words, there are always going to be some level of uncertainty in any cash-flow projection and thus careful management of cash-flow is required. You may not think that handling a spreadsheet is important for an entrepreneur, but we disagree. It is! If you fear numbers, take a stiff drink and dig into the process.

Among the key skills you will need to master are the fundamentals of building *proforma financial statements*. This includes developing of cash-flow projects that reflect the various aspects of your business, or if a new venture, what you are proposing in your business plan. Be as realistic as possible with your financial forecasts. This requires you know all of the internal operational costs as well as the marketing ones. If you manage to obtain an investor, you are going to have to negotiate deal and term sheets. If you are not familiar with these or how to read them, we always recommend finding a business lawyer who is familiar with these and can warn you of potential problems. Unlike terms for getting on a Website, which most of us ignore, this is where you will need to read the details in any deal and term sheets. This brings to mind a quote from one of Silicon Valley's classic entrepreneurs, Nolan Bushnell:

> I founded Atari in my garage in Santa Clara while at Stanford. When I was in school, I took a lot of business classes. I was really fascinated by economics. You end up having to be a marketer, finance maven and a little bit of a technologist in order to get a business going.

7.1.6 *Money Comes in Four Forms*

Another way to look at cash flow is to think of there being four types of money. We find this an easy way to help an entrepreneur understand that *not all dollars are the same*. These money types are

1. Those used for operations

2. Those restricted in their use or access

3. Those already invested by the entrepreneur and/or entrepreneurial team

4. Potential money

Each form requires you understand what they do.

Operational funds are used to keep the day-to-day activities going such as making payroll, paying various taxes, operating expenses like electricity, and when possible, debt-reduction payments. We have seen firms who literally thought they could skip paying the electricity bill or the phone bill, which is a big mistake. We remember when one consulting client wondered why he was getting no email inquiries from his Website until he realized he had ignored paying his hosting service and they cut him off.

It is critical you keep the business running. You as an entrepreneur have to try to make the best use of money you hold even if for a short time. This is often difficult given bank charges for keeping money, but you should explore asking for free checking accounts and we have found that in the United States credit unions are often more willing to do this than commercial banks. Just remember, you need to ask! Financial institutions rarely tell you ways to save money or even earn interest on short-term holdings. However, please don't do what one young entrepreneur did, which was to use money given to him as a down payment for his wedding event center to pay off the bills from prior weddings. His business was starting to look like a Ponzi scheme. This leads to our next form of money, *the restricted.*

There is one form of money, which is critical to understand and which often is not, by entrepreneurs who are often resource constrained and think that any money they have in an account is useable to any purpose. That form is *restricted money*. These are funds that are pledged for another purpose such as escrow funds, guarantee for credit, and pension or retirement funds (Carsrud and Brännback 2007). We have seen a U.S. new venture that had funds set aside to cover their payroll taxes but got into a cash squeeze and used them for something else. They were very surprised when the Internal Revenue Service (IRS) took a very dim view of that behavior. The legal bills to deal with the action cost thousands. More importantly, it is a behavior that could get you felony time in jail. Other examples of *restricted funds* are deposits, and any cash value an insurance policy may have. It is possible to use restricted money to secure lower interest rates with a bank if they are the possessors of those funds. Here again, you have to ask and negotiate.

The next form of funds is *invested money*. This is money that you as an entrepreneur have "put to work." These funds are in such things as inventory, real estate, stocks, bonds and other securities, and some type of insurance (Carsrud and Brännback 2007). We often see firms that do not use invested money well. We know of one firm that had 2 years of inventory stored in an expensive warehouse simply because they got a good deal on the volume. When one did the analysis, the deal ended up costing them 20 percent more than if they had not bought in volume. Sometimes, a good deal can get expensive and can tie up funds in inventory that is also subject to taxes in my jurisdictions.

Finally, there is a great deal of evidence that the worth of many established smaller businesses is their real estate holdings rather than in the value of the firm itself. We are reminded of one small firm in South Africa where the owner had highly a successful furniture manufacturing business. When asked what he spent his profits on, he opened the back door to his factory to show a large field full of cattle. When asked why he spent money on cattle and not on expanding his shop his answer was ". . . here we measure wealth by the number of head of cattle you own." The only problem was that the local bank would not loan on cattle and selling his cattle would reduce his perceived wealth. Culturally, he was considered rich, but business-wise he had not made the most of his *invested money*.

You need to balance risk and return by spreading the investment among various types of invested money, and we recommend not just cattle. We recognize that art is also a form of invested money, for any artist with racks full of completed paintings, it is important to take that investment and turn it into potential money by exhibiting those paintings, which hopefully will sell.

Closely related to *invested money* is the next form: *potential money*. For any new venture it is the most critical type as this is the one you as an entrepreneur can impact through the business model you adopt. You control the ultimate performance of this type of money and how rapidly you can convert it into *real money*. Potential money thus is found in accounts receivable and pending cash sales. It is also found in the value of current inventory, any credit value of customer goodwill, and in all contracts for the delivery of future goods and services. It also exists in the value of business property, equipment, and even cattle if you are in South Africa or Texas. The issue here is if you need these invested funds to make your product or service? If not, then perhaps they need to be liquidated and turned into real money.

Every entrepreneur has to focus on efficiently turning *potential money* into *real money*. A primary goal is to compress the time from when you spend money making a product and service to receiving money for that activity. This is what is meant by the "timing of turning cash into cash" (Carsrud and Brännback 2007). There are five ways to turn *potential money* into *real money*. These tricks of the trade improve cash flow. The first trick is to bill your customers sooner. The second is to collect from your customers sooner. The third is to pay your own accounts payable later (but not so late as to be costing you more). The fourth trick is to negotiate volume and/or early-pay discounts. Just don't end up with 2 years of inventory holding costs. Finally, we recommend the fifth trick where possible, and that is to encourage large orders. This requires that you can meet that large order without excessive new costs of inventory, personnel, and equipment. That is, your current operations must be able to support these approaches.

We remember one of our students who started a business in Southern California selling brightly colored beach shorts. He managed to land a major retail account who wanted 25,000 pairs of their swim wear in a month. The trouble was our student only had 2,500 pairs in inventory. The next 30 days was a mad rush of cutting fabric and sewing 24/7. Thank heaven for friends and family who pitched in to complete the order, although the last 2,500 pairs where delivered a day late because of traffic on the freeways.

7.2 Finding Money and Investors

We have seen year after year, in country after country, entrepreneurs and small business owners state that financial issues are their biggest concerns and raising outside investment including bank loans are what keep them from growing. This is reflected quite nicely in the following quote:

> An entrepreneur without funding is a musician without an instrument.   —Robert A. Rice Jr.

Most entrepreneurs start with funds they have saved or borrowed from friends and family. However, to us, borrowing your parents' life savings to start a business may be rather risky and may have consequences that ought to be avoided. Another big source of money for the venture would be entrepreneur is from suppliers who may well sell you inventory for which you do not have to pay for 30 days. We are seeing increasing use of cloud funding as well. Between 1990 and the early 2000s we saw a great deal of use of credit card debt to fund new ventures, but that has tended to wane since 2008. This is because of great recession when banks began to tighten up on their credit card lending and with credit card interest rates rather high. However, it remains one way to obtain debt financing, although with major implications for personal bankruptcy issue as banks will expect the individual to be ultimately responsible for the debt incurred.

Another source of capital can be customers who give you a down payment with the rest due on delivery of the goods and services. We see this frequently when artist do commissioned paintings or a bakery does a wedding cake for a couple. If you have a grasp on your costs that upfront payment can cover the cost of the paint and canvas for the painting or the flour and spices for the wedding cake. The upfront payment may even cover part of the labor costs. Just remember that if you take a pre-payment, you are now legally obligated to complete the task! What we are saying here is simply that people don't realize they often need less money than they thought they needed if they take the time to really understand the impact of various decisions they make and how they run the day-to-day operations.

7.2.1 More Money Sources

We often hear "... if someone would just give us the money we need we could be so successful." We frankly feel that is a bit like having the cart before the horse. Expecting others to put up money to support your venture ignores the fact that most investors, especially bankers, are going to expect you to have some *skin in the game*. Here is a list that encompasses the vast majority of typical sources of funds for a new venture, some we see used frequently, a few we have rarely seen, and a couple we only have heard about:

- Investment by family and friends
- Personal savings
- Commercial and personal loans from bank
- Governmental loan guarantees like SBA loans
- EU-regional funding instruments and similar schemes in other countries
- Credit cards
- Accounts receivable
- Angel investors
- Venture capital
- Operating a side business
- IPO
- Home equity loans
- Advances on credit card receipts
- Equipment sales and re-lease
- Selling assets like your home
- Cashing out your retirement
- Cashing out your parent's retirement
- Crowd funding
- Renting out your home or a bedroom
- Sweat equity
- Online lending schemes
- Grants from governments or even private foundations

- Winning a business plan contest

- Winning the lottery

- Playing the odds at Las Vegas

- Betting on a horse race

We have not included selling drugs, the spouse and kids as those are immoral, unethical, and in most places illegal. What we are trying to drive home in this discussion is that while money and where to find it are important, there are a lot more important decisions an entrepreneur has to make that impact financial decisions. Those decisions may well eliminate some funding options or make others more attractive. Perhaps the most important things an entrepreneur can spend time on is to develop a viable revenue model for the new venture. Any external funder will expect you to show them how you will achieve both revenues and profits.

7.2.2 The Myth of Needing Deep Pockets

The preceding discussions about starting small businesses with no viable revenue model remind us to address the myth that entrepreneurs need lots of money to start a firm. Of course, the amount of money needed is dependent on the type of business, and how long it will take before the company starts to generate revenues through sales. A biotech company developing new drugs will require very deep pockets and lots of money. We said previously that it may take 18 years before such a company generates any sales at all. Also, the amount of money needed is also dependent on how many people the company intends to hire.

In 2004 the average amount of money needed was around U.S. $54,000 ranging from U.S. $76,000 at the highest to U.S. $40,000 at the lowest (Carsrud and Brännback 2007). Those firms projecting to employ more than 10 persons within 5 years needed U.S. $113,000 on an average. These figures have changed very little in the last decade since most companies start small and remain small. The minimum legally required capital to create a limited company in Finland is €2,500. In the United States the more important figure is the average amount needed to start a new venture. Aldrich and Martinez (2001) found that most companies do not need more than U.S. $5,000 to start.

Even counting for inflation since the year 2000 the amount of money needed to start a venture remains rather low. As recently as 2009 the Kauffmann Foundation in Kansas City, Missouri, projected the average start-up cost U.S. $30,000. However, no two start-ups are the same and many home-based firms have been started on less than $3,000. Most of these are sole proprietorships with low upfront costs. Unless you attempt to find the cure to cancer or develop a new automobile like *Tesla*, many ideas for new firms require little initial investment.

However, these are just statistics and estimates from various research studies. What you should take from these is quite simple: *it does not take a lot of money to start a business if you learn to control costs*. What we have learned over the years is that the critical skill entrepreneurs need to learn is to comprehend what are their essential costs (including investments in absolutely necessary equipment, etc.) and how to reduce those costs (by leasing or buying used). Don't forget that HP began in a garage near Stanford with equipment borrowed from the university's Dean of Engineering.

This should tell you that there are usually ways to reduce the need for excessive investment. We also like to remind our students that the real goal of any venture is to *create a customer*, not just develop a product or even to produce profits. One of the cheapest things any entrepreneur can do is to provide honest and helpful customer service. It is always cheaper to keep a customer than to constantly find new ones. Artists have learned that having a collector who purchases several of their paintings becomes an advocate for that artist with other collectors, the power of *word of mouth marketing*, which is highly effective and very cheap. In the end, to be able to decide how much money you are going to need, it is necessary to understand costs. Just remember that investors don't want you to drive around in an expensive car or have an office in the most expensive building in town. Those are assets that frankly in most businesses are not income generating assets.

7.3 Understanding Investors and Bankability

At this point let us turn your attention to potential investors. You are going to need to determine whether you want any, what you are willing to do and give up to have investors, and whether you can offer your business venture to them for investment with deal terms with which you are prepared to live. There is also increasing evidence that angels and other outside investors are heavily influenced by the initial impression these individuals have of you. People use implicit personality theory and the key factors seem to be do you come across as warm and agreeable. In addition, they want to know that you are competent and have the intellectual capacity to understand the business and have cognitive judgment capability. Finally, investors want to know that you are able to act upon your intentions concerning the new venture. The less experienced your potential investors are, the more they are dependent in their judgments on first impression of you and their focus is primarily on you as an entrepreneur (and less on the business concept).

Remember, your mother is investing in you as much as she is investing in the business you are starting. The more an investor has experience in investing in new ventures, the more they have intentions to invest. But experience also impacts the perceived worthiness of the investment opportunity. In other word, pay attention to how you come across with investors. Investors get passionate about their investments and they may well see passion as an important part of the entrepreneur to demonstrate if they have obsessive passion about their venture (but don't be excessively obsessive). Remember, investors want to see that you also have the tenacity to stick with the venture, despite obstacles. Investors want to know that you also have the leadership capability to energize the entrepreneurial team and drive the business. However, the more experience investors have, the more they become concerned that if you are overly obsessive in your passion that you will burn out.

What we are saying is that every entrepreneur has to understand how investors think, be they family members, friends, venture capitalists, angel investors, or bankers. You need to understand how they make their decisions and for what in particular they are looking in terms as investors or debt holders. We know from current research that angel investors are leaving the start-up arena in large numbers for more established firms in 2015. It is more than a qualified opinion that investors are far more careful today after The Great Recession of 2008, and certainly more than they were 10 years ago. Certainly, they changed their behavior after the dot.com crash at the turn of the millennium and even more so after the Great Recession.

These changes are dependent on many other factors as well. For example, bank lending has become very difficult in the economies of Ireland, Spain, Portugal, and Greece, even with record low interest rates in Europe. As we discuss in some detail later in this chapter, you must remember that banks are asset-based lenders where they perceive start-up venture financing as extremely risky to them, even with government guarantees from programs like those of the Small Business Administration in the United States. In actual fact, to get money from any bank in the United States, Europe, Canada, Australia, or elsewhere, the punch line within the entrepreneur's elevator pitch should be that the *money is not really needed*. If the bank decides to lend you money, they will want a personal guarantee. They want to know that if they invest, they want you to show that you have been willing to invest yourself. Any investor's willingness to put money into entrepreneurial ventures is also dependent on whether there are other better and more profitable places available in which to invest.

The reality is that you, as an entrepreneur, will need to be prepared to tap multiple sources of funding other than just family, friends, and the occasional fool soon parted from their inheritance or live saving. At one time about 40 percent of new firms are funded by a single source, today that figure is much smaller. Most new ventures have multiple sources of funding and this is where institutional lenders will join the venture if they think the entrepreneur has sufficient "skin in the game." In other words, investors, not just banks, want to know whether the entrepreneur's own money has been invested. It is nice to hope you can just use *other people's money* (OPM), but the reality is that the entrepreneur will have to put up more than just "sweat equity" from his or her personal labor. Investors are going to want to know whether the entrepreneur has real money invested, even if relatively little needs additionally to be invested in the business. We know one very successful serial entrepreneur who constantly was asked to put up his used 1974 Toyota Corolla as collateral for loans, a task he found difficult to do.

Some of the sources we have listed previously are more common than others in different countries. One common source in the United States is credit card debt, something rarely used in the Nordic countries. It is very hard to get VC or angel investment in Finland, but already much easier in Sweden simply because there are more venture capitalists and angel investors. There are very few angel investors in Finland. In fact, there is little point in comparing Finland and Sweden with the United States as the United States is literarily worlds apart—not only in the number of VC and angel investors *per se* but also in the amounts of money that they invest. There are far more digits and zeros in the U.S. numbers. Although as mentioned, U.S. angel investors are moving away from start-up funding in large numbers in recent years. Moreover, not all entrepreneurs should even look for funding from venture capitalists or angel investors. Finally, very few companies these days start with an IPO and very few firms actually go through an IPO. While we discuss the IPO process and VCs in this chapter, we will not dwell on those as frankly; it is more likely you will get struck by *lightening* at your front door than you will go through an IPO or receive money from a VC. You are far more likely to have investment from friends and family.

Regardless of what country we have been in, we have found that all investors tend to look for the same things in the venture. They all look first and foremost for a good return on their investment. For that to occur, they will want to invest in a firm that operates in an area where they have expertise. They do not invest in businesses they do not understand. If they did, they would soon be out of business. Then they will all want a detailed, and to their minds a realistic financial plan. The company also has to offer a potential exit within 5 to 7 years, which is when investors hope to cash out and with a good return on the investment. Finally, the company should in some way hold elements of uniqueness—to ensure the possible exit and the good return. Even bankers providing debt want to know that there is sufficient cash flow from the business to cover debt payments. In the case of angel investors and venture capitalists while they primarily may invest money, you need to realize that investors also invest their time. A good banker will do the same to ensure the safe management of their loan funds; they often will do this via covenants in the loan documents as well as site visits. Investors also want to minimize their risk, and therefore there has to be ways of covering the risks associated with cash especially.

7.3.1 Capital

To repeat some things we have already discussed, once you have determined the amount of cash you will require, it is possible to start determining where to acquire such funds. You will need to consider what you are willing to give up in order to acquire these funds (percentage of ownership, management control, etc.). Capital can come from six sources (if you are in the United States):

1. Cash from internal operations (profits)

2. Those acquired from short-term debt financing (i.e., credit cards)

3. Liquidating non-income–generating assets (selling that used car of yours)

4. Long-term debt (mortgaging the house)

5. Equity financing (your mother investing for a share of the firm)

6. Crowd funding

It will become obvious that each of these has its limits in terms of income and each come with a variety of costs (like your mother constantly wondering how her investment is doing). The most recent addition to this list is crowd funding that we discuss later. Right now it has a lot of legal "gray areas" and seems to be basically an American phenomenon.

We briefly review these in terms of some specifics important to entrepreneurs in the following text. We will largely ignore those that are rarely used by, or available to start-ups. Entrepreneurs have access to short-term sources of debt financing that can include loans from friends and relatives, accruals, trade credits, leasing, bank lines of credit, and asset-based lending (including pledging receivables, factoring, and pledging inventory).

Sadly to say, long-term sources of debt financing (such as long-term bonds, mortgage bonds, debentures including subordinated and convertible, debentures with warrants, bonds including income, zero coupon, indexed, development, pollution control, and junk) are rarely available to most start-ups unless you are going to take a mortgage out on your home (Carsrud and Brännback 2007). The reason is simple—entrepreneurs may have access to these long-term alternatives when the venture is further along in its life cycle. We have seen, however, a few rare cases where pollution control bonds have been used to finance equipment for barbecue (BBQ) places that produce a lot of smoke. Even there, the BBQ establishments were more established businesses.

Most equity financing for a start-up will be from friends and family making investments. Some also seems to be coming from crowd funding. If you have chosen as your legal form a corporation, you could be considering issues such as preferred stock versus common stock, cumulative features, voting rights do they or don't they, and whether this stock is given as part of management compensation. These are examples of issues you face in creating your financial strategy. Finally, we want to once again state that the single biggest source of finance for a new venture is personal savings or assets. You will have to put some of your own assets into your business.

7.3.2 Debt Financing

As we have listed previously, some of the funds associated with debt can be found by including advance payments and deposit from customers. One can also borrow from family and friends (be careful there are emotional costs here). There are wealthy individuals who are "angels" and besides taking equity may provide debt. We suggest that you be careful of private placement finders and packagers as they often promise everything and deliver far less.

Sometimes debt financing can be from potential customers and suppliers. We have seen past employers provide debt financing. Rarely have we seen it from prospective employees, but it has been known to happen. The U.S. Government has programs like the Small Business Innovation Research (SBIR) grant program, which provide some financing. Likewise there are various state programs available. We have seen a few firms use Employee Stock Ownership Plans (ESOPs). Finally, there are barter arrangements. Sometimes a franchisor will provide debt financing in order to purchase the franchise. Be sure to check for any legal issues that may make this difficult or questionable.

Remember strengths and weaknesses of each of these debt methodologies and seek out professional advice before signing on the dotted line. Even VCs will offer their investment as debt convertible to equity at some point. The reason is simple, in any bankruptcy debtors are more protected than are equity holders if the firm is liquidated. That is, debtors are paid first, especially those holding senior debt.

7.3.3 Banks

While we have previously talked about bankability, we think it is important to remind you that, fundamentally, financial institutions (like banks, savings and loans, and credit unions) are *asset-based lenders*. If you want to borrow, they will want to have some collateral especially if you are a new venture. They often will ask for personal guarantees for a business loan. The business goes bankrupt, and even if it is a corporation legal format, you are on the hook for the debt personally. In some countries, like Australia, for example, if you don't own physical property, it is nearly impossible to get a bank loan for a venture. Banks want an asset as security for their loans and these might contain accounts receivable, current inventory, new equipment, property mortgages, or sales contracts. We have never seen a bank provide a loan for 100 percent of the asset value. As a new firm, you are going to come face to face with the bank's concern with the *credit-carrying capacity* of the firm. We frequently tell clients and students that you need to build a successful history with a bank of taking small loans and paying them off before asking for larger loans. Remember the old joke, *banks don't loan to people who really need money*.

7.3.4 Venture Capital

Researchers in entrepreneurship have spent a great deal of time studying venture capital and venture capitalists. While the area is certainly *sexy* as a research topic, it is in reality something many, if not most, new ventures will never receive. The reasons for this are simple. Very few new ventures are the kinds of firms in which venture capital is prepared to invest. In fact, in 2014 venture capital was doing fewer total deals than in the past and most of these are focused on firms that are already well established. Even hedge funds are starting to act as VC sources.

However, as much as the popular press and local business journals like to play up the firm that got a $5 million investment, there is the stark truth of reality. Assume there are 300,000 new ventures created in a year. Of that number fewer than 1,000 will achieve VC funding and most of those are not actually "new ventures" but those who have already started and have shown some promise. In other words, if you want VC money, you need to already be functioning. If you are one who has heard that VCs are really "vulture capitalists," bootstrapping may be the best option for you. Although we like to remind people *vultures only eat dead things*. If a VC is trying to take over your firm, you most likely have not managed the firm well.

7.3.5 Angel Investors

Angel investors are usually wealthy individuals. In recent years you will find these people have formed groups who invest in firms. While many of these are informal, some are actually organized into networks. This is especially the case in the United States and Canada. But these groups can be found elsewhere. Many angels are former entrepreneurs, but not all. We need to remind that you angels are not there to bless your start-up; rather they are in it for the money as is any investor. Recently angels are investing a lot less in start-ups than in previous years. They seem to be putting their money into expanding existing firms. There is evidence that as of 2015 angel investments are primarily in software, health care services, medical devices and equipment, information technology services, retail, and financial services. Little angel money is going into clean technology. Men still seem to be the primary recipients of angel money with women only receiving about a quarter of these funds in 2014 despite more and more women seeking investment from angel groups.

7.3.6 What Investors Look for in Any Venture

The callous truth about a new venture's money search is that there are types of investors, those individuals enamored with the entrepreneur or those enamored with the business concept. We think it is important to appreciate how VCs look at any investment because in many ways any sophisticated private investor will be expecting something very similar. These include, but are not limited to, the following:

1. The venture as it stands and the team are capable of a sustained effort.

2. The entrepreneur and team are very familiar with market.

3. In 5 to 10 years there will be a 10 times return on investment.

4. Entrepreneur has demonstrated leadership in the past.

5. Entrepreneur can evaluate and react appropriately to risk.

6. Any money invested can be made liquid.

7. The market has significant growth potential.

8. Track record relevant to venture.

9. Entrepreneur can articulate well what the venture is.

10. Proprietary protection like patents, copyrights, and trade secrets.

To sum this section up, investors are looking for people with track records and management skills. If you don't have those, the best way to achieve those is by bootstrapping a new venture. We caution you to avoid becoming slaves to adhering to any given investors' criteria. This will diminish your flexibility in trying things and fixing things that every entrepreneur needs to do constantly to make a new venture work. We have sometimes told our M.B.A. students that bootstrapping is a *real M.B.A. degree.*

7.4 Bootstrap Financing

At this point we return to the topic of bootstrap financing. In other words, how do you build a business with little or minimal external funds? One of our former students who bootstrapped his highly successful financial services firm has said:

> Perhaps because the bootstrapping necessary for entrepreneurs is about persistence, resilience, and an absolute lack of understanding of just how difficult this is going to be. If we thought through the plan well enough, we wouldn't possibly be doing this.   —Christopher Jarvis

This reflects the view many entrepreneurs hold: *Bootstrapping is the pure form of entrepreneurship.* We think bootstrapping is a very strategic approach as it makes the entrepreneur focus on the important aspects of the firm and keeps the entrepreneur very close to their customers and keeping them happy. It also means the entrepreneur is closer to the action and aware of changes in the business and its environment. It makes the entrepreneur cooperate carefully with vendors as well. This hands-on approach reduces financial risk. Most importantly, it helps the entrepreneur keep more, if not all, of the venture.

We have long preached that only viable way to finance the start-up firm without outside investment and giving up control is to *bootstrap* the start-up using as little money as possible and investing your own time, money, and energy into the venture. We are not saying that later on you will not want or need external funding. What we are saying is that you will always get better terms from investors if you can show you have started the business and made it profitable before asking for any money. By growing the new venture with profits self-generated by the firm produces a business, which is focused on a viable revenue model and whose management knows how to manage cash flow. Some evidence suggests that you can maintain an average 12 percent growth rate by using just self-generating profits from a new venture. That frankly is a nice sustainable rate. Thus, bootstrapping is a very viable option for a new venture, and once the firm is operational, it is actually easier to get investment as established business.

There are dozens of studies that show the main reason bootstrapping is chosen as a funding mechanism is that it lower costs. This is seen as the most important motivation by the entrepreneur to bootstrap. What is interesting is that while lack of capital is also seen as a reason, many entrepreneurs report two other reasons: that is fun assisting others and getting help from others. Some studies have grouped those who bootstrap into three types. The first of these are those who are cost-reducing in orientation. The second group consists of those who are capital-constrained. The final group is some call risk-reducing types. It is clear that the experience of the founder is the most significant influence for using bootstrapping. As experience is gained, the new business founder learns more about the advantages and motives for using bootstrapping as well as when external funding may be useful. The resource procurement behavior changes from initially focusing on reducing costs toward focusing on the reduction in risk in the venture.

7.4.1 Advantages to Bootstrapping

We find it interesting that *e-businesses* that started via bootstrapping over the last 20 years are still operational while most of those who took outside monies from VCs have either gone bankrupt or been purchased by others. As we have said previously, bootstrapping makes the new venture flexible and inventive, which is a useful skill in uncertain economic conditions. That means as an entrepreneur you need to be creative; have a vision for the future; and practice your selling skills with customers, employees, and vendors. Bootstrapping will hone your cash-flow management skills that we have discussed earlier. Bootstrapping makes you think of innovative ways to get things done and will make you sensitive to cost issues. In other words, you may find leasing used equipment a better alternative to buying new. The keys to bootstrapping are minimizing operational and financial risks. Here are six methods you can use to lessen the investment necessary for your venture:

1. Prepayments from clients to make or purchase merchandise

2. Negotiate vendor credit terms (start-ups usually have to pay C.O.D.)

3. Bargain for extended terms

4. Use barter to obtain products or services

5. Try to cause all costs to be variable

6. Form marketing alliances with other firms

If you decide to bootstrap, be ready and willing to move to external financial support. If you remain solely dependent on internal rates of return to fund growth for too long, you may be unable to take advantage of market opportunities. You may also fail to add new and more experienced people to the firm. However, whatever you decide, bootstrapping remains a great first approach to get the firm off the ground. We will have much more to say about developing a financial plan for your new venture as part of building a business plan. Suffice it to say, if you are reluctant to deal with numbers, as an entrepreneur you are going to have to get over that fear.

7.5 Crowd Funding

The latest addition in the United States to funding options is the increasingly popular approach called *crowd funding*. As we have said earlier, this approach seems to be primarily an American phenomenon. It has potential legal implications for offering equity investment opportunities outside of the safe guards of various securities laws that govern say an IPO. Thus, using crowd funding means you may be operating in a legal grey area. You can kind of think of crowd funding as a vote by potential customers on the viability of your business idea. Interestingly, those who actually obtain crowd funding are a very small fraction of those who ask for such funding. Typical crowd funding is online and is in the form of either donation or offering some kind in return for some reward or financial return. Let's take, for example, funding a video game, and if funded and the game is completed, you get a copy of the game for your donation. Crowd funding thus comes in two forms:

1. Equity-based funding
2. Reward-based funding

According to the available data from one website, most projects do not meet threshold on *Kickstarter*. Thus these proposed projects or products receive no funding at all. What the evidence is showing is that people who go onto *Kickstarter* and other such sites are investing in the perceived legitimacy of the product (most are actual products) in terms of seeing these pragmatic. These investors are also interested in the story being presented and its cognitive and emotional appeal. Many also seem to invest for moral reasons. There is evidence that those who are successful in obtaining crowd funding model their business on the characteristics of similar organizations that have been successful.

While very few firms actually surpass the threshold for funding on *Kickstarter*, some 90 percent who get crowd-funded do end up starting as a new venture. The big barrier here seems to be the issue getting over the threshold in the allotted time frame. Reaching that threshold seems to be dependent on media viability. Can you grab the attention of various media? One way has been to get celebrities involved help to get media attention. However, founders with prior knowledge and success are also more likely to get crowd funding. Finally, the average *Kickstarter* investment is $52,000 for commercial proposals and $7,100 for non-profit, social enterprises.

While crowd funding is not as dominant as other sources of capital currently, there are projections of $15 to $50 billion may be available via crowd funding in the not too distant future. This seems to be in partial response to the move of both Angel and VC investing to more established firms. Crowd funding thus is filling a growing gap in providing an important source for early-stage financing. However, as we have mentioned earlier, there are issues of regulation in the space of crowd funding around rewards Regulation D about who is an accredited investors under various securities laws in the United States.

We believe that there are some other relevant issues that need to be considered. While obtaining *crowd funding* could be considered a vote of confidence by the market place, it could also be an issue of group think, much like lemmings over the cliff. The real question is, can the collective action of small investors make the new venture creation process a better activity? If so, then the issue is how does one get many small investors if you want to reach the threshold? There is evidence that like Angel and VC investors, it is a matter of the reputation of the entrepreneur and those early investors. This is sometimes called the *Warren Buffett effect*. That is, if an investor has a reputation for picking winners, that reputation serves as a social cue to others as to where the so-called smart money in the market or reputational money is going. However, there is some evidence that this reputational effect may hide the risks in the venture. Interesting data suggests that low-risk deals are always funded faster.

There are crowd funding options for social entrepreneurs as well. KIVA is another micro-lending website attached to the World Bank and its associated banks. With these options loans/investments average a mere $613, but are in the range of $50 to $5,000. Unlike Kickstarter, KIVA investment options are 100 percent funded. *Start Some Good* is another non-profit crowd funding site and seems to operate much like others in this space.

One thing that these crowd funding sites have brought to attention again is the importance not only to what you say but how you say it in your appeal for funds. Words affect perceptions by your investors. If you are a social entrepreneur, the audience expects to hear different words and terms than if you were a commercial entrepreneur. In the area of social ventures, you want to reduce uncertainty on the part of investors and you want to establish a personal relationship with your investors. What research is showing is that social ventures use more collaborative and idealistic language in their funding pitches.

7.6 Exercise

While this exercise may sound simple, trust us it will take you some time to get the information together to do it. Get out your financial software or an Excel spreadsheet program and start to put together your first month's cash-flow statement. Be sure to include all income and all expenditure as well as tax payments due on any sales.

References

Aldrich, H. E., and M. A. Martinez. 2001. Many are called, but few are chosen: An evolutionary perspective for the study of entrepreneurship. *Entrepreneurship Theory and Practice*, 25(1): 41–56.

Carsrud, A. L. and M. Brännback. 2007. *Entrepreneurship*. Westport, CT: Greenwood Press.

8

How to Grow or Not to Grow Your Venture: That Is the Management Challenge

8.0 Growing Your Venture: An Introduction

> For me, the most fun is change or growth. There are definitely elements of both that I like. Launching a business is kind of like a motorboat: You can go very quickly and turn fast.

This quote by Tony Hsieh, the CEO of Zappos.com, in many ways expresses the excitement and potential dangers of growing a new business venture. It is much like riding a fast motorboat or racing a motorcycle on a dirt track in an *X Game* race. The adrenalin rush is exciting, but if you crash, you may not only lose the race but break your bones or if in a motorboat, drown.

8.1 What Is Business Growth?

Business growth is the process of advancing or increasing a given measure of a new venture's success. This growth can be achieved either by enhancing the top line (or revenue or turnover) of the business with greater product sales or service income or by increasing the bottom line (or profitability) of the operation by minimizing costs. In this chapter we are going to discuss growth from a number of perspectives and challenge you to think critically about how you want to grow your business. In this regard we are going to provide you with some mini-cases of how firms have grown. In the process we hope to make you think about how important it is to be profitable while growing. We are reminded of the following admonition when it comes to picking a growth strategy:

> Growth of the sake of growth is the ideology of the cancer cell.
> —Edward Abbey

8.1.1 Developing a Workable Growth Strategy

There are several different ways of achieving a growth strategy for a new venture and each possesses approach that has its both positives and negatives. For a new venture or an existing small business in which you have invested your own money into the firm, we strongly recommend you adopt a relatively low-risk strategy in which you adopt a slow-growth approach using internally generated funds to grow the firm. We admit this may take years to grow the firm, but it is also a sustainable approach. A faster, but clearly a risky and debt-laden, approach is to grow through acquisition, which involves buying out competitors and even moving into different markets. As it becomes obvious later in this chapter, we advise new ventures and small businesses to start out slowly and only expand once you have established the firm and its operations are stable. We know from our own experience at People Express Airlines that rapid growth often strains human, organizations, and facilities to their breaking point. We have more to say about high or rapid growth later in this chapter.

If growth is a goal you want to achieve, at the start you need to develop on what some call *intensive growth plans*. The first step, which every entrepreneur must make if they are to succeed, to any degree, is to reach your initial market. This is also one of the least risky strategies an entrepreneur can carry out. That is the strategy of market penetration. We have discussed this in some detail earlier. As we noted then, this strategy focuses rightfully upon the customer. You as an entrepreneur want to urge customers to buy more of your service or product. However, obviously a lot depends on the nature of that product or service as to the frequency at which additional ones are needed. You can also move to new areas in which to see your services and products. If you sell in one location, you could start selling in another or you could open a Website and sell off the Internet as an expansion strategy. This is sometimes seen as a *different channel* of distribution and marketing. Whatever approach you take, you will have to develop appropriate marketing tools and mechanisms to get to your new customers.

Another set of growth strategies that we mentioned in earlier chapters are *new product/service development* and *selling to new customers*. These both will help you to improve your market penetration. If you are lucky enough to have achieved a steady flow of existing customers, new product development may help you achieve in more sales. Likewise, if you want to acquire new clients, developing new products and services might prompt more attention to your new venture. We consider these approaches to be low-risk strategies that every entrepreneur should consider when you are developing your marketing campaigns as we noted in Chapter 4 on marketing.

We strongly urge any new venture to only consider growth by acquisition after you have been successful in the strategies we discussed previously. Acquiring another firm is not only an expenditure of time, but it is also one that usually requires taking on debt and taking on all the issues of integrating staff and resources. If you decide to purchase another firm, we think buying a firm in the same industry as you are in is wise. This will at least help with the marketing issues. By purchasing a competitor, you can potentially reduce some of the barriers to growth as well as potentially increase the addition of new products and services. Another approach is to purchase a supplier that can help you grow by providing better supply and hopefully at less cost, which is called *backward integration*. Another way to grow is to purchase firms that produce parts needed for your product. This is called *forward integration* and it may help grow your firm. Regardless, we do not recommend this strategy until you are both cash positive and generating sufficient profits to afford the debt that service growth often requires. We understand that, for many entrepreneurs, growth is a measure of success, which we now turn to in our discussion.

8.1.2 Growth and Success

We recognize that growth is often seen as the same thing as progress and success. Certainly this seems to be the desired relationship in many new firms. In the American culture and most countries in the world, most entrepreneurs who have achieved notable success, according to media standards, have all experienced growth and sometimes great periods of high growth. But, while growth is often recognized as an inevitability, so too is failure. Many venture capitalist consider any venture they invest in that does not "knock it out of the ball park" to be a failing venture despite the fact that the business is profitable and sustainable. The idea of success to the venture capital (VC) is certainly tied closely to rapid growth with a huge payout upon exit. Likewise, it is important to recognize that not all successful entrepreneurs view the process of growth in the same way. While we certainly do not consider Jamie Dimon, the CEO of JP Morgan Chase to be an entrepreneur, he makes an important point when he states:

> Companies that grow for the sake of growth or that expand into areas outside their core business strategy often stumble. On the other hand, companies that build scale for the benefit of their customers and shareholders more often succeed over time.

Clearly, there may be growth that is good and growth that is in fact *bad*. While we all use the terms *growth* and *growing*, what do they really mean? Is growth really a measure of success? Growth may be a bit like pornography; *you know it when you see it*. All joking aside, it is time to turn our attention to the issue of growing a new venture and what does that mean. We are also going to discuss some pitfalls of managing a small business.

8.1.3 Mini-Case on Growth by Replication

Perhaps at this point a mini-case on how one entrepreneur grew his business by creating several new firms, in the same industry, with the same model is helpful. This approach is not new. Many individuals in the restaurant industry as well as craft brewing and B&Bs have taken to using this model. We are not suggesting everyone adopt this approach, but we are using this example to show you that there are other ways to grow businesses that do not require a "bigger is better mentality." We also are using this example of growth to show you that, sometimes to grow, you have to be very careful to understand what makes your business unique. You want to make sure you do not lose sight of what made it exciting to start in the first place. In this particular case, it meant replicating the success by creating a new venture, not merely growing the older one into a bigger operation. We have known this particular entrepreneur for decades, first as an M.B.A. student, and later working in marketing at several Silicon Valley technology-based ventures.

> Bryan Kane has had a long-time passion for wines and the making of fine wines in his adopted home of northern California. This transplant from Michigan, with an engineering degree, that came to

graduate from a business school had a substantial cellar of fine wines. Upon graduating with his M.B.A. degree from UCLA and working in Silicon Valley, he had an urge to learn more about wine and how to make quality vintages. As with many entrepreneurs, he began his first venture while working full time in another job.

In Bryan's case his first entrepreneurial venture, which was in wines, came while he still was working full time in a technology firm in the Valley. Having learned a great deal about how to create boutique wines, he launched VIE (www.viewinery.com) with a couple of his colleagues who also loved fine wine. These wines had a very French focus in style, a very distinctive interpretation of what it is as a California wine. Their Syrah's wine remains exceptional for vineyard specific production. Critical to the business was sourcing the grapes for this label from specific vineyards in Sonoma and the Lake Country grape-growing regions. The focus was on quality not quantity. Rarely did the particular vintage exceed 100 cases (1,200 bottles).

Soon VIE was winning awards, and the label was profitable given the model of purchasing grapes from given vineyards and controlling costs. He was always careful about pricing, so as not to overprice the wines vis a vie the quality. Only when demand increased because of award winning vintages did the prices rise (the rule of supply and demand), but always so that value always exceeded the price but met the costs of production. Thus as that venture grew and the varieties produced by the VIE label contained white's and red's (and the occasional rosé), he knew that adding more bottles to the production runs would not maintain the quality that he wanted the label to project as a boutique winery.

Thus, he set out to launch another label, Sol Rouge (www.solrouge .com) having a very different look in label and bottle from that of VIE. The Sol Rouge winery maintained the same high standards in terms of production and quality as VIE. Bryan could expand production of wines while still keeping the cases produced small in order to control quality and maintain the boutique nature that had made VIE prize winning. To control costs, they share space and administrative functions on Treasure Island in San Francisco Bay in an event space in an old hanger called *The Winery SF*. Today Bryan is seen as one of the most creative winemakers in California.

What we hope this mini-case has shown is that growth can very much be defined in terms of an individual's personal goals and their passions. Bryan has managed to create a multimillion dollar set of ventures without the high overhead often associated with wineries. He built this set of businesses over a decade mostly by internally generated funds. Yes, we are rather proud of him and regularly enjoy his wines at home be it with Texas BBQ, steak, or just sitting on the patio.

8.2 Describing Growth Versus Defining Growth

Growth is never by mere chance; it is the result of forces working together.

We certainly agree with this quote by James Cash Penny, the great American retail entrepreneur that growth is never by chance and it is clearly the result of a lot of factors working together. The issue is that no one set of factors predict growth, and thus trying to define it for each industrial sector becomes difficult. It also depends very much on the personal goals of the entrepreneur. As we have done in other sections of this book, we will begin by trying to define the term in question, like we did with success.

Growth is often defined as an increase in some quantity over time. Growth is also defined as a stage in some process of growing in order to achieve full growth or maturity. It is a projection of a future state, like a progression of something from a simpler form to more complex one. Growth is often attached to the concept of quantity. Thus, growth can be physical as in height, or from the perspective of a business, growth as in the amount of money. Another way to look at growth from a definitional perspective is as something abstract such as a system becoming more complex or like an organism becoming more mature. In this case growth is associated with age or the aging process.

In an economic sense growth is an anticipated state such as wanting a progressive growth in capital value and income. Growth in the business arena is the process of improving some measure of a venture's success, such as growth in revenues, profitability, employees, and market share, but it could be a measure of a firm's failure such as debt, aging inventory, pension obligations, costs, etc. For most entrepreneurial firms, growth can be achieved either by boosting the top line or revenue of the business with greater product sales or service income or by increasing the bottom line or profitability of the firm. This can also be achieved by dealing with operational costs. Now that we have totally bored you with definitions, we think trying to define growth is about as difficult as trying to define entrepreneurship as it all depends on how you measure growth. Therefore, a description may prove more useful.

8.2.1 Some Descriptions and Issues

There are those within the academic field of entrepreneurship who will argue at great length that unless there is growth in a new venture, it is not entrepreneurship and does not involve entrepreneurs. To this group and others, entrepreneurship and growth are essentially the same. This view has especially been true since the publication of Birch's (1987) seminal study on growth, as we described in the beginning of this book. This is when entrepreneurship entered center stage of public awareness, a critical part of policy makers' agenda, and gained the attention of business school professors. This convergence of attention on the importance of entrepreneurship became a growth industry in itself (Brännback et al. 2014).

Moreover, growth has often been regarded as something good. For example, often growth is associated with better firm performance. Since growth is considered good, it is easy to see that growth frequently is used as an indication of success. But as we showed in Chapter 2 on success with its varied meanings, even growth can mean so many things as well. If growth means getting bigger, does being bigger mean the firm is better? Not always if we look what happens to the very fastest growing firms over time. But if your new venture grows *too fast*, what are you to do? There are limits to size in nature and in business. There are also structural issues that limit exceptionally fast growth rates. A 100 percent annual growth rate of two to four employees may be reasonable. But is a 100 percent annual growth rate of 100 to 200 employees going to be as easily achieved and can the firm support such increases with its current revenues?

What we are trying to say is that from years of working with entrepreneurs, and from the challenges we have addressed in previous chapters, growth is not always easy to achieve and may not always be good. There are many boutique wineries that the last thing they want is to produce more. Growth to them is not about making more bottles of a given vintage. To these vintners and to us, growth in demand can be a huge problem. Actually, we are highly cautionary about a strategy of rapid or high growth as it is usually problematic in several areas, the least of which is operational. Rapid growth puts excessive demands on suppliers, marketing, personnel, distribution, manufacturing, and obviously finance. What we are trying to make clear is that growth can be dysfunctional and especially so when we speak of *high growth*. However, we want to point out that high growth is extremely rare and to sustain that is even rarer (Brännback et al. 2014).

In 2005 the Global Entrepreneurship Monitor Consortium published a study on High Expectation Entrepreneurship (Autio 2005), this is another nice bureaucratic word for high-growth entrepreneurship. This study showed that in most Western countries a very low number of entrepreneurs were aiming to create a high-growth company. In fact, the number was ranging between 0.5 and 0.8 percent. Spelled out directly this means that in order to have *one* high-growth firm, 200 firms have to be created. High growth in this report meant that entrepreneurs indicated they were going to hire 20 persons or more in the next year. Again, what we would like to call an academic head count exercise. From our experience, this is not how entrepreneurs plan ahead, that is, in terms of how many they will hire next year. Usually, they will tell us how much more they intend to sell next year. Although we are aware of one example where we were told of a Chinese start-up, which started with 2,000 persons, however, here we still think numbers got confused and lost in translation. At the same time we agree with the scientist, publisher, raconteur, and statesman of the late 18th century, Benjamin Franklin who said:

> Without continual growth and progress, such words as improvement, achievement, and success have no meaning.

Some growth is thus necessary. The real question any entrepreneur must ask once they get over the initial excitement of the thought of growing their venture and bring a new product or service to market is: "When is high growth even something to avoid?" In their *Harvard Business Review* article, Churchill and Mullins (2001) point out that:

> . . . few people understand that a profitable company that tries to grow too fast can run out of cash—even if its products are great successes. That is the biggest threat to a growing company is its

own growth rate or in our words: "Nothing will kill you deader than your own success!"

When we talk about entrepreneurial growth, there are several dimensions. To us there are five fundamental dimensions:

1. Employment growth

2. Growth in sales (turnover or revenues)

3. Growth in profitability

4. The time it takes to achieve growth and high growth

5. Growth in firm value

In the following sections we discuss some of these in some depth.

8.2.1.1 Growth in Number of Employees

Birch's (1987) study seemed to clearly show that growth in employment through the creation of new companies seemed to be the secret to national wealth creation. This very much legitimized entrepreneurship as field of research, but even more so as something very important in society at large. In a sense that is a correct observation as an increase in employment indeed is growth: growth in employment. But, at the same time we need to ask what else does an entrepreneur want to grow in their business, and is growth in number of employees always necessary or desirable? To us growth is so much more than bodies hired. From our experience as we have already said, most entrepreneurs do not measure their success by growth in the number of employees. Perhaps, if you are a social entrepreneur looking to provide employment to the unemployed, such a measure might be appropriate. To us employment growth is only one way of measuring growth. Here is why we consider it is not the best measure to use.

If it is the number of people we are keeping track of, it is easy to see that relative growth (expressed as percentage) is very high at first in most start-up companies. A start-up company usually starts with a very small number, for example, two persons, unless you start on the premise of employing yourself, when the number is 1. For the sake of illustration, let us assume that the firm starts with two persons, and after 1 year of operations hires yet a third to the firm. The company has now in relative numbers grown 50 percent, which is seemingly a high number. However, a company with 100 employees, which adds on one person, will show 1 percent growth, a very small number. Yet, in absolute terms both companies have contributed equally to employment, that is, one person.

From this illustration, using numbers, it is easy to see that small companies, even when adding on less than a handful of employees, will show enormous relative growth rates because the base rate was in itself so small. Now, the tricky part here is as we have shown in previous chapters, that adding on employees is an act which generates costs and these costs need to be covered with additional revenues or investment. We mentioned the rule of thumb that in order to be able to add on one person, revenues, that is, sales should increase threefold; otherwise there is a real risk that the increase in cost is too high for a start-up to be able to carry. We still stick to this rule of thumb.

Growth in employment is interesting from other stakeholders' perspectives. From a politician's perspective, it is growth in employment that most politicians or policy makers want to see, thus their interest in entrepreneurs and having entrepreneurs hire people. However, for the entrepreneur, growth in employment is risky as much as it may be necessary for the sake of firm's operations as shown by Churchill and Mullins (2001) and one of our recent books (Brännback et al. 2014). We urge any entrepreneur to really be careful when becoming involved in a governmental program that encourages the firm to hire. Make very sure that is what you want and that the firm needs at that point. We are not saying don't use such programs, but use them wisely.

We have also seen entrepreneurs who write business plans to get into such programs in which the grant is aimed at growing local employment. We have over the years seen far too many such business plans suggesting that their growth in employment will be nearly exponential, that is, growth from 2, to 4, to 8, 16, 32, 50, etc. Once the firm is up and running and just how much an employee will cost the firm, this number series usually is heavily revised and remains an unrealistic dream at best. This ends up disappointing the governmental agency but also may force the company to hire simply to meet the obligations for receiving such funds. When we look at national statistics, we find that 98 percent of the firms regardless of which country we look at employ no more than 10 persons, more than 90 percent will employ only 5 persons.

As we mentioned in Chapter 6 on building an entrepreneurial organization, many entrepreneurs want to keep their firm small because having a lot of employees will require organizational structures that few entrepreneurs want. We also know that the issue of cost is one very efficient constraint here as well. Once again as with governmental funding, be aware of the demands of venture capital or angel investors to rapidly expand your business in terms of market share as those demands can be just as prohibitive and costly as hiring new employees. We strongly agree with the Secretary General of the United Nations, Ban Ki-moon, when discussing sustainable economic growth:

> Sustainable development is the pathway to the future we want for all. It offers a framework to generate economic growth, achieve social justice, exercise environmental stewardship and strengthen governance.

We have said it a few times in this book already—we have rarely met an entrepreneur that tells us they created their company so that they could hire a lot of people. Digging through our files, we actually found one example: a Vietnamese refugee in the United States who started a food business selling egg rolls in carts near a major public university campus. He wanted to grow the firm in terms of new employees, but was not going to hire just any kind of employee. He wanted to hire his family and get them visas to move to the United States following the fall of the South Vietnamese government. We realize that not everybody has this kind of an agenda, not even the policy makers.

For most entrepreneurs, we have met, this does not seem to be a reason for becoming an entrepreneur at all. However, if you talk to a politician, they firmly believe that hiring people is the driving force. Entrepreneurs may want to hire family, but head count is then just a consequence of really wanting to support a family or get them a visa. In many cases it is not even a question of whether an entrepreneur *can*, rather it is about *not wanting to*. We say this even if there are those who argue that working for a fast-growing business is more fun. Once again, this is the adrenaline junkie usually talking. From our own personal experience, managing a fast growing firm is more *like riding a bucking bull in a rodeo, one in which you know you are going to get thrown off and maybe gored in the process.* So if growth by adding on employment is problematic, then how should we look at growth?

8.2.1.2 Growth as Sales Growth and Profit Growth

Most of practicing entrepreneurs that we know will want to talk about *sales growth* or *growth in turnover* also known *as growth in revenues*. How much more has the firm sold since this time last year? However, many entrepreneurs also know that when there is a growth in revenues, there is always also an increase in costs. The trick then again is to balance the two so that revenues are greater than costs. This is something we discussed in Chapter 7 in which we talked about cash-flow management.

Any practicing entrepreneur, after having created a new firm, will soon realize that cash flow and profitability are among the most important measures of firm performance. This will occur despite the public jargon, and obsession, with growth in market share. We argue that sustainable growth is what is ultimately important. With sustainable growth, we mean that growth does not jeopardize profitability of the firm. *The firm grows and remains profitable at the same time.* We dislike the popular myth that rapid growth is the same as success. If one really bothers to dive into entrepreneurship theory, one will very soon find that profit is the ultimate aim of entrepreneurship, and important to all firms, regardless of size. To re-cite, from that chapter on entrepreneurial finance, the late great management guru Peter Drucker (2001):

> Profit is a condition of survival. It is the cost of the future, the cost of staying in business.

Quite a number of entrepreneurs we know and have researched are also prepared to discuss growth in term of *growth in profits*. However, for some reason, which is still unclear to us, academic researchers rarely discuss or even study entrepreneurial profitability. To us, profitability or growth in profitability is essential to any viable venture. Few companies can exist without profit for too long. *Without profits, you will be dead as a nail.* Growth in profits is necessary also because usually there is a cost increase in operations even if the firm does not hire additional persons. That is, with respect to firm survival growth in profits is important. What we suggest at this point is ignore what many of our academic colleagues and the popular media say. Focus your business on the growth of profits and far less on the growth of market share.

8.2.1.3 Growth in Terms of Length of Time

In yet another way, growth can also be understood as how long it will take to get to growth. As we have discussed in previous chapters, it is our experience that most entrepreneurs will underestimate the time it takes to get their first sale. It usually takes a lot longer. Then there is length of time until you reach break-even (out-flow is same as in-flow). Partly this is because entrepreneurs are what we call pathological optimists, which means that when somebody thinks an idea is nice (which really means only just that), the entrepreneur takes it as *a customer who bought the product*. The other reason for the delay is that few start-up entrepreneurs have been involved in sales, so they are not able to estimate the effort that needs to be involved. Here is a mini-case example from Finland, but it could have easily happened in Texas, California, or Sydney.

Recall the company we briefly described in Chapter 6 about having problems hiring the right skills. This company is in the business of selling software to public hospitals and private clinics. Now, when selling to public institutions, those public agencies have to put out a call to the general public for bids for service. That allows every interested company to then send in quotes for providing that product or service. Once the quotes have been received, they are analyzed and usually there are a number of decision levels within the buying organization that the whole issue has to pass before the final decision to buy is taken. Sometimes, depending on the agency, the final bid must be approved by another governmental agency.

In this particular case at one point in the process, the secretary who was handling the paper work was taken ill and had to take a 3-month sick leave. This meant that nobody was pushing the matter ahead. The process stood still for 3 months, as nobody else would touch the secretary's piles of paper. Then once she returned to work, it took another 4 months to reach a final decision on approval. That is, it took 7 months before the sale was completed. That means 7 months of potential cash flow was lost and income was not earned. It also meant that there was 7-month period when the entrepreneur had to figure out how to pay salaries. This example is not unique. As the company soon found out, this is a completely normal procurement process by public institutions, and it has to be built into growth projections, budgets, strategy, and the business plan.

Typically, when we discuss growth, especially with start-up companies, the issue of how long it takes before a company begins to grow is often raised but rarely fully understood. External events can cause all sorts of problems even for your potential investors who likewise can get caught up in events. We know of an investment company, on whose board we sat, which was impacted by the 9/11 disaster in New York City, because its operations were across the street from the destroyed Twin Towers. It was months before the firm could return to normal operations in funding minority-owned fast food and casual dining establishments. Sometimes you have to learn to realize growth is never easy and often subject to situations beyond your control and can impact your suppliers and investors as well as your customers.

How long it takes to make a sale and how long it takes to grow is very much dependent on the kind of company you are, what you are selling, who are your customers, as well as the industrial sector in which the firm operates. As we mentioned in Chapter 7 on entrepreneurial finance that if period of time is 18 months, give or take a couple of months. However, for some industries the time frame could be a lot longer. For example, a biotechnology company may well show growth in *losses* for up to 18 years before being able to generate any revenues.

8.2.1.4 Growth in Firm Value

One of the most important ways we feel you can measure growth is by looking at the firm's value. We are not discussing the very rarely achieved initial public offering (IPO) value of a firm, which is often very illusive and highly dependent on some estimate of both future earnings and excessive hype of market share. Here we are talking about the firm's value as it is a critical and fundamental source of an entrepreneur's wealth. Too often, we have seen this value based primarily on the value of the real estate owned by the firm. This is a bit like our example earlier of the furniture manufacturer in Africa who determined the value he had created by the number of cattle he had managed to purchase with the profits from the firm. Here we are talking about the value of the firm based on its positive cash flow and projected earnings going forward. You can think of this as an exit value or the cash value of the firm. We are hopeful that this value is not all in the real estate that houses the firm or cattle.

Firm value is entirely different from all measures of growth. It is the growth factor, which is often what entrepreneurs and shareholders in particular want to see. A firm's value is a measure of *discounted expected value* (what one thinks the company will be worth some years ahead). As we have said earlier, it is not just a measure of the real value of actual cash flow, but it uses that as a part of determining the firm's value. Usually, this is a measure used when discussing publicly traded firms, but it exists among privately held firms also. However, it is fair to say that this view of value is usually not the primary measure of most start-ups where the primary concern is cash flow and sales.

Projections of cash flow are best done when there is some past history in which to ground those projections. We have seen way too many business plans for a new venture that have projected the value of the nascent firm in 5 years to be worth more than Apple is now. What we say to every entrepreneur is don't fall for your own PR or thinking your future projections are reality now, disregarding profitability. We remember too many young entrepreneurs who argued with us that profits were passé and it was all about market share. This was during the dot.com boom, before the turn of the millennium, when the *new economy* was thought to emerge, where cash and profits were not important anymore. Well, it turned out that cash and profits were key components of the new economy too, and most of those people are now no longer in business.

We realize that *an unprofitable high growth strategy* can be a strategy of convenience for a start-up as a way of raising finances from demanding VCs and angels. These demands are usually tied to an exit strategy determined by the external investor. Often, the entrepreneur tries his/her best to implement such a strategy, but the result is way too frequently heavy debt or shrinking margins. This is a short-term strategy for investors to try and drive the return on their investment up, but it is not a recommended strategy for an entrepreneur seeking to create a sustainable and profitably growing firm.

Needless to say, there are more ways to measure growth; growth in margins, growth in market share, growth of an industrial sector, growth in competition, and growth in potential market. But from an entrepreneur's perspective, who is struggling with creating a viable company and the very issue of firm survival, the dimensions we have discussed previously are the most important ones to keep your eyes on. What is problematic here is that these measures of growth are associated with firm performance as well. This means that firm performance and growth are often treated as synonyms. Nevertheless, it is absolutely crucial that you understand that all ways to measure growth are in fact very different entities. This tells us that growth occurs over time on any one of the three dimensions: employment, sales or profits. This should tell you that growth is a *process* and is dependent on the entrepreneur. As the following quote from Anne M. Mulcahy, the former Chairperson and CEO of Xerox Corporation, points out:

> Turnaround or growth, it's getting your people focused on the goal that is still the job of leadership.

8.3 Growth and Competition

Finally, a few words about growth with respect to competition. There is always competition. We have heard too often that there is no competition. To this we always respond in two ways: either you have not looked or there is no market. It may look like there is no competition, but there is always some kind of a solution to the same problem being addressed. It may not be as good or identical to the solution you are about to launch, but there is always something. Remember, Thomas Edison was not the only one working on the light bulb, but he was the one who knew how to commercialize the invention. In other words, he knew how to innovate and make money from it.

Competition, however, is sooner or later going to affect your venture and in particular your growth ambitions and projections and usually in a negative way. Large firms often make the mistake of ignoring incumbents until it is too late. Conversely, small start-up firms fail to realize the sensitivity of the "big guy's toes they are stepping on." No matter how brilliant an idea, a large firm may retaliate in a number of ways. Competition is never pretty and sometimes it can become really ugly.

For example, a medium-size pharmaceutical company in Finland had a very potent treatment for breast cancer already in the late 1990s. They wanted to enter the U.S. market and needed a partner to help them. They found such a partner and a license agreement was made together with what seemed like a good royalty agreement based on units sold once the partner company had commercialized the treatment on the U.S. market. It turned out this new treatment would cannibalize on the partner company's own product. The partner company was chosen because they had experience of this market, as they too were active in this area. What the Finnish company failed to realize was that their product was in fact threatening the sales of an existing product. The partner company, once the agreement was signed, literally put the Finnish product on the shelf and let it sit there. No royalties ever came from this agreement and obviously no growth.

A similar pattern almost happened at the University of California, Los Angeles, when it developed a laser light device for hair removal. When the university tried to shop the patent for commercial development a razor manufacturer wanted to purchase the patent. But, the university wisely realized that what that firm would do would be to shelve the patent to keep this competition to razor sales out of the market.

Competition can also change slowly. Let us look at Nokia and Apple. These are not start-up companies but will serve as a good illustration. In many cases large organizations may not realize the magnitude of a threat or may fail to see that markets are changing, especially customer preferences. One can never take the luxury of being complacent or thinking you are the best, because that is when you will take your eye off the ball in terms of constant improvements. Or as Jack Welsh, the longtime CEO of GE said: "You should constantly argue with success!" (This was to his mind the secret to GE's success.) We are reminded of when IBM had the best electric typewriter with 1,200 moving parts, but failed to see the rise of digital word processing. Today an IBM Selectric typewriter makes a wonderful boat anchor.

Most of us are familiar with the success of Nokia mobile phones in the late 1990s and early 2000s. As you know one of the authors of this book is from Finland, so there is a very real close-up to this story. It was nice as a Finn to travel the world and notice that almost everybody was using a Nokia mobile phone. Annual sales were growing in double digits. The technology was outstanding and the design was for a while the best one could get—almost. In the spring 2005 she was in London and riding the Underground. Anyone who has been in the London Underground knows there are a lot of people riding it almost on any hour of the day. It didn't take long before a particular phenomenon struck her. *Everyone in the Underground was wearing white headphones*—everyone except for she. For the next few days she just looked at these white headphones. She returned home without thinking about this anymore until she was going for a conference in Singapore a year later in 2006 and her daughter, then 12 years, asked her to bring her an iPod. Needless to say, these white headphones were everywhere, in Finland too. But, as we know iPod was just a music device and soon to be followed by the iPod touch. Both of these devices found their way into her home.

At the same time Ericsson had launched a small mobile phone that you could fold and it became very popular. Nokia did not quite notice that customers liked this smaller thing that would fit into a pocket. Nokia was debating which operating system they should switch to in their next-generation phones, and in their world mobile phone was still about technology sold at low cost. As you may remember Nokia phones were not expensive and they had solid technology, if not state of the art.

Apple launched the iPod Touch and that too, as we know, was also successful. This gadget had the same design as what was to be launched as the iPhone. People were lining up in endless lines to lay their hands on this new mobile phone. This smart phone was clearly a word of the web success. In 2008, once again at a conference in the United States, she noticed that everybody was using an iPhone, no longer a Nokia-made phone. And, so was she. She had bought her own in the fall of 2007.

The rest is history, but it serves as a brilliant example of how competition can sneak up over a number of years. While Apple was building up a brand loyalty with iPod and iPod Touch through ingenious design and understanding that it could compete on *technology* and *design* in a way that price no longer was a critical success factor, Nokia basically lost their competitive position by failing to realize that growth was no longer based on technology at low cost. Low cost was not an issue when competition and growth suddenly was based on design and branding. That is, the rules of competition had changed, which had every impact on future growth—it killed it! Today, we watch Samsung starting to take market share from Apple in the cell phone market; history repeats itself. So, growth and growth projections always have to be considered against the existing competition and a careful scanning of potential competition.

8.4 Growth as Metamorphosis

Too often, we think of growth as some linear function that is ever increasing at some rate. However, there is yet another way to look at growth and that is as a process of evolution. You grow, you morph, change, transform the business into something different than it was when it first started. Just like a butterfly starts as an egg, then it becomes a caterpillar, then into a chrysalis, and finally a butterfly. We are not saying that biological analogies are always appropriate for looking at growth of a firm. However, from years of observations we have noticed something about a large number of entrepreneurial firms that become family businesses and survive for generations. They change in a large number of areas besides age.

While some remain in the initial industry in which they began (like hospitality or beverages), we have also seen another pattern. This is one we think of as the *metamorphosis approach* to growth and survival. Go into any city anywhere in the world and you will find firms that started out decades if not centuries ago that over the course of their existent moved from being in one industry to another, often because of changes in technology or in many cases because of new opportunities becoming available. We can think of no better way to demonstrate this change than to give you a mini-case. In this case it is a story of a business in Austin, Texas that has spent over 140 years reinventing itself as a business. One of us has actually had the privilege of using the services of this firm during one of its stages as Miller Blueprint.

In 1876, following the Civil War, R. C. Lambie and his partner Francis Fischer started a general contracting business to fill the increasing need by individuals to be able to build an ever-expanding Austin, the capital of Texas. They built many of today's historic structures that still stand in the city and gave the city area much of its historic character. The firm built the Elizabet Ney Museum in Austin, the Old Main Building of St. Edward's University, as well as many of the iconic courthouses in Texas. Lambie was famous for his elaborate woodwork in the buildings he and Fischer built. Some of these structures they built in Austin housed various businesses which members of the family started and some buildings are still owned by branches of the family. Mr. Lambie had a daughter, Agnes Louise, who went to the still new University of Texas at Austin where she obtained two degrees. Even today one can say the family bleeds burnt orange and loves longhorns.

While at UT-Austin Louise met John Miller and they married. They had a son named Robert Lambie Miller in 1922. With her father's blessing she and her husband started Miller Blueprint in 1920. Clearly she used her father's connections in the general contracting business to build their initial customer base. The business continued to grow for the next 90 years keeping pace with the construction boom that has engulfed Austin and expanding into various related businesses. The firm sold typewriters, mechanical business calculators, as well as making blueprints for builders. John Miller worked every day till he died at age 89. Their son, Robert worked at Miller Blueprint till age 85. Robert Miller married Anna Buchanan who was the first female student body president at UT-Austin. It is their daughter, Luci, who now is president of the latest incarnation of the family firm: Miller Imaging and Digital Solutions.

With the advent of new digital technology, the firm did not need the prior amount of space and employees to handle their graphics business. They took this opportunity in 2014 to rebrand and reimage their business. John Miller's grandson now runs G4 Spatial Technologies, a spin-off of the family firm's surveying business, which started as a part of their construction business. The Millers started Southwestern Aerial Surveys prior to World War II, which was terminated when the U.S. government requisitioned their airplane for the war effort. The family-owned firm adapted to that change as well. The firm survived and changed. Today many of the siblings from the third generation of the family work in the family firm as are some of the children in the fourth generation.

In the process of running Miller Blueprint, John and his wife continued the family tradition of investing in Austin real estate. While they did the typical Texas thing of betting on oil and gas, it was real estate that provided the foundation of the family wealth. Today, downtown Austin real estate remains a critical part of the family's business activities. The family saw the businesses they ran as something that allowed them to live well and buy real estate in downtown Austin. They saw real estate as a "savings account or investment" for the future. The businesses provided the *living*, while the downtown real estate provided their *future* in what has become the 10th largest city in the United States.

If you have read this mini-case carefully, you will see that this entrepreneurial family has reinvented the family firm multiple times, expanding into new products and services, and then taking opportunities in digital technology to move into new areas as well are rebrand the Miller brand. All along they have used the wealth the business generated to invest in real estate in the city they have called home for 140 years. In many ways real estate in Texas is like cattle in Africa; it is measure of wealth. It is clear this firm grew, changed, moved into new sectors, transformed itself to fit the technologies of the time, and yet through all of it has been successful in supporting the family and impacting their community.

8.5 Conclusion

We hope that in this chapter on growth we have encouraged you to seriously examine how you want your firm to grow and mature, regardless of whether it is a commercial or a social venture. We have tried to provide you with some different ways to think of growth and growing your venture from thinking of growth as market share, to number of employees, to growth in profits. Every firm will grow at some rate and also will, at times, even contract. This is just a natural part of the life of a venture. If you are lucky, the firm may last 20 years, which is average for many nonpublically traded firms. If you are really lucky, you may end up like some Italian family firms in the wine industry that are over 1,000 years old and still owned by the descendants of the founding family. In other words, firms can have a life of their own in many ways. The vitality of that life all depends on how well the managers act as stewards of their inheritance. Some do quite well in keeping the firm viable; others make a real mess of it. Early on, be aware of the challenges these changes bring to the firm and to the entrepreneur as its manager. You are the one to make the choice of how you want to deal with these, so be aware of those who have agendas that may be in conflict with your goals for growing the firm. Thus let's turn now to an exercise for you to do.

8.6 Exercise

We want you to think of entrepreneurs that you know personally. Ask yourself what kinds of skills, knowledge, contacts, and resources they brought with them in creating their venture. If you don't know for sure, go and ask them. While you are there, ask them whether they saw changing patterns in the market place. Now we want you to ask whether they wrote a business plan. Many entrepreneurs often will say they did not write a formal plan, or they did only for an investor. Now ask them whether they had a plan in their mind that they followed and updated as they went along especially when they started to grow. Ask your entrepreneur friends if they had to revise, retrench, and reinvent their business to sustain its success. How did they react to the challenge? Did your friends become frustrated and were they concerned with the possibility of failure?

References

Autio, E. 2005. GEM 2005 High Expectation—Entrepreneurship Summary Report. www.gemconsortium.org.

Birch, D. 1987. *Job creation in America: How our smallest companies put the most people to work*. New York: Free Press.

Brännback, M., A. L. Carsrud, and N. Kiviluoto. 2014. *Understanding the myth of high growth firms: The theory of the greater fool*. New York: Springer.

Churchill, N. C., and J. W. Mullins. 2001. How fast can your company afford to grow? *Harvard Business Review*, 79(5): 135–142.

9

Planning: Should You, When Do You, and How Do You?

9.0 Overview of Plans and Planning

Plans are nothing; planning is everything.

Perhaps no quote better sums up our fundamental position on planning than that from the Supreme Commander of Allied Forces in Europe during World War II, the president of Columbia University, and also the president of the United States, Dwight D. Eisenhower. To us it is not the plan that is critical as much as it is the process and "doing" associated with planning. It is the learning how to gather the information. It is seeing and understanding how different parts of the business affect other parts. As the great scientist, statesman, philosopher, and raconteur Benjamin Franklin stated:

If you fail to plan, you are planning to fail.

At this point it is also appropriate to reveal what we mean when we say planning. It is the act or process of making or carrying out plans. We are explicitly talking about the *establishment of goals, policies, and procedures for starting a new venture*. We freely admit there are times you will need to write a plan. For example, they are usually for bankers, investors, or even to attract key employees. But to us, business plans are really about *business planning—the process of putting it all together, which involves thinking and doing*. There is a considerable debate in entrepreneurship education and research of the usefulness of business plans. There are studies that will claim that business plans really do impact the future success of a firm and those that will show that a business plan had no impact what so ever. Then there is the issue of whether it makes any sense to teach courses on how to write business plans. We happen to belong to the category, which thinks business plans are good and useful for certain things. But, we too have our reservations when the focus on the plan becomes obsessive.

Let us take an analogy in food recipes. Most of us have sometime in our lives had to consult a cookbook when attempting to bake a cake or make something so simple as spaghetti Bolognese. The first time we have notoriously followed the recipe; that is, when the recipe has wanted us to take a tablespoon of something and a pound of something else, we have done precisely that. Some of us may still cook that way, by carefully reading and obeying. But, some of us have diverted from the recipes in every possible way—the use of spices in particular or put in something else, so that one could even say that it is no longer Spaghetti Bolognese we are making but really something else—absolutely delicious as well. So too, do we see business plans. Business plans give us a structured procedure of putting together something delicious. We can alter the ingredients along the way, but basically we will follow the same structure, perhaps digress from the order of putting the ingredients together, but still arriving at the same end—something delicious.

Perhaps this view is reflected best in the following quote by the professional boxer, Mike Tyson:

Everyone has a plan till they get punched in the mouth.

To us this quote reflects the harsh reality that once you start the venture, every plan becomes a work in progress. It has to constantly be modified to keep up with the day-to-day reality of the business and the ever-changing nature of the contexts in which a firm operations (economic, financial, social, etc.). Otherwise, reality will throw you a knockout punch. Long-term planning is not universally applicable nor even wise in certain circumstances; say if you are running an event, but planning even in this situation occurs. We know from entrepreneurship and strategic management research that some people are more likely to plan than others. This is true regardless of the firm's focus. While this may be related to personality traits like locus of control, we know that highly educated people are more likely to plan.

Before we go further, we need to make something very clear, while a business plan is a form of a strategic plan for a venture, not all strategic plans are in fact business plans. In general strategic plans are usually written for larger firms and are often lacking in the very specifics that are critical to the start-up of a new firm. Often, strategic plans are written with lofty terminology and generalities. Mission statements often are so general that they can easily be moved from one firm to another or one industry to another. A mission statement of "Being the leading firm in the industry" clearly is not the same thing as a business concept statement that we discussed earlier in this book. To us, business plans are about knowing how you are actually going to behave. To us a business plan is where the "rubber hits the road." Strategic plans are usually way too ephemeral. Let us turn now to what we know about the role plans play in ventures.

The outcome of the business plan and the planning process should be a clear vision of the purpose of the firm. Earlier we have cited Peter Drucker in saying that the purpose of a firm is to create a customer. Therefore, business planning and execution are the starts to real M.B.A. degree in that you are stating *how the firm is going to create a customer and how it will make money.* Planning tells the reader what the company is now and what it will become. This is where the entrepreneur states what the real customer needs are and how the company will serve real customer needs. Look at the business plan as a *managerial game plan* on how to get the new company up and running. In summary a business plan is

- A communication tool to different readers
- An analytical tool first and foremost to the entrepreneur and the entrepreneurial team
- An operating tool spelling out how the venture will get up and running

9.1 Why Plan?

First you have to realize that it is not about writing a single business plan, or many. As we said at the first of this chapter, it is the process and activities associated with making a plan that are critical. That is one reason we do not believe it is useful to really have someone else write the plan for you. Next, anyone who intends to create a company has to be prepared to write several plans depending on the audience and to revise those plan many times as events evolve during the life of the venture. As with strategic plans, we have seen far too often entrepreneurs, when they have written "their plan," lean back and say "here it is!" As if it is done and it is engraved in stone like some religious tome. Realize that it most likely is not done. Every business plan is a living document subject to frequent changes. It is not at all unusual that revisions start almost immediately. What we are saying is that it is really essential to understand that business planning is an ongoing process of the constantly evolving venture. As the company progresses, one has to constantly ask whether this is good and reflecting what we intended.

A business plan is not a tombstone carved in granite that is meant to hold for thousands of years ahead. Perhaps the last business plan written in stone was the Ten Commandments and even ultimately Moses broke those. Since then we have been using various forms of word processors like pen and ink and now computers. Why this shift from stone? The answer is simple. Every plan is out of date by the time it is finished, but that does not mean it is not useful.

Then, we would like to raise one other issue here and that is the notion of *writing* a plan. As we have said, to us *planning* (the act of thinking and doing) is critical. You are wise to write down something. If the actual business plan is intended for raising more financial funds, you will have to write a formal plan in writing *and* to orally present it; that is, sell the content of the text convincingly to those you want to invest in your venture. This is also known as pitching a venture. For the purpose of the actual pitching, the plan then also becomes the screenplay of that pitch— particularly the executive summary of that plan. At any rate, most investors are rather conservative and expect a plan to look in a certain way. That, to them, is one way of minimizing the risk of investing. We have heard investors say: "Oh, but the plan looked good and I was convincing it would work, and still the venture did not take off."

But, to create a venture and the act of planning does not require a good hand in writing. Creating a venture is rarely an act of writing an academic thesis. This is probably one reason some academic colleagues argue that writing a plan is not helpful. If you are not good at writing, and a lot of entrepreneurs abhor writing, draw pictures on a piece of paper or on a napkin at a restaurant as we have known to have happened. Or why not speak (pitch) your idea and thoughts on a video, and play it to yourself. Keep on revising until you are satisfied and firmly believe somebody else will believe in your venture as much as you do. It is not the form that is essential. What we are saying here is that we use the expression *to write a business plan* to mean *planning*. Video versions of plans have been funded, especially when pitching thinks like movies, television series, etc.

As we said, we firmly believe that some planning is necessary for the simple reason that a business plan becomes a way of becoming prepared for almost whatever can occur. It is far better to be prepared for good and for bad, than not! This is not the same as listing all things that can possibly go wrong; it is also for preparing for what to do if you hit on a box office success. Remember, nothing will kill you deader than your own success. We argue that it is important to be prepared, because the odds of succeeding are still to date not very favorable and being prepared will increase the likelihood of success. The harsh reality is that 85 percent of businesses are no longer in business after 5 years. This does not necessary mean that all have failed—they may have been acquired and continue their second life. It means that the original business concept did not quite fly by the original ideas. A business plan will therefore also be a tracking tool to be able to follow how the firm is doing relative to original assumptions. For a tracking tool to work, something needs to be archived somewhere and since the human memory has a nasty tendency of being selective especially when things do not evolve as anticipated, even a napkin will do, but preferably something more.

9.1.1 Hooked on a Feeling

Not too long ago, one of the authors was contacted by a young entrepreneur who had entered the construction business. The business had set off like many do—three young guys with degrees in house building, plumbing, and electrical engineering who wanted to work for themselves and not for somebody else. First, it was small scale, but soon the company needed to hire additional people to be able to deliver and complete their undertakings. In the phone the entrepreneur summed up his problem: "I have a feeling more money is going out the door than coming in." He had a feeling! So, the author visited the company and heard the full story, which was a company about to become a rapidly growing company and clearly needed advice on how to manage this without wrecking the venture. The *feeling* the entrepreneur had in the pit of his stomach told him that failure was a probable future unless something was done. The author then asked to see the budget to get an understanding of the cost structure. The response he provided to the request set off all alarm bells: "Oh, we don't do budgeting in this company!"

In actual fact that meant they did no planning at all. They were driving with the autopilot, hoping that it all would work out. But, now *a feeling* was indicating that the autopilot was not working properly. They got their budget and their plans for the future done, and today the firm is successful and expanding with more than 20 employees. And it is no longer run on *a feeling or by the seat of their pants*. A budget is perhaps the minimum requirement of a business plan and critical to the *planning process*, although by itself it is not sufficient.

9.2 When Do You Plan?

In this section we are very briefly going to review what we know from research literature about planning besides the fact that the more educated you are, the more likely you will be to plan. We know that there are positive effects of formal plans on the viability of new ventures and their sustainability. The effect of planning on firm performance would seem obvious. However, this seems to be a finding that has a number of caveats. A lot of these are related to when you write the plan, how long you take to write a plan, and when in the process of planning you actually write a plan.

For example, from numerous research studies, there seems to be a curvilinear relationship between the relative amount of time spent planning, as well as when in the process you plan and see subsequent outcomes. If you start your business by writing a plan firmly, you will be less effective. We conjecture that the entrepreneur can plan too early and fail to take advantage of purposeful planning because of fuzzy information at the start. We strongly believe as you are doing something, like marketing, that you write the marketing section of the plan when you collect that information. This will make the data input a bit less fuzzy. There are real differences in plans that are done in the front of starting a venture and those that are written when the firm is operational or at least starting operations. The latter seems to be more grounded in reality. Based on research, you will want to syncretize your activities as you are doing with your planning and your plan writing. For example, you write the product plan as you are developing your product/service. We also know from research that if you wait till you have done a lot of activities to then write a plan and have taken longer, the positive effects of planning seem to be reduced. The longer you are in the process of starting a business does not seem to make your venture any more successful.

There are a series of findings from the research, and from our personal experience, we find most helpful when you consider when to start in on writing a formal plan. First, when writing a business plan one tends to assume that things don't change over time, but we know that they do. Be prepared for those changes and don't be afraid to go back into the plan to make modifications, even minor ones. Do not take this as a sign of failing to make good plans from the start, but more as an actual fact of business reality: *business is constantly changing*. Modifications are inevitable, which is much more a rule than the exception. We have some evidence that individuals will make upward of 20 plus versions of their plan before they get to a workable document. Remember that planning is not done in isolation for the activities you are undertaking. If we have not made it plain enough, we do not recommend "flying by the seat of your pants" planning. You need to take time to think.

9.3 How Long Will It Take?

What we have found interesting is the confirmation of our belief with research that there is a limit to the time period in which to start a venture. If you have taken less than 3 to 4 months between the time you thought of starting a business and starting it actually, you are asking for failure. If you take longer than a year, you most likely are taking too long and the opportunity has been lost. This is what some in our field call the *window of viability*. Your best chances for launching a venture and writing a successful plan are best between 5 and 12 months from inception, with the average being 10 months. That is, those who plan do better than those who don't. If you are much earlier or later, simply writing a plan at the very start will not be effective in creating a viable venture. Between the period of months 7 and 10 seems to be when there is a 2-month window in which writing a plan can have an effective impact on the venture, but it is you who need to have the practical knowledge of doing things for the venture. Think of writing a plan as making a commitment. Here is where a quote by the great business management guru Peter Drucker makes sense: "Unless commitment is made, there are only promises, hope, and nice intentions; but no plans."

9.4 For Whom Do You Plan?

The reason why an entrepreneur ends up writing several versions of a business plan has multiple causes. One is you begin to see how things fit or don't fit together like your marketing and operations. Thus revision becomes necessary. Another reason is that plans written for internal operations are going to emphasize something very different from plans written for say investors. That is, how a plan is written and what is emphasized in it depends on *for whom* the plan is written. Is the plan for convincing funders, is it for potential stakeholders, is it for attracting potential alliances or collaborators, or perhaps is it something for showing future employers? Conversely, we believe that any person seeking employment in a start-up company should really ask to see a business plan in order to get an idea of what may lay ahead, to make an informed judgment over whether the firm will survive.

At the very beginning the business plan is written for the entrepreneur and the team as documentation of their intentions. It is an internal roadmap. The plan should say what the management team is going to do, how they are going to do it, and why they care so much about doing it. The plan becomes a blueprint of reasons and justification of choices that the entrepreneur and the team make. Regardless while the various plans will be different, they still have to be consistent from a financial standpoint. Don't go changing numbers in various versions of your plan to make something look better than it really is. In the process of business planning, there are four factors that are absolutely critical:

1. The people
2. The opportunity
3. The context
4. The risks and rewards

Who are on the start-up team? From our experience, the people are probably the most critical. A great idea can be thoroughly ruined by the wrong people. It is absolutely essential to get the right people on the bus. We have seen far too often a group of friends become anything but friends, and this usually occurs when problems lie ahead and money or shortage of money becomes the issue. How committed are the members of the founding team, and how will the other team members react if one team member decides to move ahead elsewhere? It is during the business planning process that these sorts of events also have to be processed—to be prepared. The *people* involve not only the founding team but also outside parties such as key service providers, suppliers, and those taking care of the accounting as well as legal and insurance services.

You have to be clear on what is the company selling and to whom. You need to show that you understand if the company should grow, how fast, and what could possibly stand in the way of success. Here is where the founding team needs to consider the business environment. If there are special regulations that will affect the venture, you need to acknowledge them. For example, if the entrepreneur intends to venture into food production or restaurant business, there are a whole set of regulations as how to store and handle food. Dairy products or meat will require specific refrigerated storage. These regulations will vary across national borders, but also in the United States across states. For example, in Sweden or Finland somebody growing berries, from which one could make juice and perhaps alcoholic beverages, will face considerable restrictions. In Sweden and Finland it is not possible to sell alcoholic beverages from the producer's operations. That can only take place through the state monopoly. In Finland you are allowed to serve the drinks at the operations, but the customer cannot buy bottles to take home. In addition, you need to demonstrate you know if there are governmental regulations that impact operations.

Finally, are there factors that constantly change that cannot be controlled by you and the entrepreneurial team? Yet, these require some form of reaction. We have said that to be prepared is not only about listing what can go wrong but also listing what can go right. These lists should be carefully discussed by the team as to how they will deal with the good, the bad, and the really ugly. Now that we have finished being "bitchy" about what bugs us with most business plans and their presentations, we will turn to what should be in every section of a decently written business plan. Please remember that even the best-written business plan depends on a decent product/service and a management team that can deliver. No plan can guarantee success.

9.5 What Goes into a Business Plan?

Through all of our chapters we have tried to provide you with the fundamentals of being a successful entrepreneur. One of those that we have alluded to is the ability of entrepreneurs to see opportunities and exploit them. One way to do this is to not only create a business plan but more importantly implement it. As we have pointed out several times, the plan itself is less important than the process of gathering the information necessary and understanding how decisions in one area like marketing affects human resources and operations. When writing a business plan document for an investor, some of the pieces you should include are

1. An executive summary (you may need a standalone executive summary as well)

2. A clear description of the business concept be it for a service or a product

3. A detailed market analysis and a marketing penetration plan for the first year

4. An analysis of the current and potential competition as well as a discussion on how the industrial sector you are in operates and where your venture fits

5. An introduction to the management team, their experience and expertise, and how it fits the venture

6. A reasonable outline for start-up operations including who makes or does what for the venture

7. A discussion on the critical risks the venture will face, and these can be integrated in the various divisions of the plan

8. Finally, a detailed financial plan, with assumptions and cash-flow projects

9.6 Detail Content of a Written Business Plan

In this section we are going to walk you through what ought to be in each section of a typical business plan in a written format or even in a video version. Please note, depending on to whom you are giving the plan and depending on certain sections of your industry may be more critical and expensive than others. While there are some general guidelines as to what is in a good plan, each will be different as each is telling a different story about how a group of individuals are going to create and run a new venture. These are true for both for-profit ventures as well as non-profit ones.

9.6.1 Executive Summary Content

When writing a business plan, remember that focus and being succinct is critical. If an executive summary is to be attached to a full business plan, you need to keep this section to two pages. If it is a standalone document (and you will need these too), you should keep it to five pages. Now here comes the fun part, you need to be able to do each of the following in those two to five pages. And please remember that the executive summary is also the screenplay for your pitch, in other words, the oral presentation of the venture.

- First, state the intent of the venture. Is it retail, manufacturing, distributor, or a service?

- Now very briefly tell the reader as to the current stage of development for the venture. Is it a start-up, doing initial operations, starting an expansion, entering rapid growth, at a stable operation level or some other operational stage?

- Now describe what is unique about the venture including its product/service mix, and tell the reader about any patents, licenses, royalties, distribution rights, or franchise agreements the venture possesses.

- Next, tell the reader what is the legal form of organization, and whether it is a proprietorship, partnership, LLC, limited partnership, S-corporation, or corporation.

- Next, you need to tell the reader quickly about the management team, their skills, and what they bring to the new venture. Complete resumes of team members should be placed in an appendix.

- Tell the reader of key support groups like attorneys, accountants, consultants, and don't forget Board of Directors or Advisors.

Now that you have done the above in a paragraph or two, you continue the following:

- Briefly tell the reader about the industry in which you are operating.

- Then tell them about your customers, their needs, product benefits, target markets, and market penetration plan. You should give the reader on overview of the marketing plan.

- Now tell them about your competitor including direct competition and indirect competition. Show you know their strengths and weaknesses.

- Now in your executive summery tell the reader how much investment the venture needs for product/service development, marketing, salaries, and operations. In other words, tell the reader how much money is needed and how it will be spent. *Be sure to tell when the business will reach break-even and then turn a profit.*

- Tell the reader what type of financing you are looking for, such as debt, equity, and/or grants. Explain how investors be paid back either by stocks, warrants, or loan payments. Indicate what has been invested to date and from whom.

- Then tell the reader about any potential innovation of your products or services that can contribute to long-term sustainability or growth.

- Then tell the reader about anything that makes it difficult for competitors to enter into your target market.

- Finally, if there are any contracts, existing employee contracts, noncompete agreements, and buy/sell agreements you need to state these.

We know we have suggested you to put a lot into two pages of an attached executive summary. We even admit it is hard to do when you have five pages. However, by forcing you to be clear, succinct, and highly focused, the less difficulty potential investor has to encounter in understanding the business, the more likely they will read the document, which is the first stage in getting their attention. This will also make doing oral elevator pitches easier as there you have a very short time. That is, in the executive summary you are short of *space* and in the pitch you are short of *time*. Expect to write and rewrite your summary every time you complete a section of your business plan. It should *not be cut-and-paste job*, but it must be consistent with the all the sections of the plan. The executive summary takes a lot of word crafting and we have seen some go through 20 to 30 versions.

9.6.2 Marketing Plan Content

To us, one of the most critical parts of any new venture is marketing your product and service and making sales. Here is where you can take the exercises we asked you to do in Chapter 7 and put them to work. Often, investors and even distribution partners will want to see a very detailed marketing plan, sometimes even a standalone marketing plan. With a business plan, marketing will be what drives production and financial plans as we have noted in earlier chapters. As we have said before, you write a marketing plan you are going to need to have a very clear and deep understanding of your target market with both data and focus group support. You will need this before you write the executive summary. It is mandatory that the venture's marketing plan demonstrates a real understanding for the target market's needs and that the firm obviously understands its potential customers. Some of what we suggest you include may not be relevant to your industry, but if they are, you need to address them.

- Give the reader some general information on the market in which your venture is competing including the current market size, its growth potential, as well as any geographic location limits.

- Tell the reader about any critical industry trends as well as any seasonal factors that can affect sales.

- Tell the reader whether you will be doing single, bulk, or direct sales and how you will achieve these, including website sales. You need to be clear about what is the profit potential for each of these marketing channels. Let the reader know about the development of any new products/services as well as new customer groups and markets.

Now you need to provide some details about your customers or various customer groups, such as age range, gender, professional backgrounds, income levels, any psychographic and geographic information, and any other demographics.

- Be sure to describe the benefits your products and services provide customers.

- Be sure to explain if these benefits differ for different customer groups and how. We recommend, if possible, provide a cost-benefit analysis for the customer. Remember, customers here could be other businesses and not just individuals. Whether you are talking about individuals, groups, or firms, tell the reader what problems you are solving. Remember our earlier discussion about needs, wants, and fears.

- Be specific about the customer's need for your products or services in terms of how much they will save in either time or money.

- Let the reader know what will be the customer's return on their investment.

- Be sure to explain whether customers will have to significantly change their behavior in doing things. Will the customers have to purchase something else to be able to use your product or service?

- Most important, tell the reader that the users will have to change how they are used to do things (changing habits is usually very difficult, even when your product or service is for the better. Humans like routines!).

If you can describe customers' reactions to the products and services, include any testimonials, market surveys, or focus group studies in summary in the body of the plan and in detail in an appendix. In the body of the plan

- Now you need to tell the reader the particular niche you are within the market and its appeal to that niche. Be sure to mention the target market's potential dollar volume, do this for each target market, and prioritize. Remember your target market might not be the end user but instead your specific distribution channel for a market.

- Now tell the user the approaches you will be using for selling the products or services to an end user, including distribution channels, such as sales representatives, using a direct sales force, utilizing direct mail, trade shows, engaging telemarketing, internet websites, and cell phone applications. Be sure to discuss the costs of each of these approaches in terms of dollars, people, and lead times.

- You will also need to describe to the reader the advertising and promotion materials you will give to distributors and end user customers. Be very specific. If you are going to use radio, newspaper, trade journals, magazines, and television, explain why with examples and costs. Or are you going to use viral marketing tools and have everything on Facebook, Twitter, and YouTube? Please show why this is going to be more efficient (not just cost efficient) for reaching your customers. In consumer business that is most likely true but suppose your business will be in *original equipment manufacturing* (such businesses still exist!), then something of the "old school" might still be needed.

- Show how logos, color schemes, and packaging are going to enhance the firm's identity and brand. You should attach examples if possible. If you are going to provide warranties and guarantees, make sure that these are clear and show how you will promote these and how they may affect profits. State why and how your marketing efforts are unique or different from competitors. Let the reader know if you are using trade shows, how many, and their costs.

- Finally, explain any anticipated new opportunities in future markets and be sure to include their size, proposed method of penetration, and costs.

9.6.3 *About Competition*

It may seem strange to be talking about your competition in your business plan, but the reader will expect you to acknowledge that there is competition for the customers you are seeking and their money. If you say you have no competition either you have not looked, or there are no customers. Everyone has competition, even if they don't have the exact same product or service you provide. You need to list your direct and, of equal importance, indirect competitors by product/service and note their geographic market. You need to also note the emerging competitors entering your industry and market. We suggest you produce a list

---

of these competitors with their strengths and weaknesses, and put it in an appendix or at least study it very carefully to stay prepared. For an investor it will show you know what is going on in your industry and will demonstrate your own strengths as a manager.

In the body of the competition section, you need to discuss how you are going to deal with competitors, especially the big ones.

- Try to estimate the competitors' share of the market by product or service and how they compete; for example, do they compete on product superiority, price, advertising, brand name, or some other dimension?

- Show how you are superior to your competitors and on which dimensions like operations, management, products and services, price, or delivery. Show how the competition is seen in the eyes of customers. Here, if available, try to include customer reactions.

You need to tell the reader that you understand how your venture could manage the strategic objectives of the competition. Show that you understand what will cause the competition to want to attack your venture. If they attack your position in the market, explain how you respond will. In other words, tell the reader what kinds of marketing tactics you expect the competition to make. You also need to show on what basis the industry typically competes like price, quality, promotions, personal selling approaches, constant innovation, legal battles, or other approaches. You should show you know how the industry typically treats new entrants. Tell the reader how easy or hard it is to enter your industry as a firm and what has typically happened to new firms. In other words, tell the reader about the barriers to entering and exiting your industry. That is, here is where you will convince the reader that you understand your business and the ecological system in which it exists. Remember that for most entrepreneurs everything is new and the entrepreneurs face what is known as *the liability of newness*. The only way to battle the unfamiliar is with *more proof*.

9.6.4 *Management and Organizational Plan*

Any business plan is as good as the people who are going to execute it. You want the reader to understand the strengths of the entrepreneurial team and how those individuals are organized and led.

- Here you need to discuss the contribution of each of entrepreneurial team members in terms of experience, talents, any prior experiences or their track records, training or education, money they are investing (not sweat equity), and the amount of time they will devote to the business. In fact, a very brief CV of each team member is needed but very brief. Longer versions can be attached or made available.

- Today, it is also necessary to describe the total compensation packages for the entrepreneurial team in terms of salaries, benefits, stock options, and bonuses. You need to show adequate rewards for team members. But, you may also have to explain how you will handle a situation where revenues are so low that you cannot pay salaries for a period of time. Even if you do not write this into the plan, make sure you have somewhere discussed and documented this. Do not expect you can move in with friends if hell happens as this is usually when friends cease to be friends.

- Next, if there are any special contracts with other team members such as noncompete agreements, and buy-sell documents. If there are these need to be briefly discussed in this section and then place detailed contracts in an appendix.

Now here comes the difficult part to describe. You can't just say they are a wonderful team and work perfectly together. You need to somehow demonstrate how the entrepreneurial team determines the strategic objectives of the firm and who they are committed to making the new venture a success. You are going to need to show the ability of the team to acquiring necessary resources for the venture, this can be done by showing their past history in this regard, or by what they have achieved so far in the venture. Through the plan and how you discuss the team, you need to establish they have the capabilities to manage the needed resources for the venture. Somehow you are going to need to show that the team can manage complex interactions. You need to demonstrate that the team is committed to the firm and can work together to achieve a set of goals. Make the reader believe that your venture will perform up to its potential with this management team in place.

When it comes to human resource policies, in the business plan you need to demonstrate that there are clearly defined roles using job descriptions that specify responsibilities, authority, and accountability. When you read this, you might think, is this all necessary for a start-up with only three persons where everybody has to do everything? Again, this is certainly needed when you ask for other people's monies, but you do well to have some agreement among the team members on who is expected to do what in the first place. This becomes absolutely necessary when you start to hire additional employees. In other words, you will need clear specification of job qualifications. You need to state what your anticipated hires should have in terms of professional competencies, job-related skills, and experiences. Very few persons looking for jobs will fall over themselves to get a job as "jack of all trades." Therefore, show what you have done to find the best applicants for positions in your firm. You need to be sure of how you will elucidate expectations in advance of hiring and how you will provide appropriate incentives, rewards, and opportunities for advancement in the firm. This is also important as a potential employee is likely to want answers to all of these above questions and it is better to once again be prepared. Remember that when you are hiring and interviewing, you are essentially also being interviewed by the applicant.

9.6.5 *Financial Plan Content*

This section uses the homework that we gave you in Chapter 7 on entrepreneurial finance. We strongly believe that as you develop prior sections of your business plan, each produces a financial footprint. For example, your marketing strategy has financial costs and so does your management section with salaries and benefits. You need to take each of these kinds of notes and prepare to use them in writing this section of your plan. You are also going to need to get on a spreadsheet program, be it Excel, or another spreadsheet/accounting program. Even if you never show your plan to another person, you need to do this for yourself so you have some idea of where your venture stands financially currently and what you project rationally for it to be.

Before you do any spreadsheets, you need to verbally explain your various assumptions about what is going to happen to you in terms of sales volumes, production, how you are dealing with accounts receivable and payable (delays etc.), and what is going on with various overhead expenses like leases, power, and travel. You need to discuss what capital expenditures you plan on making and how you will handle depreciation.

Now you need to build the plans and budgets for the first year in terms of sales, production, all operating expenses, the number, and salaries plus benefits for all employees. Be sure to include your headcount plan for future hires. You should also list all capital expenditures as well as all start-up costs, including fixtures, equipment, and space. Now you can prepare a cash-flow statement for the first year and then until the venture cash break-even. These cash flows should be done by individual months. Make sure you have considered any start-up expenditures. Remember to reflect your previously stated accounts payable and receivable procedures and any delay due to collection periods. Also remember that there may well be a delay in receiving cash from a sale unless your business is cash-only. Credit cards may pay you weeks after a purchase, so you need to plan for these delays. We think that the important thing during the first year is to have at least a month cash-flow project that you can track. We know some firms that do weekly cash-flow projects and in movie productions we have seen daily ones. The point is until you are cash positive, you need to keep a *very close eye* on all monies going in and out. By doing this, you will see how accurate your projections are and can adjust future ones based on experience.

Building on your first year cash flows, you now need to prepare a 5-year cash-flow spreadsheet using quarterly projections. Remember not everything is linear, so avoid using straight line projections. Make sure you have identified all business expenses that you will expect over the 5 years. Now you can prepare your first-year profit and loss statement (P&L) and one that reflects the 5-year P&L. You can do years 2 through 5 annually. Now you can do a balance sheet for each quarter for the first year of operation. Make sure you have realistic projections and they coordinate with the P&L. Now do a yearly balance sheet for the first 5 years and be sure they are consistent with the P&Ls. Be prepared to show how your projections compare with any industry norms. Are your costs, revenues, and profits higher or lower than industry standards?

Please don't forget to calculate and show your break-even, using the formula we gave you in Chapter 7.

$$\frac{FC}{(\text{Price} - \text{VC})}.$$

9.7 General Comments Concerning Plans

A typical business plan will be 25 to 30 pages, not counting financial spreadsheets or any needed supplements. While this seems too short to do justice to your brilliant business concept, just remember that no one is going to read a long business plan. You will be lucky if they get through the executive summary and are still interested. If you have to capture their attention with the summary, follow up with short and sweet discussions of the remaining issues and at least begin the process. We have learned that if individuals have to trudge through a large volume of reading to find out critical information, they will simply move on to the next plan. We are strong believers in short and sweet plans who get to the point. You are not writing the great American or Finnish novel, nor are you telling the history of the world. You are, however, telling a short story about how you are going to start your venture and how you are going to make it succcssful.

We have found the same thing to be true for any visual presentation of a plan. If your presentation is more than 15 PowerPoint slides and/or 10-point font, you are going to lose the listener, and never put in copies of the spreadsheets because no one can read them on a screen. If people want to see greater detail on a given area, you should be able to provide longer description, especially marketing and operational plans. The most frequently included appendixes include management resumes, product materials, and tax returns, if available. Put the detailed plan in an order consistent with the executive summary. Be sure to include a cover page including logos and contact information as well as a "Table of Contents" with page numbers. The final product should be in a binding that allows the reader to turn pages easily. Finally, in your writing avoid terms like *state of the art* or *world class*, or any other *jargon* that is frankly just filler.

9.8 Final Words on Planning and Success

You have now read a great deal about how to become a successful entrepreneur and how to create a viable business concept and entrepreneurial organization. What we have tried to do in this book is to show you how various aspects of entrepreneurial actions help create a successful entrepreneurial venture. We are also trying to deal with one of the side effects of being an entrepreneur: *overconfidence*. Realize you may be able to walk on water, but you will get your shoes wet.

First of all, you need to have an idea that you are passionate about. That to us means that you are realistically crazy about it, so that you are prepared to work very hard to get it going. And you have to be prepared to feel passionate about the idea and the actual venture even when things get difficult.

To be successful again depends on how *you define* success. It does not have to mean that you become filthy rich; it is not always about earning lots of money and very rarely about hiring a lot of people. As we have shown here, for many it is about doing something meaningful, and that usually is also what many employees want to do. Perhaps, *happy* would be a better expression, and we hope we have shown you how to become a happy entrepreneur!

Planning again is about trying to prepare for the good and the happy, but needless to say also for the bad and the really ugly. Hopefully only the good will happen, but as the Boy Scouts say "Be Prepared." Planning is not just a writing exercise, which a lot of academic scholars think because they are trained that way. Planning is about putting your words into action and running the venture *for real.*

9.8.1 Mini-Case on Chocolate Pralines

We would like to end this book with a sweet little story. In one of our training classes for start-up (those who had recently started) and nascent entrepreneurs (those who were thinking of starting a firm, but had yet not made the final decision), we had a lady who wanted to start a chocolatier making pralines and a café.

> She was passionate about this idea. She knew how to make the most delicious pralines, so the skill was in place. However, how to turn this into a viable business still needed a lot of help and advice. As we have said often in this book, many entrepreneurs we have met are what we call pathological optimists. Here we had one too. One who was thinking

a little like technology entrepreneurs—if we build it, they will come. She too was thinking if I make the world's most delicious pralines, *they* will come. She had previously run a small café where she also had sold some of these so she knew people liked them. Now, she wanted the pralines to be the main business and the café to be the add-on.

At one of the classes the participants were to present us with their business ideas. This lady had been so excited about her idea that she presented us with a very detailed description of the venture. Here we had the size of the chocolatier to the square foot, the equipment she needed, raw material in terms of the quality of the cocoa, the design of the boxes the pralines would be sold (they were going to be sold in boxes of 2, 4, and 8, but no idea of the price), opening hours, number of employees, interior design, etc. Essentially, she had everything in there that we asked for with respect to marketing, operations and even the competition. But, one very critical part was missing; the cash flow in and out. She had now presented us with a very detailed plan of the *out*, the costs, without actually calculating the costs. What we were reading, however, was costs, more costs, and even more costs. We asked her how many pralines she had to sell every day to cover for these costs. The reply was, she didn't know. Voilà was then the critical task on which she had to focus. Until she did that task, she had no idea whether it was even feasible to open up a café. It turned out it was, and 6 months later she opened up the venture and the candies are wonderful.

Figure 9.1 A conceptual model of building a successful firm.

This is a typical example of how many entrepreneurs start and what we have also wanted to convey in this book. She was turning a dream into reality and she was prepared to work very hard for it to come true, but to get to the venture going, she had to do some basic structuring and calculating. This required: *thinking, planning, and doing*. To summarize the fundamentals of becoming a successful entrepreneur, it takes a number of factors, both internal to the entrepreneur and the entrepreneurial team as well as external factors to create success. Perhaps the best way to demonstrate this is by this graphical representation seen in Figure 9.1 of how different factors in a business plan drive success.

Index

E

eBay, 122, 128, 129

e-businesses, 195

e-commerce, 128–130

economic development, of regions (Birch's study), 9–10

economic wealth creation, 46. *See also* wealth creation

Economist, 1

economy, 51

economy, informal, 163

Edison, Thomas Alva, 2, 6, 41, 70, 216

education, marketing approach and, 104

Einstein, Albert, 43, 66, 70, 123

Eisenhower, Dwight D., 223

electric car, 127

electricity, invention of, 6

Eliot, T.S., 123

e-mail, 100, 105, 153

employees, hiring new, 146–151
  big errors, 147–148
  buy-sell agreement, 148
  case example, 150–151
  characteristics of good, 148–150
  decision-making about, 151–153
  firing and, 152–153
  rejection and, 152

employees/employment
  growth in number of, 209–211
  self-motivated, 149–150

employee stock ownership plans (ESOPs), 191

endangered elephants (Babineaux's painting), 24

entertainment, 60

entrepreneurial management, 165–166

entrepreneurial mindset, 3

entrepreneurial team, 142–144

entrepreneurial team structure, 158–162
  informal structure, 161–162
  line form, 159–160
  project approach, 161

entrepreneurial venture, 25

entrepreneur(s), 1–2. *See also specific entries*
  biographies, 3
  as capitalist, 17
  characteristics, 14, 26
  copycats, 124
  defined(ing), 13, 16–17, 25
  as dreamer, 68–70
  failed, 19
  identifying, 12–13
  incubators and accelerators, 11–12
  made or born, 12
  marketing approaches, 94
  mindset and attitudes, 14–16
  myths and stories, 1–2, 8
  national innovation systems for, 10–12
  necessity, 12–13, 20, 21, 29
  opportunistic, 12–13
  opportunity and, 28–29
  as opportunity creator/innovator, 17
  overconfidence, 243
  personality factors, 13–14

Musk, Elon, 114, 122, 173
myth(s), entrepreneurial, 2

N

O

venture creation, 142–145
    entrepreneurial team, 142–144
    other issues, 144–145
    outsourcing, 145
    start-up team, 142
venture's money search, 193–194
viable business concept. *See also*
  business concept model
    creativity and, 65–66, 71–72
    designing, 76–77
VIE (www.viewinery.com), 205
von Goethe, Johann Wolfgang,
  142, 146

W

Wagner, Richard, 23
Walker, Madam C. J., 2, 3
walking-around market re-
  search, 95–96
    examples, 96–97
Wal-Mart, 88, 121, 133, 143, 154
Walt Disney, 67
wants/desires. *See also* fears;
  needs
    identification, idea generation
    and, 59–61
Warby Parker, 78, 173
Warhol, Andy, 23
Warren Buffett effect, 198
Waterford Crystal, 5
Watson, Thomas, Jr., 38, 153
Wayfair, 100
wealth
    defined, 46
    economic, 46–47
    success and, 46–47

wealth creation
    economic, 46
    as entrepreneurial goal, 16,
    19, 26
websites, 101
Wedgwood, Josiah, 4, 5
Wedgwood china, 4, 5
Wedgwood pottery, 5
Welsh, Jack, 217
West Side Story, 124
Wiebe, Richard, 129
WiFi technology, 131, 173
Wikipedia, 72–73
Winfrey, Oprah, 3, 4, 97
women entrepreneurs, 3.
  See also entrepreneur(s)
women's World Banking, 8
word-of-mouth advertising,
  106
    power of, 118
word-of-web advertising,
  106–107
    power of, 118
World Bank, 198
World Wide Web, 129
would-be entrepreneur,
  2, 68–69, 169. *See also*
  entrepreneur(s)
    exercise for, 68–69
    information resources for, 95
WWRD group, 5
www.booking.com, 129

X

Xerox Corporation, 216
X Game, 201